The Claims
of Truth

The Claims
of Truth

John Owen's Trinitarian Theology

Carl R. Trueman

paternoster
press

Copyright © 1998 Carl Trueman

First published 1998 by Paternoster Press

04 03 02 01 00 99 98   7 6 5 4 3 2 1

Paternoster Press is an imprint of Paternoster Publishing,
P.O. Box 300, Carlisle, Cumbria, CA3 0QS, U.K.

British Library Cataloguing in Publication Data

A catalogue record for this book is available from the British Library.

ISBN 0–85364–798–4

⅂ 1001260823

Typeset by WestKey Ltd, Falmouth, Cornwall
Printed in Great Britain by Clays Ltd, St Ives plc.

For Catriona

Sine qua non.

CONTENTS

Preface

A few brief comments are in order as a preliminary to the main text. First, while this book will no doubt be understood in some quarters as a defence of Owen's theology, such an interpretation would, in fact, represent a misreading of my argument. I wish at the start to make it clear that I write as a historian of ideas, not as a systematic theologian. My interest is not to discover whether Owen was right or wrong, but to see what he said, why he said it, whether it was coherent by the standards of his day, and how he fits into the theological context of his own times and of the western tradition as a whole. Of course, I do have personal intellectual convictions about the theological value of Owen's writings, but I have tried to be aware of my own theological commitments and to keep them as separate as humanly possible from my analysis. Several of my Nottingham colleagues, unconvinced by my protestations of objectivity, have pushed me on this point on a number of occasions, and I have had to confess to them that the 'truth question' often haunts me like Banquo's ghost at Macbeth's feast. If my powers of exorcism have let me down at any point in the following pages, I ask the reader's indulgence.

Following from the first point, I have used terminology in this book which normally has certain dogmatic and evaluative connotations but which I have employed in a way which is not meant to imply either endorsement or criticism of certain ideas. For example, I have used the word *heresy* and its cognates not to cast aspersions on particular positions but to reflect the fact that certain ideas stood outside of the creedal and confessional traditions of mainstream western Christendom. I have also used *orthodoxy* with a small case *o* to refer to ideas which are historically consistent with the western catholic tradition devolving from the early church Creeds, and *Orthodoxy* with a capital *O* to refer to ideas consistent with the historic confessional tradition of the Reformed churches. One reviewer of my earlier book, *Luther's Legacy*, objected in a rather bad-tempered fashion to my use of the term 'Catholic Church' when referring to the church which looks to the Pope as its authority. I still prefer this title to the anachronistic Protestant phrase 'Roman Catholic Church' and have used it again in this book, although occasionally I have had recourse to the inelegant word 'papist'. Again, this is not intended as a pejorative term.

The most delightful part of writing a book is thanking those who have helped to make the project possible. First, thanks are due to Pieter Kwant and the staff at Paternoster Publishing for giving advanced support to the project and seeing it through the press. I also owe, once again, a great debt to my friend, Peter Stephens, Professor of Church History at the University of Aberdeen. It was Peter who first taught me the importance of not using my own theological convictions as criteria for historical analysis, and who, through many telephone calls and letters, has over the years been a source of constant encouragement and advice. He will note, with some amusement, I hope, rather than disappointment, that the pupil is in this book rebelling against the teacher on various points of style and presentation; but it remains true that all I learned about the methodological content of church history, I have learned from him. Scott Clark, of Wheaton College, has been similarly supportive, and has offered constructive criticism on a number of sections of the work. Thanks too to Paul Schaefer Jr. for giving me a copy of his excellent Oxford DPhil thesis.

At Nottingham Tony Thiselton and Douglas Davies, as heads of department, both gave help and support at various times, and Ed Ball provided an absolutely invaluable taxi service to the Cambridge University Library. Seth Kunin, my colleague in the 'Aristotelian Annex' of the Nottingham Department, has helped to keep me sane with his dry, rabbinic wit and with regular pints of real ale. My postgraduate, Steve Griffiths, deserves mention as the one human being in Britain to whom I can talk about Owen without his eyes glazing over within 30 seconds. John Heywood Thomas has also been a key influence. It was he who first alerted me to the central importance of medieval philosophy for subsequent theology, and who gave up valuable time to talk to me about Aquinas and to comment on some of my theories about Owen.

In addition to my Nottingham colleagues, I have been fortunate enough to spend over six months at the Meeter Center, Calvin College, Grand Rapids, where most of the writing up of this project was carried out. The staff there were wonderful, providing me with a home and an office, allowing me full use of both the Library and the Inter-Library Loan System, and even paying for certain rare materials to be microfilmed. I am particularly grateful to Connie Bellows, Director of Human Resources at Calvin College, for being such a great landlady; and to the Director of the Meeter Center, Rick Gamble, to the Center's Librarian, Paul Fields, and to the Secretary, Susan Schmurr, for all their help and for countless acts of personal kindness towards myself and my family. In addition to the Meeter Center, another attraction of the Calvin College campus was the dynamic presence of Richard Muller. My intellectual debt to his work is immense, and the time I spent with him and his postgraduate student, Raymond Blacketer, was both stimulating and entertaining.

Research, of course, costs money. I would like to thank the following for their help: the University of Nottingham for granting me a semester of study leave in 1996 and for the award of a New Lecturer's Research Grant to facilitate work on Thomas Aquinas and on Reformed theology; Mary Charles Murray, my colleague, and Terence Wilkerson, Reader in Philosophy at Nottingham, for providing crucial references; the British Academy for the Small Personal Research Grant which enabled me to stay at the Meeter Center; and the Governing Body of the Meeter Center for the award of a Stipendiary Fellowship for 1996.

I would also like to thank Dr Alan Clifford for his work on Owen, and for the numerous conversations we have had over the years. When I read his book five years ago I realized that sooner or later we would have to cross swords in print. The following book contains much sharp dissent from his work, but I hope he will understand it as an attempt to criticize his views which yet takes them seriously.

Finally, I would like to thank the many people from outside the academic world who made my study leave possible: my parents for administering my finances etc. in my absence; Arthur Johnson for constant, if sometimes slightly bemused, support and encouragement; Neil and Bethan Parmenter for friendship and for help with moving to the States; John and Pauline Horry, good friends, the latter of whom put some real 'va-va-voom' into our American trip; the Barham family for help with the logistics of our return; my two sons, John and Peter, for helping me to keep my work in perspective; and my wife, Catriona, who for the last three years has listened to my sometimes very angry outbursts about Owen, the secondary scholarship, and my own work. She was also willing to leave home and friends and travel to the other side of the world just so that I could pursue the project. The book is dedicated to her in thanks for all that she has given up, materially and emotionally, over the years so that I could pursue my goals.

Carl R. Trueman
Nottingham

Abbreviations

ANF	*Ante-Nicene Fathers*
BSABR	*Bibliotheca Sacra and American Biblical Repository*
CD	Barth, *Church Dogmatics*
CH	*Church History*
CTJ	*Calvin Theological Journal*
DLGTT	Muller, *Dictionary of Latin and Greek Theological Terms*
EQ	*Evangelical Quarterly*
HTR	*Harvard Theological Review*
JEH	*Journal of Ecclesiastical History*
JHI	*Journal of the History of Ideas*
JMRS	*Journal of Medieval and Renaissance Studies*
NAKG	*Nederlands Archief voor Kerkgeschiedenis*
NCE	*New Catholic Encyclopedia*
NPNF	*Nicene and Post-Nicene Fathers*
OC	*Opera Calvini*
PRRD1	Muller, *Post-Reformation Reformed Dogmatics 1*
PRRD2	Muller, *Post-Reformation Reformed Dogmatics 2*
RC	*Racovian Catechism*
SCJ	*Sixteenth Century Journal*
SJT	*Scottish Journal of Theology*
ST	Aquinas, *Summa Theologiae*
WCF	*Westminster Confession of Faith*
WTJ	*Westminster Theological Journal*

One

Owen in Context

Introduction

John Owen is, in many ways, the forgotten man of English theology. In his own day he was chaplain to Cromwell, preacher to Parliament, Chancellor of Oxford University, leading light of the Independents, and the pre-eminent Puritan theologian – by any standard one of the most influential men of his generation. He was also immensely learned: even a cursory reading of Owen's works reveals a mind steeped in patristic, medieval, and Reformation theology, and phenomenally well-versed in contemporary theological literature, Protestant, Catholic, and heretical. Yet the scholarly interest in his work since his own day has been minuscule, even compared to that in his contemporary, Richard Baxter.[1]

There are a number of reasons for this neglect which immedi-

---

[1]   There is an excellent modern biography of Owen: P. Toon, *God's Statesman: The Life and Work of John Owen* (Exeter: Paternoster, 1971). Also worth consulting is A. Thomson's 'Life of Dr Owen', in *The Works of John Owen*, 24 vols. (London: Johnstone and Hunter, 1850–55), hereafter cited as *Works*, 1, pp. xxi–cxxii. Even work on Baxter has been slight until fairly recently. A good discussion of the progress made in Baxter studies can be found in Hans Boersma's fascinating analysis of Baxter, *A Hot Peppercorn: Richard Baxter's Doctrine of Justification in Its Seventeenth-Century Context of Controversy* (Zoetermeer: Boekencentrum, 1993), pp. 1–24. While I disagree with Boersma's reading of Owen, this book is the most significant contribution to the study of Baxter's theology since J. I. Packer's (sadly) unpublished DPhil thesis, 'The Redemption and Restoration of Man in the Thought of Richard Baxter' (Oxford University, 1954). Other more recent works on Baxter's life and cultural contribution include G. F. Nuttall, *Richard Baxter* (London: Nelson, 1965); and N. H. Keeble, *Richard Baxter: Puritan Man of Letters* (Oxford: Clarendon Press, 1982).

ately suggest themselves – none of which have anything to do with the intrinsic merit of Owen's work as an example of seventeenth-century English theology or Reformed Orthodoxy. The first is the fact that theology within English universities has been, until fairly recently, the monopoly of an established Church for whom Reformed theology was simply not a major interest. The Great Ejection of 1662 effectively removed from the Church, and thus from the intellectual establishment, the vast majority of those ministers committed to a more thoroughly Reformed faith; it therefore surrendered both the Church and, as a result, the academy to a group whose theological concerns were generally more latitudinarian. In the twentieth century the Anglican monopoly of higher education has gone, but Anglicans have continued to set much of the scholarly agenda within university theology departments, and so have also determined that the subjects studied reflect their own ecclesiastical concerns. Consequently, the Puritans, and Owen among them, suffered the neglect which their separation from the Church made inevitable.[2]

In addition to this ecclesiastical dimension, the scholarly neglect of Owen is affected also by the nature of the Anglo-American interest in Puritanism. This interest has tended to emphasize the social, political, and, more recently, psychological aspects of Puritanism rather than its theological dimensions, as is clearly seen in the works of, amongst others, Perry Miller, Christopher Hill, and Patrick Collinson.[3] Such scholars have done much

---

[2] The work of Packer is a notable exception to this Anglican trend, but the majority of his contributions since his dissertation have been aimed exclusively at ecclesiastical, not scholarly, constituencies: see, for example, the collection of essays entitled *Among God's Giants: The Puritan Vision of the Christian Life* (Eastbourne: Kingsway, 1991).
[3] See P. Miller, *The New England Mind: The Seventeenth Century* (Cambridge: Harvard UP, 1939); C. Hill, *Society and Puritanism in Pre-Revolutionary England* (London: Secker and Warburg, 1967); P. Collinson *The Elizabethan Puritan Movement* (Oxford: Clarendon Press, 1967). For articles surveying the way in which Puritan studies, particularly those concerned with New England, have changed over recent decades, see the following: M. McGiffert, 'American Puritan Studies in the 1960's', *William and Mary Quarterly*, Series 3, 27 (1970), 36–67; L. B. Ricard, 'New England Puritan Studies in the 1970's', *Fides et Historia* 15 (1983), 6–27. For an assessment of Perry Miller's contribution to Puritan studies, and a critique of his underplaying of the role of the Bible and theology in Puritanism, see George M. Marsden, 'Perry Miller's Rehabilitation of the Puritans', *CH* 39 (1970), 91–105. Also worth consulting in this context is the bibliographical essay in Charles L. Cohen's *God's Caress: The Psychology of Puritan Religious Experience* (Oxford: OUP, 1986), pp. 275–89.

magisterial work and greatly expanded our knowledge of the
Puritan tradition, but they have inevitably tended to focus on
aspects other than the theological. The strength of the non-theological tendency within Puritan studies is evident from the fact
that most of those engaged in studying British and American
Puritanism do not do so from within university theology or
religion departments but under the auspices of other disciplines:
Miller, for example, was a literature professor; Hill and Collinson
are historians.

While the gains made by such non-theological studies of Puritanism have been immense, the lack of interest in the theological
dimension has created a situation where seventeenth-century
studies compare somewhat unfavourably with the related discipline of sixteenth-century studies. In the latter field, the last thirty
years have seen an immense amount of work which has sought
to understand Reformation thought against the background of
medieval and Renaissance patterns, and which has also attempted to synthesize the intellectual dimensions of the age with
underlying social and political concerns.[4] The result has not been
a simple reworking of the old-style history-of-ideas, but an increasingly rich and diversified crop of works which has greatly
illuminated our understanding of the age. Indeed, through the
early work of Heiko Oberman, and the studies of exegesis which
have emerged from his pupil David Steinmetz and his students
at Duke University, there has occurred a revolutionary change
in the way in which the theology of the Reformation is viewed.[5]
No longer can the subject be studied in terms of a straightforward
reaction to the Middle Ages: the relationship between Reformation thought and its precursors has been shown to be highly
complex and to defy classification in the simplistic partisan terms
advocated by earlier generations of scholars, both Catholic and

---

[4] The work of Heiko Oberman has been particularly significant in this context: see
his *The Harvest of Medieval Theology: Gabriel Biel and Late Medieval Nominalism*
(Durham: Labyrinth, 1983); *The Masters of the Reformation* (Cambridge: CUP, 1981).
[5] See Oberman, *The Dawn of the Reformation* (Edinburgh: T and T Clark, 1986); D.
C. Steinmetz, *Luther and Staupitz: An Essay in the Intellectual Origins of the Protestant
Reformation* (Durham: Duke UP, 1980); S. E. Schreiner, *The Theater of His Glory:
Nature and the Natural Order in the Thought of John Calvin* (Grand Rapids: Baker,
1995).

Protestant. This development in scholarship, exciting though it is, finds few counterparts in the field of the seventeenth century, partly because there is no tradition of intellectual history with regards to Puritanism corresponding to that upon which Oberman and others were able to build, and partly because those studying Puritanism have neither the interest nor the theological training to pursue such a course. This is not to denigrate what has been done – far from it – but simply to explain why there is such a dearth of studies on seventeenth-century theology, and to point out that, just as social and political studies can no longer claim to be exhaustive in scope with reference to Reformation history, so they should not claim the same with reference to the seventeenth century.

Given the above, it is not surprising that Owen features in the narrative of scholarship on Puritanism only occasionally, a fact which belies his significance, intellectually as well as politically, in his own day. Owen has not been singled out for such neglect: as yet, there are scarcely any published monographs on any leading Puritan thinker, and many of the studies which do deal with Puritan theology tend, in the tradition of Miller, to focus on sermonic material as their basic source; but it is simply not an adequate approach to focus all the attention on sermons as the basis for understanding the Puritan mind. The sermon is where the Puritan mind touched the Puritan pew and thus where theology and society came, as it were, into contact, but the content of those sermons was determined to a large extent by the large theological tomes and works of exegesis that lined the walls of Puritan studies: of these works, many of which would have been written by Owen, scholars have said almost nothing.[6] Until

---

[6] In his fascinating account of New England preaching, Harry S. Stout describes as the most surprising result of his research his discovery that the content of sermons remained remarkably stable during the period which he studied: see *The New England Soul: Preaching and Religious Culture in Colonial New England* (Oxford: OUP, 1986), p. 6. This may indeed be surprising from the perspective of a historian interested in the changing social function of sermons, but is easily explicable from a theological perspective, where the continuity in theological framework can be seen as playing a significant role. Of course, in order to show this, one must study the theological systems and commentaries that lie behind the sermons, and not simply the sermons themselves, and there has been little work in this area.

extensive work has been done on the theological convictions of the Puritans in a manner which parallels that of the work on the Lutheranism and Reformed theology of the sixteenth century, the kind of work which scholars such as Oberman have pioneered with reference to the sixteenth century will simply not be possible with reference to the seventeenth.

While Owen has been all but forgotten by scholars, his name is, however, very much alive within certain Christian circles, and this too has not helped to bring him to academic attention. His works are indeed highly thought of today by some, but these supporters are generally very conservative, even fundamentalist, Christian groups who are interested in Owen not because they wish to understand him within his historical context, but because his writings are seen as an important source for their own brand of conservative theology and as normative for today. This pietistic tradition is most clearly symbolized by the fact that his works are kept in print by the Banner of Truth Trust, a group that has done tremendous work in keeping Puritan writings available but which is also committed to a particular doctrinal position that renders any book which it publishes suspect, often unfairly, to many in the academic community. As a result, Owen is perhaps regarded by others (if they have heard of him) less as a seventeenth-century thinker and more as an obscurantist precursor of some fearful brand of fundamentalism.[7] Such a picture is reinforced when one of the few pieces of significant scholarship on Owen to emerge in recent years is, in its stated purpose, an exposé of the errors in his theology and thus a contribution more to contemporary debates within the British neo-Calvinist movement than to seventeenth-century studies.[8]

Finally, while there has been a steady growth in interest in

---

[7] Even given the partisan approach of this tradition, it has nevertheless produced a number of articles which, through their uncritically descriptive approach to Owen's thought, actually produce more historically accurate portraits than some of the more tendentious scholarly readings: see, for example, Jack N. MacLeod, 'John Owen and the Death of Death', in *Out of Bondage*, Proceedings of the Westminster Conference (Nottingham, 1984).

[8] A. C. Clifford, *Atonement and Justification: English Evangelical Theology 1640– 1790, An Evaluation* (Oxford: Clarendon Press, 1990), esp. pp. vii–ix.

seventeenth-century Reformed theology over recent years,[9] two further factors have continued to marginalize Owen. First there has been the tendency in continental theological scholarship to exclude, whether by intent or accident, Puritanism from its discussions. Indeed, when looking at books on the seventeenth century, one could be forgiven for thinking that Orthodoxy and Puritanism are discrete phenomena. The paucity of British authors cited in Heppe's famous collection symbolizes this separation from the side of Orthodoxy,[10] while, on the Puritan side, the tradition of scholarship which takes its cue from M. M. Knappen has tended to assume that the origins and development of Puritanism lie in England's medieval reform movements and that it is therefore an essentially English phenomenon.[11] Only in the work of Richard Muller is some real attempt to overcome this problem being attempted.[12]

---

[9] There are a number of fine studies of Puritan theology in existence, but on the whole these tend to study the Puritans in terms of their contemporary context and of the Reformed tradition, ignoring the impact of patristic and medieval sources upon their thinking: see J. S. Coolidge, *The Pauline Renaissance in England* (Oxford: Clarendon Press, 1970); G. F. Nuttall, *The Holy Spirit in Puritan Faith and Experience* (Chicago: University of Chicago Press, 1992); J. von Rohr, *The Covenant of Grace in Puritan Thought* (Atlanta: Scholars Press, 1986); D. D. Wallace, *Puritans and Predestination: Grace in English Protestant Theology* (Chapel Hill: University of North Carolina Press, 1982).

[10] H. Heppe, *Reformed Dogmatics Set Out and Illustrated from the Sources*, trans. G. T. Thomson (Grand Rapids: Baker, 1978). For other classic studies of Reformed Orthodoxy which take little or no account of Anglo-Saxon developments, see P. Althaus, *Die Prinzipien der deutschen reformierten Dogmatik im Zeitalter der aristotelischen Scholastik* (Leipzig: Deichertsche, 1914); E. Bizer, *Frühorthodoxie und Rationalismus* (Zurich: EVZ, 1963); H. E. Weber, *Reformation, Orthodoxie, und Rationalismus* (Gutersloh: Bertelsmann, 1951).

[11] See his *Tudor Puritanism* (Chicago: University of Chicago Press, 1939); also *idem*, *Two Elizabethan Puritan Diaries* (Gloucester: Peter Smith, 1966), p. 1; his lead is followed, for example, by E. F. Kevan, *The Grace of Law: A Study in Puritan Theology* (Ligonier: Soli Deo Gloria, 1993), p. 42. More recently, Patrick Collinson has attacked the insularity of Puritan studies by pointing to the interaction, both economic and intellectual, between English Puritanism and parallel Reformed movements on the continent: see his 'The Beginnings of English Sabbatarianism' in *Godly People: Essays on English Protestantism and Puritanism* (London: Hambledon, 1982), pp. 429–43; also his 'England and International Calvinism 1558–1640' in *International Calvinism*, ed. M. Prestwich (Oxford: Clarendon, 1985), pp. 197–223.

[12] See, for example, his *Christ and the Decree: Christology and Predestination from Calvin to Perkins* (Durham: Labyrinth, 1986).

The second tendency has been the willingness of those few scholars who are interested in Puritan theology to accept the 'Calvin against the Calvinists' thesis.[13] In such a world, Owen, as one of those terrible scholastic perverters of Calvin's own thought, is demonized and doomed to have importance only in relation to sixteenth-century antecedents.[14] Such scholars need only look at Owen to find proof texts which confirm their a priori analytical model and they consider their task completed. Indeed, Owen almost seems in some works to fulfil a role analogous to one of the poor wretches in Hilaire Belloc's *Cautionary Verses*, a salutary lesson to any tempted to feel that Calvin's thought was not the last word in Christian theology.[15] This tradition, dominated to a large extent by scholars with personal theological agendas and a vested interest in driving a wedge between Calvin and the Reformed Orthodox, has tended to bypass the work of Oberman etc. and to pursue an agenda which probably confirms the deepest suspicions of most social historians about the presuppositions, purpose, and value of intellectual history.[16]

---

[13]   This thesis finds it most concise statement in B. Hall's essay, 'Calvin against the Calvinists' in G. E. Duffield (ed.), *John Calvin* (Grand Rapids: Eerdmans, 1966), pp. 19–37. Other such work includes R. T. Kendall, *Calvin and English Calvinism to 1649* (Carlisle: Paternoster, 1997); and H. Rolston III, *John Calvin versus the Westminster Confession* (Richmond: John Knox Press, 1972).

[14]   See, for example, Alan Clifford's notion of 'authentic Calvinism': *Atonement and Justification*, pp. 69–94.

[15]   Perhaps the scholar who most persistently portrays Owen in dark colours is James Torrance. For him, Owen has a doctrine of God which completely undermines assurance and makes God essentially justice and only arbitrarily love, and is the Puritan whose theology is most vitiated by the Western *ordo salutis*: see 'The Concept of Federal Theology – Was Calvin a Federal Theologian?', in W. H. Neuser, (ed.), *Calvinus Sacrae Scripturae Confessor* (Grand Rapids: Eerdmans, 1994), pp. 15–40, 36; 'The Incarnation and "Limited Atonement"', *EQ* 55 (1982), 83–94, 84; 'Strengths and Weaknesses of the Westminster Theology', in A. I. C. Heron, (ed.), *The Westminster Confession in the Church Today* (Edinburgh: St Andrew Press, 1982), pp. 40–54. What is most intriguing about Professor Torrance's criticisms is the complete lack of specific primary source citation and discussion – two passing references in the above articles to the whole of *The Death of Death* scarcely count as documentary proof of particular charges.

[16]   The picture is not all black, however. On the positive side, Owen has proved a moderately popular subject for research dissertations among students interested in the Reformed theology of the seventeenth century, although few of these have ultimately found their way into print; perhaps this last fact is an indicator of the lack of wider scholarly interest in the intellectual life of seventeenth-century Puritanism.

In light of the above, there is a clear need to study the thought of individuals such as Owen in order to shed light upon the intellectual dynamics of the seventeenth century, in a manner which avoids the unhistorical pitfalls represented both by those who attempt to isolate English Puritanism from the tradition of continental Reformed Orthodoxy and by those who adopt the 'Calvin against the Calvinists' model of interpretation. The approach taken towards Owen in this work is determined by the conviction that he was one of the most significant English Reformed theologians of the *seventeenth century* and that is how he must be interpreted. Therefore, the criteria used to explicate and evaluate his work will not be those of the sixteenth century, or even of the twentieth century – such approaches are nonsensical in terms of historical method, and usually tell the reader more about the author's own beliefs than about those of the subject.[17] Instead, Owen's thought will be described and explained in terms of the various theological traditions of Christianity to which he belonged and upon which he drew, and of the particular intellectual and polemical contexts within which he found himself working. The result may well be too descriptive for some, but, when one surveys the scholarship on Reformed Orthodoxy, it often seems that attempts to indulge in dogmatic evaluation of the

---

Footnote 16 (*continued*)   Nevertheless, the last decade has seen the publications of four books which did start life as dissertations and which do pay significant attention to Owen and his thought: Sinclair Ferguson's *John Owen on the Christian Life* (Edinburgh: Banner of Truth, 1987); Alan Clifford's *Atonement and Justification*; Joel Beeke's *Assurance of Faith: Calvin, English Puritanism, and the Dutch Second Reformation* (New York: Peter Lang, 1991); and Randall Gleason's *John Calvin and John Owen on Mortification* (New York: Peter Lang, 1995) (pp. 177–80 of this last work contain a very useful list of unpublished dissertations on Owen and related subjects). All four make significant contributions to the field, and, while Ferguson, Beeke, and Gleason take a generally positive view of Owen's work, the somewhat negative assessment of Clifford raises a number of interesting questions for future students of the Puritan's theology.

[17]   A good, if not slightly amusing, example of an unhistorical statement about seventeenth-century theology is that made by J. B. Torrance when he alleges that it is the 'nature-grace' model of the Westminster Confession which prevents it from saying anything 'about race relations': see 'Strengths and Weaknesses', p. 50. To the historical mind, it is more likely to be the fact that race relations were not an issue in seventeenth-century England that is to blame for such an oversight.

relevant theology has led to an obscuring and distortion of the canons of historical method and objectivity. Those who wish to argue about whether Owen is right or wrong may do so, but that is not a game played within this book, and to read it in such a way is to mistake my intention. The task in hand is one of explication and clarification. After all, even if one wishes ulti-mately to make the case that Owen was either a perverter or a preserver of the Reformed tradition, one must first establish exactly what he said and why he said it.

The Importance of the Theological Context

The word 'Puritan' has proved notoriously difficult to define, and it remains true to say that it is easier to give examples of Puritans than give a precise and fully adequate definition of Puritanism.[18] That Owen was a Puritan is beyond all doubt, but as a label for him it is somewhat limited in its usefulness. Indeed, because of its cultural and historical connotations, it places a perhaps undue emphasis upon Owen's position as a seventeenth-century Anglo-Saxon which, while obviously true, is only part of the story. In order to understand Owen and his theology, it is vital to see him as part of an ongoing Western theological tradition which has historical roots back beyond the Reforma-tion, beyond even the Middle Ages, and which is closely allied to parallel movements on the continent.

Recent scholarship on the sixteenth century, while not blind

---

[18] The literature debating the definition of Puritanism is vast. The following represent a good sample of the variety of views on this subject: J. C. Brauer, 'Reflections on the Nature of English Puritanism', *CH* 23 (1954), 99–108; Collinson, *Elizabethan Puritan Movement*; B. Hall, 'Puritanism: The Problem of Definition' in G. J. Cumming (ed.), *Studies in Church History* 2 (London: Nelson, 1965), pp. 283–96; W. Haller, *The Rise of Puritanism* (New York: Columbia, 1955); Hill, *Society and Puritanism in Pre-Revo-lutionary England*; Miller, *The New England Mind: The Seventeenth Century*; Jens Møller, 'The Beginning of Puritan Covenant Theology', *JEH* 14 (1963), 46–67; L. J. Trinterud, 'The Origins of Puritanism', *CH* 20 (1951), 37–57. For a good recent discussion of the issues, see Paul R. Schaefer, Jr., 'The Spiritual Brotherhood on the Habits of the Heart: Cambridge Protestants and the Doctrine of Sanctification from William Perkins to Thomas Shepard', unpubl. DPhil diss. (University of Oxford, 1994), pp. 1–33.

to important areas of discontinuity, has brought attention to the important continuities that exist between Reformation thought and the patristic and medieval intellectual background.[19] As noted above, this approach to the history of doctrine has been taken up and applied with great success to the development of Reformed Orthodoxy in the late-sixteenth and seventeenth centuries, most notably in the work of Richard A. Muller.[20] Such scholarship has emphasized the need to interpret individual theologians as existing and working within established theological traditions (exegetical, doctrinal, philosophical, etc.), and to understand specific formulations of doctrine historically rather than dogmatically. This approach simply reflects sound historical methodology but is, of course, possible only when the question of the ultimate truth or falsehood of the points at issue is left on one side, something that has apparently been particularly difficult, perhaps understandably, for scholars in the field of doctrinal history.

Much of the small amount of work on Owen has not apparently benefited in any significant way from the more historically sensitive work on the sixteenth and seventeenth centuries, and little attempt has been made to set him within the broader ongoing intellectual tradition. Instead, to give one example, Owen has been judged by one scholar almost solely by his fidelity to the theology of John Calvin.[21] While the systematic theologian may possibly be happy with this, from the historian's point of view the underlying presuppositions of such an approach are highly problematic for a number of reasons. First, the choice of Calvin, a sixteenth-century theologian, as the criterion for judging seventeenth-century theology is, historically speaking, an entirely arbitrary move. Even in the sixteenth century, Calvin was

---

[19] E.g. see H. A. Oberman, *The Impact of the Reformation* (Grand Rapids: Eerdmans, 1994); D. C. Steinmetz, *Luther in Context* (Grand Rapids: Baker, 1995); J. P. Donnelly, *Calvinism and Scholasticism in Vermigli's Doctrine of Man and Grace* (Leiden: Brill, 1975).

[20] R. A. Muller, *Christ and the Decree; PRRD1* and *PRRD2; God, Creation, and Providence in the Thought of Jacob Arminius* (Grand Rapids: Baker, 1991).

[21] Clifford, *Atonement and Justification*, where a chapter entitled 'Authentic Calvinism' sets the benchmark by which Owen, Baxter *et al.* are to be judged.

at best first among equals; his theology did not represent the entire Reformed tradition and was not the only model available to subsequent theologians. Of course, some scholars argue that Calvin's theology represents the truth and can therefore function as a basic criterion for analysis of theology in any subsequent era. In fact, this claim should immediately be subject to suspicion: what these scholars usually mean is that Calvin (or their interpretation of Calvin) agrees with their own beliefs. Such an approach is therefore highly subjective, unhistorical, and inappropriate as a framework for an historical analysis of seventeenth-century thought.

In the case of Dr Clifford's study, the comparison between Calvin and Owen takes place only across a very narrow range of doctrinal points; atonement and justification to be precise. This raises the question as to why atonement should be regarded as the acid test of fidelity to Calvin, and not church-state relations, sacramental thought, polity, views on the ministry etc. It also raises the equally valid question of whether it is possible to isolate the issue of atonement in either Calvin or Owen from broader doctrinal concerns, such as the doctrine of God, Christology etc. If one wishes to adopt continuity with Calvin as the basic criterion for judging the development of Reformed theology during the century-and-a-half after his death, one must do so over the whole range of theology in a manner which does not arbitrarily isolate one or two doctrines from the whole theological complex. In fact, as is clear from the first objection above, the question of such continuity between Calvin and the 'Calvinists' is, from a historian's point of view, something of a red herring anyway.

A further problem is that this approach completely isolates 100 years of Reformed theology from the rest of the Western theological tradition. Anyone with even a passing acquaintance with patristic and medieval theology will realize upon reading Owen that he cannot be reduced to the simplistic categories suggested by the 'Calvin against the Calvinists' school. Calvin himself never imagined that his own work would provide the single necessary starting point and criterion for any future theological reflection – that honour was reserved for Scripture alone – nor did he consider his writings to have drawn a line under everything which preceded them. Thus, to seventeenth-century Reformed theologians, Calvin's writings are one (admittedly important) resource among many, alongside which must be placed not only other Reformed writers but also the works of the Fathers and the medieval schoolmen. Those who think they have understood Owen and his Puritan contemporaries simply in terms of the Reformed tradition of the sixteenth and seventeenth centuries have not really understood him at all. Other branches of the Western tradition also play vital roles in his theological work, and to ignore, generalize about, or dismiss these on the basis of aprioristic prejudices about Scholasticism, medieval theology etc. is to do a fundamental injustice to the work of a highly sophisticated thinker.[22] Nothing so separates the thought of the Reformed Orthodox such as Owen from some of the fundamentalists who today claim their authority as the Orthodox understanding of, and dialogue with, the whole Western tradition. The point is made with elegant eloquence by Paul Tillich, not a name one usually associates with a sympathetic reading of Reformed Orthodoxy:

> [I]t is a pity that very often orthodoxy and fundamentalism are confused. One of the great achievements of classical orthodoxy in the late sixteenth and early seventeenth centuries was the fact that it remained in continual discussion with all the centuries of Christian thought . . . These orthodox theologians knew the history of philosophy as well as the theology of the Reformation. The fact that they were in the tradition of the Reformers did not prevent them from knowing thoroughly scholastic theology, from discussing and refuting it, or even accepting it when possible. All this makes classical orthodoxy one of the great events in the history of Christian thought.[23]

This description of Orthodoxy fits Owen perfectly. As will become clear, he was throughout his theological career engaging in a critical interaction with, and appropriation of, the Western

---

[22] For an exposé of the many nonsensical presuppositions which underlie the 'Calvin against the Calvinist' school of interpretation, see the two-part article by Richard Muller, 'Calvin and the "Calvinists": Assessing Continuities and Discontinuities between the Reformation and Orthodoxy', *CTJ* 30 (1995) 345–75; 31 (1996), 125–60; also the ecellent analysis by W. J. van Asselt, 'Studie van de Gereformeerde Scholastiek: Verleden en Toekomst', *Nederlands Theologisch Tijdschrift* 50 (1996), 290–312.

[23] P. Tillich, *A History of Christian Thought*, ed. Carl E. Braaten (New York: Simon and Schuster, 1968), p. 306. A similar description of Orthodoxy is provided by Otto Weber, *Foundations of Dogmatics*, trans. Darrell L. Guder, 2 vols. (Grand Rapids: Eerdmans, 1981), 1, pp. 112 ff.

tradition as a whole. To attempt to explain his thinking in terms of one or two 'big ideas' is to reduce to the level of the sound-bite something that is in itself extremely complex and incapable of such reduction.

The Reformed Orthodox Background

Having drawn attention to the need to look beyond the immediate Reformed milieu in order to gain a proper understanding of Owen's theology, it may seem slightly odd then to move straight to a discussion of the Reformed background rather than adopting a chronological approach and dealing first with patristic and medieval influences. On the issue of influences it is indeed important not to fall into the error of reducing everything to Reformed theology, but it is also necessary to understand that Owen's appropriation and utilisation of patristic and medieval sources was determined by the theological context in which he found himself. It was the issues with which he was confronted as a *Reformed* theologian of the *seventeenth century* that drove him back to church tradition and which shaped and influenced which works he read, how he read them, and what ideas he drew from them. It is therefore important to know what the specific concerns of the seventeenth-century Reformed were in order fully to understand the manner in which they used their sources.

A key point to make about Owen's immediate Reformed context is to reiterate that he should be understood not simply as part of an English or even as part of a British movement, but as part of an international movement. In terms of theology, the English Puritanism of those such as John Owen, while having its own distinctive emphases and experiencing its own peculiar doctrinal controversies, was essentially the local manifestation of Reformed Orthodoxy.[24] Were it not so, it would be possible to

---

[24] This is not to argue that Puritanism was essentially a monolithic theological movement. As said above, it is easier to give examples of Puritans than to find a core definition of Puritanism, and the existence of such heterodox 'Puritans' as John Milton is a clear indication that the category cannot be simplistically reduced to certain theological beliefs. In this work, however, I will use the term Puritan and its cognates as equivalent to 'English Reformed'.

drive a distinct wedge between the kind of theological work being conducted by the Puritans and that being done by the continental Reformed, but all of the evidence points in the opposite direction.[25]

Of particular importance was the intellectual traffic between England and the continent, particularly Holland. From the early days of the sixteenth century, the constant uncertainty about which direction ecclesiastical policy would take in England had meant that there was an almost constant stream of exiles passing back and forth between England and the continent, helping to import new ideas into English theological life. The presence of significant theologians such as Martin Bucer and Peter Martyr at Cambridge and Oxford respectively had also reinforced continental influences.[26] Then, during the various persecutions of Puritans that took place during the latter part of the sixteenth and the first half of the seventeenth centuries, many English divines found themselves again forced into exile on the continent, with such influential intellectual leaders as William Ames fleeing to Holland as the most accessible and safe haven for those of

---

[25] Contrast this with the view of E. F. Kevan, standing in the tradition of the arguments of M. M. Knappen, that '[t]he theology of Puritanism was essentially British', *The Grace of Law*, p. 42. While it is true that Britain produced a significant number of Reformed theologians, their work was full of positive citations from continental sources, was framed in dialogue with continental thinkers, and was widely and appreciatively read by continental authors. It is true that Puritanism was not the first English movement for ecclesiastical reform, and that such can be traced well back into the Middle Ages, but this scarcely allows us to claim it, as does Kevan, as part of a positive, continuous and peculiarly British, doctrinal tradition. First, movements for reform were scarcely unique to Britain, and, more importantly, the historian must be able to document the connection by showing specific textual, or conceptual, dependence. In fact, there is at times something almost tragicomical about attempts to find some kind of definite point of influence between the theology of English Protestants and English medieval reform movements. For example, D. D. Smeeton has written an entire book based upon a speculative and entirely undocumentable connection between the theology of the Lollards and that of William Tyndale. Such a connection *may* exist, but it simply cannot be proved on the basis of empirical evidence in the way that, say, Tyndale's use of Luther can, especially when many of the allegedly distinctive 'Lollard' themes are present in works of Augustine, Erasmus and others, Tyndale's knowledge of which can be easily documented: see his *Lollard Themes in the Reformation Theology of William Tyndale* (Kirksville: Sixteenth Century Journal Publishers, 1986).

[26] See Carl R. Trueman, *Luther's Legacy: Salvation and English Reformers, 1525–1556* (Oxford: Clarendon Press, 1994), *passim*.

Reformed convictions.[27] In the years of Laud's ascendancy the more liberal Dutch presses also provided English theologians with the means to disseminate their views.[28] The relationship which this encouraged between intellectual life in Holland and that in England led to a significant interchange of ideas. One needs only to look at the number of English books translated into Dutch to see the size of the Dutch appetite for English works, particularly those dealing with theology.[29] Indeed, theological works account for 75–80% of all such translations, most, though not all, of which can be broadly categorized as being of English Reformed works by authors such as Perkins, Baxter, etc.[30] It is surely not insignificant that, according to Cornelis Schoneveld, the tradition of Dutch translations of English books was started 'almost single-handedly' by the writings of William Perkins.[31] Dutch theologians were also open, albeit sometimes slightly grudgingly, in their praise of the work of their English Reformed counterparts.[32]

The 'intertraffic of the mind' was not, however, all one-way: contemporary continental thought also provided a significant source for English Reformed theologians. A glance at the libraries of Baxter and Owen reveals that they had significant numbers of continental books upon their shelves, and this is reflected by

---

[27] On Ames, see K. L. Sprunger, *The Learned Doctor William Ames: Dutch Backgrounds of English and American Puritanism* (Chicago: University of Illinois, 1972).

[28] For example, William Twisse, later prolocutor of the Westminster Assembly, had his *Vindiciae Gratiae, Potestatis, ac Providentiae Dei*, one of the most extensive Puritan treatments of its theme, printed by Johannes Jansonius at Amsterdam in 1632. For a comprehensive study of the English Puritans' use of Dutch presses, see K. L. Sprunger, *Trumpets from the Tower: English Puritan Printing in the Netherlands 1600–1640* (Leiden: Brill, 1994).

[29] On the interchange of ideas between England and Holland in the seventeenth century, see Cornelis W. Schoneveld, *Intertraffic of the Mind: Studies in Seventeenth-Century Anglo-Dutch Translation with a Checklist of Books Translated from English into Dutch, 1600–1700* (Leiden: Brill, 1983); also K. L. Sprunger, *Dutch Puritanism: A History of English and Scottish Churches of the Netherlands in the Sixteenth and Seventeenth Centuries* (Leiden: Brill, 1982).

[30] Schoneveld, pp. 121–4, 167–257. Latitudinarian authors, such as Lancelot Andrewes and John Tillotson, are also well represented.

[31] Ibid., p. 124.

[32] Ibid., p. 123, where he mentions Wittewrongel, Oomius, Ridderus (apparently no natural Anglophile), Voetius, and Koelman.

the numbers of citations of such authors in their writings.[33] English theologians also frequently chose continental theologians as their specific opponents in various polemics: for example, Perkins and Twisse with Arminius; Owen with Grotius and various Dutch Arminians, to name but a few. In this way, continental developments helped give specific shape to English Reformed theology. Furthermore, the nature of international politics at the time led to significant English involvement in the Synod of Dordt which culminated in one of the classic statements of Reformed Orthodoxy.[34] The Synod itself then appears to have acted as something of a catalyst in English theology, stimulating the bringing into the open of doctrinal tensions that had simmered just below the surface.[35]

The Canons of Dordt themselves provide a convenient way to assess the fundamental compatibility of English Reformed thought with continental Orthodoxy during the early part of the seventeenth century. A comparison of the Canons (1619) with Ussher's Irish Articles (1615) and the Westminster Confession

---

[33] For Baxter's library, see G. F. Nuttall, 'A Transcript of Richard Baxter's Library Catalogue: A Bibliographical Note', *JEH* 2 (1951), 207–21; 'A Transcript of Richard Baxter's Library Catalogue (Concluded)', *JEH* 3 (1952), 74–100. For Owen's library, see the auction catalogue of his books, a source which has apparently not been used in previous studies of Owen: *Bibliotheca Oweniana* (London, 1684). Nothing better serves to indicate the massive gulf that exists between the intellectual approach of divines such as Owen and Baxter and the attitude of those modern fundamentalists who frequently cite them as spiritual ancestors than a brief glance at their libraries. The former men were not by any account obscurantists: they were conversant not only with contemporary theology in all its forms, Reformed, Lutheran, Catholic, and heretical, but also with modern, medieval and classical philosophy, and with medieval and patristic thought.

[34] On English involvement at Dordt, see J. Platt, 'Eirenical Anglicans at the Synod of Dordt' in D. Baker (ed), *Reform and Reformation: England and the Continent c.1500–c.1750* (Oxford: Blackwell, 1979), pp. 221–43; N. Tyacke, *Anti-Calvinists: The Rise of English Arminianism c. 1590–1640* (Oxford: Clarendon Press, 1987), pp. 87–105; P. White, *Predestination, Policy and Polemic: Conflict and Consensus in the English Church from the Reformation to the Civil War* (Cambridge: CUP, 1992). For the Latin text of the Canons of Dordt, along with English translation, see P. Schaff (ed.), *The Creeds of Christendom* 3 (Grand Rapids: Baker, 1983), pp. 550–97.

[35] Tyacke, p. 87, 101–5. On tensions over predestination within the Anglican hierarchy from the mid-sixteenth century, see Trueman, *Luther's Legacy*, passim; White, pp. 39–59.

(1647) reveals fundamental agreement on each of the famous 'five points', although the two confessional documents inevitably cover far more theological ground than the more narrowly polemical Canons.[36] The Irish Articles themselves provide an important part of the background to the work of the Westminster Assembly, which had a specifically international reference in its brief. While the Thirty-nine Articles were open to a Reformed interpretation, in practice they had proved somewhat more open to alternative interpretations than many were happy to allow, and so Parliament had convened the Westminster Assembly in order to make the Church of England into a more thoroughly Reformed body and bring it doctrinally closer to its counterparts in Scotland and on the continent. While the delegates were drawn exclusively from English and Scottish divines, the intention was to make a church which reflected the international Reformed consensus. In this, it was, on paper at least, largely successful.[37]

The significance for Owen of the Westminster Confession, and of the international theology which it embodied, can scarcely be overestimated. Owen was not himself one of the delegates, and, while initially Presbyterian on matters of church polity, he became an Independent through reading the works of John Cotton.[38] Nevertheless, his substantial agreement with the

---

[36] For the text of the Irish Articles, see Schaff, pp. 526–544.

[37] While the Dutch did not play a formal role in proceedings at Westminster, their views were earnestly sought after by the delegates, particularly in the debates about church government. This is a clear sign that the Westminster assembly in no way considered its theological deliberations to be *sui generis* and isolated from continental movements: see Sprunger, *Dutch Puritanism*, pp. 364–8. The Canons of Dordt were, of course, subject to a variety of interpretations in England, with such apparently different theologians as William Twisse and Richard Baxter both claiming to represent their authentic teaching.

[38] Toon, *God's Statesman*, p. 27. There seems to be some evidence to suggest that Owen may have returned to his Presbyterian convictions shortly before his death, based on statements in the *Inquiry into Evangelical Churches* (1681) and the posthumously published *True Nature of a Gospel Church* (1689). The evidence is outlined in *Works* 16, p. 2, and the editor's cautious comments to the effect that Owen's view differed on points from both classical Independency and Presbyterianism, but that his views fit more naturally into the Independent camp would appear to be sound. The validity and authority of supra-local bodies such as synods in particular circumstances was something which only the most radical of Independents would deny: see, for example, the section of the Savoy Declaration entitled 'Of the Institution of Churches, and the Order

Westminster Confession is clear from the Savoy Declaration of 1658, for the drafting of which he was largely responsible.[39] Intended as the Independents, equivalent to the Westminster Confession, it follows the latter almost verbatim, except for a number of relatively minor additions and a thorough revision of the section on ecclesiology. In the more strictly theological areas, the two documents are in full agreement.

Owen, then, can be located within this developing tradition of European Reformed Orthodoxy that included Dordt and Westminster, and which represented an international Reformed theological consensus. Indeed, as will become clear, his theology reflects the broad parameters and concerns of the Reformed tradition: a high view of Scripture as the epistemological basis of theology; an understanding of salvation rooted in the divine covenants; an historical economy of salvation focused on the person and work of the Lord Jesus Christ; and a basic concern to bring out the Trinitarian nature of God's creative and saving activity. In all of these areas, Owen's thinking is, in the broadest sense, not original but rooted in a tradition which extends back to, and developed out of, the Reformed theology of the middle decades of the sixteenth century.[40]

Nevertheless, while Owen's theology can be seen as standing in such a tradition, it would be wrong to posit a simple, static connection between the theology of 1550s and that of the 1650s. While Reformed theology did not undergo significant development in terms of its broad scriptural and Trinitarian concerns during this time, it did experience considerable formal and meth-

---

Footnote 38 (*continued*) Appointed in them by Jesus Christ', sect. 26 in Schaff 3, p. 728, where synods are permitted in situations where this would be helpful to a church in difficulty. While the Declaration explicitly denies that these synods have any ecclesiastical power in the proper sense of the word, it does nevertheless provide a picture of Independency which is somewhat different from the caricatures presented in popular Presbyterian polemic.

[39] The other guiding hands behind the Declaration were Thomas Goodwin, Philip Nye, Joseph Caryl, William Greenhill, and William Bridge, all of whom had been delegates at the Westminster Assembly.

[40] For a discussion of the development of Reformed theology from the Reformation to the end of the sixteenth-century which focuses particularly on Christological and Trinitarian themes, see Muller, *Christ and the Decree*.

odological change as it sought to meet the changing polemical and pedagogical needs of the church. Indeed, Owen's theological career, running as it does from *c.* 1640 to 1683, covers much of the period which Richard Muller has called 'High Orthodoxy', and which witnessed 'the full and final development of Protestant system prior to the great changes in philosophical and scientific perspective that would, in the eighteenth and nineteenth centuries, utterly recast theological system into new forms'.[41]

Muller characterizes this period of High Orthodoxy as a time when the inherited systems of earlier Reformed thought were elaborated both in terms of an increasing precision with regard to theological language and doctrinal distinctions, and in terms of the need to engage polemically with a new host of opponents. The creative days of Reformed theology were over; the task now in hand was one of elaboration, consolidation, and defence; and controversies were no longer confined to the old Catholic and Lutheran chestnuts, but involved new opponents, such as the Arminians and the Socinians, who were, in many ways, superficially much closer to the Reformed camp in terms of stated presuppositions and who were consequently that much more dangerous.[42] Such a broad picture fits Owen perfectly: his theology was, more often than not, developed in the heat of controversy, and it is to this polemical context that one must turn if a clear understanding of his work is to be gained.

The Polemical Context

Owen's theological opponents can be grouped into three broad categories: Papists, Arminians, and Socinians. Of these three, the Papists were the least important to Owen and took up proportionately less of his time. His library, and the citations sprinkled throughout his writings, indicate that he was well-acquainted with Catholic theology, in terms both of its past history and its

---

[41] *PRRD2*, pp. 37–8.
[42] *PRRD1*, pp. 36–7.

contemporary controversial literature.[43] Indeed, as we shall see, Owen is able to use Catholic theology positively when it suits his purpose without this overturning the Reformed or Protestant nature of what he is saying. While he does allow that Catholic thought has some positive contribution to make, however, his attitude to the Catholic Church as an institution is completely negative. His major statements on the Roman Church can be found in three treatises: *Animadversions on a Treatise Entitled 'Fiat Lux'* (1662); *A Vindication of the Animadversions on 'Fiat Lux'* (1664); and *The Church of Rome No Safe Guide* (1679).[44] In all three, he sees the ultimate point at issue between Catholicism and Protestantism as one of authority: is authority grounded in

---

[43] Owen was particularly interested in the conflict between Molinists and Jansenists over the nature of grace, and planned to write a book surveying all the relevant literature, as the following statement in *Vindiciae Evangelicae* (Works 12, p. 560) makes clear: 'As I have in the preface to this discourse given an account of the rise and present state of Socinianism, so I thought in this place to have given the reader an account of the present state of the controversy about grace and free-will, and the death of Christ, with especial reference to the late management thereof amongst the Romanists, between the Molinists and Jesuits on the one side, and the Jansenians or Bayans on the other, with the late ecclesiastical and political transactions in Italy, France, and Flanders, in reference thereunto, with an account of the books lately written on the one side and the other, and my thoughts of them; but finding this treatise grown utterly beyond my intention, I shall defer the execution of that design to some other opportunity, if God think good to continue my portion any longer in the land of the living.' He never did this, although he did write a 'Preface' to TG's *The True Idea of Jansenisme* (London, 1669), which contains the following statements (pp. 18–20) which shed interesting light on Owen's view of Catholic theology, particularly that of Thomas and the Dominican Order: 'The system of Doctrines concerning the Grace of God, and the wills of men, which now goes under the name of *Jansenisme*, as it is in general agreeable unto the Scripture; so it had firmed it self in the common profession of Christian, by the Writings of some excellent persons, especially *Augustin*, and those who followed him, unto such a general acceptation, as that the belief and profession of it could never be utterly rooted out from the minds of men in the *Roman* Church itself . . . Moreover, one whole Order of their Fryers, out of zeal for the Doctrine of *Thomas*, (who was less averse from the sentiments of the Antients in this matter, than the most of that litigious crew of Disputers, whom they call Schoolmen;) did retain some of the most material Principles of this Doctrine, however not a little vitiated with various intermixtures of their own. Not a full Age since, as will appear in the ensuing account, after the lesser attempts of some more private persons, *Jansenius*, a Bishop in *Flanders*, undertakes the explication and the vindication of the whole doctrine of the Effectual Grace of God, with the annexed Articles principally out of the works of *Austin*.'

[44] All three treatises can be found in *Works* 14.

the teaching office of the church, or in the internal witness of the Holy Spirit to the truth of Scripture? For Owen, the two are mutually exclusive, and Catholicism's choice of the former is the basic foundation for all her subsequent errors. In this, his views are typical of the Puritans of his day.[45]

While Owen was utterly opposed to papal Catholicism, it was not his most important polemical target. Of far more concern to him were the doctrines of the Arminians and Socinians, and he devoted considerably more space to attacking their doctrines than to his disagreements with Rome. There are good historical reasons for this. In the years during and after the Civil War, it was radical Protestant theology, not the Roman Church, which posed the greatest immediate threat to the theological and political stability of England. Compared to some of the wild groups which flourished during this time, such as the Seekers and the Ranters, Arminians and Socinians might seem to the twentieth-century mind to be comparatively orthodox; but to Owen they denied some of the basic tenets of the faith and were thus to be regarded as deadly heretics. Indeed, Arminians and Socinians, by their very approximation to the Orthodox in terms of their emphasis upon the Scripture principle – the use by the Reformed of Scripture as the sole cognitive foundation for theology – and the frequent sophistication of their arguments, were a proportionately greater threat to Reformed theology than those radical sects which rejected outright the basic presuppositions of Orthodoxy in favour of the 'inner light' or whatever. Thus, while England in the mid-seventeenth century was a breeding ground for the weird and wonderful in terms of religion, the more extreme sects are scarcely mentioned by Owen; for him the real threat comes from the Arminians and the Socinians.[46]

---

[45] E.g. William Twisse, *The Scriptures Sufficiency* (London, 1656), p. 7; J. Ussher, *A Body of Divinitie* (London, 1653), pp. 20 ff.; Richard Baxter, *Catholick Theologie* (London, 1675), Preface p. 22 (no pagination in original).

[46] Knowledge of the teachings of radical religion in seventeenth-century England is hampered by a lack of documentary evidence. How many sects there were who wrote no books we shall never know. Nevertheless, the magisterial works of Keith Thomas and Christopher Hill have provided a wealth of fascinating insights into this area: see K. Thomas, *Religion and the Decline of Magic* (New York: Scribners, 1971); C. Hill, *The World Turned Upside Down* (London: Pelican, 1975). Hill has also attempted to

Owen's writings are full of allusions to, and direct quotations from, Arminian and Socinian works, and his library catalogue shows that he had a considerable number of such writings on his shelves. In addition to the continental authors, such as Episcopius and Vorstius, he also engaged specifically with domestic manifestations of Arminianism, particularly the writings of John Goodwin, whose *Redemption Redeemed* (1651) provided Owen with an opportunity to explicate his view of perseverance in great detail.[47] The problems raised by Arminianism focused upon the relationship between God and creation, pushing to the forefront of discussion issues such as the relationship between the persons of the Trinity, the role of Christ in predestination, and the nature of God's foreknowledge.[48] On each of these issues, Owen saw the Reformed faith as under threat from the Arminians, both in terms of the direct contradiction between Reformed and Arminian views, and in terms of the wider systematic implications of the Arminian modifications for Orthodox theology as a whole.

On the Socinian side, Owen's library catalogue, and the references in his writings, show that he was clearly aware of the major continental writings both for and against Socinianism. As in his battle with Arminianism, when he came to address Socinianism, specifically in his massive *Vindiciae Evangelicae* (1655), he again chose to focus most of his energy on a domestic opponent, John Biddle, whose *Twofold Catechism* had been published in 1654.[49]

Footnote 46 (*continued*) show the influence of radicals upon such individuals as the essentially orthodox Bunyan and the more free-spirited Milton: see *A Turbulent, Seditious, and Factious People* (Oxford: OUP, 1988); *Milton and the English Revolution* (New York: Viking, 1978). Thomas's work should be read in conjunction with the moderate critique of some of his central theses in L. Godbeer, *The Devil's Dominion: Magic and Religion in Early New England* (Cambridge: CUP, 1992).

[47] John Goodwin (*c.*1594–1665), a graduate of Queens', Cambridge, was a militant Republican and Parliamentarian as well as a theologian whose Arminian writings constantly brought him under suspicion of Socinianism. Even by the high standards of his time he appears to have been an exceptionally controversial character, and Edmund Calamy declared that he 'was a man by himself, was against every man, and had every man against him'. For Owen's refutation of *Redemption Redeemed*, see his *The Doctrine of the Saints' Perseverance Explained and Confirmed* (1654) in *Works* 11.

[48] On these issues, see Muller, *Arminius*.

[49] On John Biddle, the so-called 'father of English Unitarianism', see H. J. McLachlan, *Socinianism in Seventeenth-Century England* (Oxford: OUP, 1951), pp. 163–217. For Owen's *Vindiciae Evangelicae, see Works* 12.

This is in part due no doubt to the fact that he was undertaking this project at the request of Parliament which was then concerned with the growth of this heresy in England. Nevertheless, perhaps because of the lack of sophistication in Biddle's work (it was little more than a catechism of questions with brief comments and relevant biblical proof texts written in answer), Owen also dealt extensively in this work with the *Racovian Catechism*, which was the major confessional writing of the Socinians at that time, and which provided him with a more sophisticated level of argument with which to engage.

In Owen's mind, Socinianism and Arminianism were intimately related. This arose from the fact that he understood both as arguing for doctrinal positions which granted human beings a level of autonomy and self-sufficiency which he regarded as unbiblical. In his earliest extant work, *A Display of Arminianism* (1642), he starts by listing the points upon which the Arminians deviate from the Orthodox position: in their attempts to free themselves from God's jurisdiction, they reject the unchangeableness of God's decrees, they question God's prescience, and they deny all-governing providence and the irresistibility of God's will; then, in order to clear human nature from the imputation of sin, they deny predestination, original sin, the original perfection of Adam, and the efficacy of Christ's death, while asserting free will and the active role of that will in salvation.[50] Those who have read any Arminian writings of the period will realize that Owen's case is somewhat overstated and overgeneralized, but the passage nevertheless gives a clear picture of the areas of doctrine which he felt were important and necessary to defend. Two concerns are obvious: the logical, causal priority, and unchangeableness, of the divine plan to save; and the efficacy of Christ's work in the historical execution of this plan. These are the two poles around which Owen's response to the Arminians and Socinians is constructed, and it is the Arminian rejection of the Orthodox position on these issues which renders its teachings so unacceptable to Owen and so close in his mind to those of Socinus and his followers.

---

[50] *Works* 10, pp. 12–14.

Underlying these two concerns in his debates with his opponents is the fact that, for Owen, both the divine plan of salvation and Christ's work in accomplishing that salvation rest ultimately upon a thoroughgoing Trinitarianism. The Trinity does not have the status of an optional extra in his theology, but represents the necessary ontological framework of his entire soteriology. This is why he regards Socinianism, with its basic denial of orthodox Trinitarianism as such a pernicious heresy: to reject the Trinity involves the wholesale rejection of Christian theology. Furthermore, it also points to another reason for the close link in Owen's mind between Arminianism and Socinianism: it was easy to see in the modifications of Trinitarian perspectives required by Arminian soteriology a decisive move towards the anti-Trinitarianism of the *Racovian Catechism*, John Biddle and co.[51]

In conflict with the Arminians and the Socinians, we shall find that Owen is forced again and again to reflect upon his Reformed heritage and both to work out the implications of the innovative heretical teaching for Orthodoxy and to elaborate thereby in more explicit detail the presuppositions of his own soteriology. In such a context, it is not only unreasonable to expect his doctrinal formulations and statements to mimic those of an earlier generation, it is also totally unhistorical. The inadequacy of the earlier codifications in themselves to deal with these issues is obvious from the very fact that such doctrinal deviations as Arminianism and Socinianism gained significant followings. The questions they raised about the principles of scriptural interpretation, the nature of God, and the content of salvation drove the Orthodox to greater levels of precision in their explication of Reformed doctrine in order to defend the tradition, and Owen was no exception to this general tendency.

While Arminianism and Socinianism provided the major targets of Owen's theological work, theirs were not the only views

---

[51]   See Ch. 3. There are, of course, also good historical reasons for linking the two, as many Arminian theologians were regarded as crypto-Socinians. A good discussion of the controversies surrounding the Remonstrants can be found in J. Platt, *Reformed Thought and Scholasticism: The Arguments for the Existence of God in Dutch Theology, 1575–1650* (Leiden: Brill, 1982).

with which he engaged and which helped to shape his thought. English Reformed theology too had its own specific emphases, against some of which Owen reacted, although in a somewhat less violent fashion than his responses to his more obviously heretical contemporaries. Preeminent among Owen's more orthodox domestic opponents was Richard Baxter, a theologian whose thought is so eclectic and so individual that he defies classification.[52] Owen's primary engagement with Baxter was over the extent and intent of the death of Christ, and on the nature of justification. It was Baxter who first took the field against Owen, attacking the latter's *Death of Death in the Death of Christ* (1647) in his *Aphorismes of Justification* (1649).[53] While Baxter was a year older than Owen, he was at this point by far the junior man in terms of reputation, and later apparently regretted the personal note in his attack.[54] After the Restoration, there was a certain amount of *rapprochement* between the two

---

[52] It is worth qualifying this by noting Nuttall's observation that, while Baxter was *sui generis* in his own day, his thought did enjoy some popularity among non-conformists in the eighteenth century: see G. F. Nuttall, *Richard Baxter and Philip Doddridge: A Study in Tradition* (London: OUP, 1951). On Baxter's theology, see Packer, 'The Redemption and Restoration of Man in the Thought of Richard Baxter'; Clifford, *Atonement and Justification*; G. J. McGrath, 'Puritans and the Human Will: Voluntarism within Mid-Seventeenth Century English Puritanism As Seen in the Thought of Richard Baxter and John Owen', unpubl. PhD diss. (Durham University, 1989) ; Boersma, *A Hot Peppercorn*; Carl R. Trueman, 'A Small Step Towards Rationalism: The Impact of the Metaphysics of Tommaso Campanella on the Theology of Richard Baxter', in Trueman and R. S. Clark (eds.), *Protestant Scholasticism: Essays in Reassessment* (Carlisle: Paternoster, 1997). Three earlier studies still worth consulting are G. P. Fisher, 'The Theology of Richard Baxter' and 'The Writings of Richard Baxter', *BSABR* 9 (1852), 135–69 and 300–29 respectively; and the anonymous 'Richard Baxter's "End of Controversy"', *BSABR* 12 (1855), 348–85.

[53] For Baxter's specific attack on Owen on the issue of atonement and its relationship to justification, see *Aphorismes: Appendix*, pp. 137 ff.

[54] 'I was young, and a stranger to Mens tempers, and thought others could have born(e) a Confutation as easily as I could do myself; and I thought I was bound to do my best publickly to save the World from the hurt of published Errors, not understanding how it would provoke men more passionately to insist on what they once have said. But I have now learned to contradict Errors, and not to meddle with the Persons that maintain them. But indeed I was then too raw to be a Writer.' *Reliquiae Baxterianae* 1, p. 107, quoted in F. J. Powicke, *A Life of the Reverend Richard Baxter 1615–1691* (New York: Hought Mifflin Co., n.d.), p. 239. Powicke's biography is a standard work, but for a more recent life, see Nuttall, *Richard Baxter*.

men, but their relationship never appears to have been particularly warm.[55]

On atonement and justification, Owen regarded Baxter's views as approaching those of the Arminians and thus as open to similar strictures. Nevertheless, the breathtaking learning of the self-taught Baxter with his seemingly encyclopedic knowledge of medieval theology and his penetrating philosophical acumen, combined with his apparently limitless appetite for polemical disputation, made him an especially significant opponent. The clashes between Owen and Baxter reveal the depth and sophistication of English Reformed theology in the seventeenth century, and the extent to which its protagonists, particularly Baxter, drew upon the language and structures of medieval Scholasticism. Indeed, any attempt to drive a wedge between Owen and Baxter by arguing that the former is scholastic while the latter is not, or that the former is more scholastic than the latter, cannot stand up to scrutiny.[56] If Scholasticism is a method, then both have clear scholastic tendencies and, as the writer of the *Methodus Theologiae* (1681), the English Puritan work which bears the closest resemblance to medieval scholastic antecedents – an intricate, subtle, and comprehensive system of theology which makes extensive use of scholastic categories and language – Baxter is without doubt the more scholastic of the two! His reputation for warm piety reflects the fact that his devotional works were to enjoy extensive reprintings after his death, while his doctrinal works, upon which he himself wished his reputation to rest, were never very popular.[57] In his doctrinal works, par-

---

[55]   There is some surviving correspondence between the two men, dated January/February 1669, over the possibilities of increased concord between Independents and Presbyterians. The letters give an interesting insight into the differences between the two men, with, among other things, Owen arguing for a tighter doctrinal basis which would explicitly exclude the Socinians, and Baxter maintaining that the Scriptures and Apostles' Creed, 'this old sufficient Catholick Rule', should be enough. The letters are reproduced in *The Correspondence of John Owen* (Cambridge: James Clarke, 1970), pp. 136–45; and summarized in the *Calendar of the Correspondence of Richard Baxter* (Oxford: Clarendon Press, 1991), nos. 769 and 771.

[56]   *Pace* Clifford, *Atonement and Justification, passim.*

[57]   As Fisher so eloquently expressed it ('The Theology of Richard Baxter', 135–6), '[I]t is not as a theologian that Baxter is chiefly known. He is least indebted for his reputation to those works on which he most relied for fame. The volumes which are

ticularly the *Catholick Theologie* and the *Methodus Theologiae*, the reader encounters discussion of the most rarefied and precise doctrinal distinctions, such as that between *solutio eiusdem* and *solutio tantidem* which forms a key part of his debate. In light of claims about the necessarily deleterious effects of Scholasticism and Aristotelianism on Owen's theology, and attempts to separate the two men on this issue,[58] it is worth noting at the start, however, that the appropriateness of using scholastic method or of Aristotelian causality and logic within the theological task is never a point at issue between Owen and Baxter; indeed, it could not possibly be otherwise, as both men used these within their theology. Their arguments are rather over the content of the theology which these tools, of which both men self-evidently approved, were used to express.[59]

While Baxter represented tendencies within English Reformed theology which pointed in an Arminian direction,[60] there were

---

Footnote 57 (*continued*) the fruits of his most severe toil and were written "chiefly for posterity," repose, in dust and silence on the shelves of antiquaries; while the "Call to the Unconverted" and the "Saint's Rest" are found with the Pilgrim of Bunyan, wherever our language is spoken.' Nuttall (*Richard Baxter and Philip Doddridge*, pp. 17–18) cites Doddridge, one of those who held Baxter's theology in high esteem, as considering the *Methodus* to be 'unintelligible'. As one might expect, the devotional works too are marked by the impact of Aristotelian language and Scholasticism, pointing to the fact that piety and Scholasticism are not mutually exclusive categories. See, for example, his definition of 'rest' in *The Saint's Everlasting Rest* as 'the end and perfection of motion', Baxter, *Practical Works* 3 (London, 1707), p. 10.

[58] See Clifford, *Atonement and Justification*.

[59] Clifford, *Atonement and Justification*, p. 98, quotes Baxter to the effect that 'They that are so confident that Aristotle is in hell, should not too much take him for their guide in the way to heaven', *The Reformed Pastor* (Edinburgh: Banner of Truth, 1974), p. 120. Read in context, the passage is not advocating the rejection of Aristotle and philosophy in theology, and certainly not explicitly attacking Owen, but stressing that it must keep within the bounds determined by faith: 'philosophy must be taught to stoop and serve, while faith doth bear the chief sway.' *Ibid.* With such a statement, Owen would have no disagreement; the problem arises in determining where these bounds are. As we shall see, it is arguable that philosophy is subject to more explicit restrictions in the theology of Owen than in that of Baxter, particularly in light of Baxter's break with the Reformed tradition on the relationship of the Trinity to metaphysics: see Chs. 2 and 3 below; for a more detailed discussion of this problem in Baxter, see Trueman, 'A Small Step Towards Rationalism'.

[60] I am not, of course, arguing that Baxter was an Arminian, but merely indicating that there are tendencies in his thought which point in this direction. As Boersma argues, his theology is too complex and eclectic for simple categorization: see *A Hot Peppercorn*, pp. 25–33.

tendencies even within the most orthodox of the Orthodox which Owen also found himself having to oppose. As in his conflicts with Baxter, the most obvious points of conflict were on the issues of atonement and justification. On the former, Owen came to reject the view, common among the Orthodox, that Christ's death was necessary to salvation only because God had decreed that it be so.[61] Among the Orthodox, the two men he chose to single out for criticism on this issue were William Twisse and Samuel Rutherford.

On the matter of justification, English Reformed thought had developed a certain emphasis that seems to be confined to English and Dutch speaking traditions, that of eternal justification. Indeed, the whole idea of 'eternal justification' does not seem to be reflected in the broader Continental tradition of Reformed Orthodoxy at all. Eternal justification was the idea that the elect were not only elected in eternity, but were also justified in eternity. While the doctrine is generally associated with the so-called Antinomians, such as Tobias Crisp, it also found support among the more traditional Orthodox, such as Thomas Goodwin.[62] On such a view, faith became the realization of one's prior justification, the acknowledgement of one's eternal status before God, and not in any way, constitutive or otherwise, a part of that justification. While the issue of justification is not of immediate relevance to this study, it does provide a significant part of the theological context of Owen's discussion of the atonement in his debates with Richard Baxter.[63]

Such, then, was the contemporary intellectual context of Owen's work: on the positive side, the tradition of Reformed Orthodoxy which sought to restate and clarify the doctrinal gains of the Reformation; on the negative side, the assaults of Arminianism, Socinianism, and the development of unbalanced emphases within Reformed Orthodoxy itself. Anyone who reads Owen's writings, however, will soon become aware that his

---

[61] For discussion of this, see Ch. 3 below.
[62] See Tobias Crisp, *Christ Alone Exalted*, ed. J. Gill, 2 vols. (London: John Bennett, 1832); Thomas Goodwin, *Of Justifying Faith* in *The Works of Thomas Goodwin*, 12 vols. (Eureka: Tanski Publications, 1996), 8.
[63] For a fuller discussion of the issues involved, see Ch. 5 below.

theology cannot simply be understood in terms of contemporary conflicts and concerns, for Owen is self-consciously striving to be a catholic theologian in the full and proper sense of the term. Like his Reformer predecessors, he does not see his work as innovating, as presenting new discoveries to the world, but as drawing upon the theological legacy of the past in order to present contemporary formulations of true Christian doctrine.

Owen and the Western Tradition

Patristic, Medieval and Renaissance roots

As examination of Owen's writings will show, his thought represents in many ways the attempt of a seventeenth-century theologian to work out the implications of Reformed theology in terms set by the classic Trinitarian and Christological formulations of the early church. For example, throughout his work the notion of the unity of the three persons plays a key role in his understanding of revelation, creation, and redemption. It will also become clear that the specifically Western notion of the dual procession of the Spirit is, among other things, central to Owen's arguments for the unity of the economy of salvation, his view of the relationship between Christ's two natures, and to his understanding of the importance of Scripture as the medium for knowledge of God. In light of the importance of such basic patristic doctrinal formulations in Owen's theology, it should be no surprise that his library contained very many patristic tomes, and that his writings are littered with allusions to, and quotations from, such luminaries of the early church as Augustine, Hilary, Athanasius and others. Indeed, his theology is constructed with self-conscious reference to the catholic patristic tradition.

The catholic nature of Owen's theology can be seen quite clearly from the letter which he wrote to Baxter in 1668/9 concerning the latter's basis for a proposed concord between Independents and Presbyterians during the Restoration. In response to Baxter's notion that the Scriptures and the Apostles' Creed would be adequate as a doctrinal basis, Owen argues that the first four ecumenical councils should also be included in order to make it impossible for Socinians to slip through the net.[64] The implication is obvious: the Scriptures, interpreted within the framework of Nicene orthodoxy, should provide a sufficient safeguard against error. This should not be taken to imply that the Creeds have any ultimate normative authority for Owen. It is only because he regards them as faithfully reflecting the position of the Scriptures themselves that they have any role to play. Nevertheless, in the light of Socinian claims to reject the Trinity etc. on the basis of *sola scriptura*, the Creeds are useful as a practical test of orthodoxy. It is quite clear from this that Owen was not so naive as to hold to the view that theology as a discipline could be pursued simply in terms of the reader, with an empty mind, engaging with the bare text of Scripture and thus somehow automatically imbibing pure doctrine. That was the professed approach of the Socinians, and the results were neither catholic nor orthodox. Owen's position is far more subtle: what lies behind his argument at this point is his understanding that a critical relationship exists between the great human formulations of the faith and the words of Scripture. While the latter are the ultimate norm for theology, the former are useful in providing a working doctrinal framework within which the theological task of scriptural interpretation can take place, although not in such a way that Scripture is ultimately subordinated to the Creeds. The Creeds act as heuristic devices which facilitate the unlocking of Scripture's teaching. The result is that Owen's theology, far from being a radical break with the earlier tradition is rather a critical appropriation of that tradition for contemporary needs.

While this adherence to early catholic orthodoxy will surprise no one familiar with the Reformers' claims to be restoring the church to its early doctrinal purity rather than bringing in innovative new doctrines, what may surprise some is the more positive attitude which Owen has to medieval theologians than is apparent in the writings of Calvin and many of the early Reformed writers. While Owen's specific use of medieval theology will be

---

[64] *Correspondence*, p. 137; *Calendar of the Correspondence of Richard Baxter*, nos. 769 and 771. The exchange also gives an interesting insight into the different approaches of the two men, with Owen being the more narrowly doctrinal.

discussed at greater length where relevant in future chapters, it is worthwhile making a few preliminary comments on this issue. The first thing to note is that Owen's use of scholastic theologians is typical of the time, and reflects not only a general characteristic of the Reformed Orthodox but also, and more specifically, the growth in interest in scholastic theology which was evident in England from the latter part of the sixteenth century.[65] To describe a theology as 'scholastic' is, of course, to make a descriptive statement about its structure and methodology, not a value judgment about its content, a fact known by Catholic writers for many years but which has only recently started to find acceptance among Protestant scholars.[66] Indeed, for many Protestant scholars, the word 'scholastic' is a profoundly pejorative term, implying an overly-rationalistic and disputatious approach to theology.[67] In fact, the word and its cognates had a double meaning for seventeenth-century Reformed thinkers. On the one hand, the words could be used in just the negative way in which many modern scholars use it; thus, Samuel Rutherford refers to 'needle-headed schoole-men'.[68] On the other hand, the word was also used as a value-neutral descriptive term referring to a particular way of approaching a theological topic; thus, the same Samuel Rutherford is quite happy to write a work with the title *Disputatio Scholastica de Providentia*.[69] The word therefore pos-

---

[65] On the growth in interest in Scholasticism, and its role in reinforcing the scholastic nature of the university curriculum, see W. T. Costello, *The Scholastic Curriculum at Seventeenth Century Cambridge* (Cambridge: Harvard UP, 1958).

[66] Cf. J. A. Weisheipl 'Scholastic Method', *NCE* 12, 1145–6, and W. H. Crilly, 'Scholastic Philosophy', *NCE* 12, 1146–7, with the now classic definition given by Brian Armstrong, *Calvinism and the Amyraut Heresy* (Madison: University of Wisconsin Press, 1969), pp. 30–1. For the appropriation of the Catholic insight by Protestant scholarship, see, for example, Muller, 'Calvin and the "Calvinists"', pp. 126–9.

[67] See, for example, the work of Donald McKim which speaks of Scholasticism as 'rigid' and of the Reformation as 'dynamic': 'John Owen's Doctrine of Scripture in Historical Perspective', *EQ* 45 (1973), 195–207. McKim is drawing on the work of Brian G. Armstrong, whose definition of Protestant Scholasticism now enjoys the status of a textbook definition.

[68] *Christ Dying and Drawing Sinners to Himselfe* (London, 1647), p. 2 of the introductory epistle (no page number in original).

[69] Edinburgh, 1643. On Rutherford's ambiguity, see P. G. Ryken, 'Scottish Reformed Scholasticism' in Trueman and Clark, *Protestant Scholasticism*.

sessed a certain elasticity of meaning for the seventeenth-century Reformed Orthodox which it has tended to lose in modern scholarship.

In terms of pure method, Owen's theology exhibits some distinctly scholastic traits: for example, a passion for topical subdivision, and the use of questions and objections as a way of refuting his opponents and drawing out the full implications of his theology. Nevertheless, in terms of overall structure, Owen's theology is not as scholastic as that of his great contemporary, Richard Baxter, whose massive *Methodus Theologiae* represents perhaps the greatest application of the medieval *quaestio* method to the theological task which Puritanism produced.[70] When Owen comes to make his most systematic statement of doctrine, it is a more historically focused covenant scheme which he chooses to supply the organizational principle underlying his argument, probably a sign more of the impact of federal theological schemes on his thought than of any specific medieval antecedent. In contrast, Baxter's *Methodus Theologiae* represents perhaps a more traditional scholastic pattern, moving synthetically from prolegomena to the doctrine of God and so on.[71]

Owen's use of medieval Scholasticism does not stop at the level of *quaestio* and detailed subdivision, but also incorporates extensive use of the terminology which had been developed during the Middle Ages for the precise expression of doctrine. As we shall see in later chapters, much of Owen's use of medieval writers can be referred to in this linguistic and terminological category, and does not therefore in any way represent blanket approval of the overall content of their work, or uncritical adoption of that content into his own writings. There are a number of obvious reasons why Owen borrows some of the language and conceptual argumentation of medieval Scholasticism for the articulation of Reformed theology, of which the most significant would appear to be that of relating to the polemical context within which he was working: faced with a series of heresies which raised extremely difficult questions about the structure of predestination,

---

[70] London, 1681.
[71] See Ch. 2.

the nature of the Trinity, the hypostatic union, etc., and which, in the case of the Arminians and Socinians, frequently used the language and shibboleths of the Reformers concerning, for example, *sola scriptura,* etc. in a way that actually subverted the Reformers' original intentions, Owen and his contemporaries were forced to expand their theological vocabularies in order to clarify concepts and doctrines in a manner that made such equivocal use of their traditional language by opponents increasingly difficult. A good example of this is provided by his *Dissertation of Divine Justice* (1653), in which, as we mentioned above, Owen attacks, among others, William Twisse and Samuel Rutherford for their view of the atonement's necessity. Here, Owen uses a wealth of vocabulary drawn from Catholic Scholasticism, both medieval and Renaissance, in order to make the precise, fine, and unambiguous distinctions which he needs in order to establish what is a particularly subtle point. Indeed, near the beginning he uses Suarez's definition of vindicatory justice as his point of departure. In so doing, Owen is careful to distance himself both from much of Suarez's method and from some of his conclusions, but nevertheless describes his definition as 'deservedly famous'.[72] Owen is not therefore giving unconditional approval to the Jesuit's work – far from it – but he recognizes his definition of vindicatory justice as something which can be deployed within a Reformed framework to clarify his own views on the relationship of God's absolute attributes to the created realm.

As this last example shows, the borrowing from Catholic theology, medieval and Renaissance, does not stop at the level of vocabulary. As I have argued elsewhere, the same treatise in which he borrows from Suarez also depends for its cogency upon an acceptance of the analogy of being, that foundation stone of the Thomist approach to theology.[73] Indeed, in his discussions of God, creation, and providence, we will see that time and again Owen has recourse to such sources for both the vocabulary and the metaphysical framework which he needs to defend Reformed

---

[72] *Works* 10, p. 502.

[73] See Carl R. Trueman, 'John Owen's *Dissertation on Divine Justice*: an Exercise in Christocentric Scholasticism', *CTJ*, forthcoming.

theology against the assaults of Arminians and Socinians. It comes as no surprise, then, when we find that his library catalogue contains extensive listings of Catholic authors of the Middle Ages and the Renaissance. These books were not there for curiosity value, or even simply as sources to allow Owen to build an informed case against Rome: they were also important positive resources for the articulation of his own theological convictions.

Owen's 'Aristotelianism' in context

Owen's use of medieval scholastic theology points to one other area of his thought which has been regarded as the most problematic and damaging aspect of his theology: his use of Aristotle.[74] According to popular scholarly mythology, Aristotelianism and the theology of the first and second generation Reformers are mutually exclusive, and so to the extent that later theologians rely on Aristotelian and scholastic methodologies, rather than the allegedly more humanistic and biblical approaches of the Reformers, to that extent they betray and pervert the Reformation gospel.[75] This idea has become something of a factoid,[76] and now possesses the status of a self-evident truth, rather like the principle of non-contradiction.[77]

Since the early 1960s, the work of Paul Kristeller, Charles Schmitt, and Heiko Oberman has served to debunk many of the myths surrounding Aristotelianism and Scholasticism. The findings of these scholars have been taken up, fruitfully applied, and verified by others, with the result that, since the early 1970s, with

---

[74] Clifford, *Atonement and Justification*, *passim*.

[75] Cf. the comments of Clifford, *Atonement and Justification*, p. 95 with the nuanced analysis of David Bagchi, '*Sic et non*: Luther and Scholasticism', in Trueman and Clark, *Protestant Scholasticism*.

[76] The term is, I think, derived from Norman Mailer. A factoid, he said, was a piece of nonsense repeated so often that everyone believed it.

[77] An example of this is the way in which Clifford assumes at the outset of his work that Aristotle is a bad influence on theology: 'Owen's early regard for Aristotle perhaps explains his inability to be thoroughly and exclusively scriptural.' *Atonement and Justification*, p. 98. This might be a legitimate *conclusion* for a systematic theologian, depending on the evidence, but it is scarcely a legitimate *presupposition* for a historian. Cf. James B. Torrance, 'The Incarnation and "Limited Atonement"'.

the publication of Robert Preus's two volumes on *The Theology of Post-Reformation Lutheranism*, there has been a growing body of scholarly opinion which both rejects the approach to Protestant Scholasticism which presupposes that it is a betrayal of the Reformation approach to theology, and also questions the necessarily deleterious effects of using Aristotle.[78] Clearly, any work which intends to focus upon Owen's Aristotelianism must take the findings of this new stream of scholarship into account.[79]

Historically speaking, it is important to remember that Aristotelian thinking provided the dominant scientific and philosophical world view in the seventeenth century. In this regard, the comment of Paul Kristeller is enlightening:

> Aristotelian natural philosophy, rich in subject matter and solid in concepts, could not possibly be displaced from the university curriculum as long as there was no comparable body of teachable doctrine that could have taken its place. This was not supplied by the humanists, the Platonists, or the natural philosophers of the later Renaissance, who could dent but not break the Aristotelian tradition. The decisive attack came from Galileo and other physicists of the seventeenth century.[80]

Kristeller's point is extremely important, and one frequently

---

[78] R. D. Preus, *The Theology of Post-Reformation Lutheranism* (St Louis: Concordia, 1970–72); also O. Fatio, *Méthode et Théologie: Lambert Daneau et les debuts de la scolastique reformée* (Geneva: Droz, 1976); J. Raitt, *The Eucharistic Theology of Theodore Beza* (Chambersburg: American Academy of Religion, 1972); Muller, *PRRD1*.

[79] One point which must be made at the start concerns the Reformers' rejection of Aristotle. It is quite clear that their attack on the use of Aristotle in theology must be seen against the specific background of medieval Scholasticism and not against later developments within the Reformed (or Lutheran) tradition. To do the latter is to indulge in the kind of unhistorical speculation which says more about the views of the contemporary scholar than about the views of the Reformers themselves. Of course, one could argue that the Reformers' objection to Aristotle represented a kind of dogmatic a priori which has universal relevance for any theology which wishes to claim fidelity to their views, but this simply will not do, representing as it does a misreading of much of the evidence and basic confusion of the related, but separate, methodological tasks of historical and systematic theology.

[80] *Renaissance Thought: The Classic, Scholastic, and Humanist Strains* (New York: Harper and Row, 1961), p. 44. It is worth remembering, however, that not even the work of Copernicus and Galileo was able to bring about the immediate end of the dominance of Aristotelianism: see the essay of Charles B. Schmitt, 'Towards a Reassessment of Renaissance Aristotelianism' in *Studies in Renaissance Philosophy and Science* (London: Variorum Reprints, 1981), pp. 159–93.

missed by those eager to dismiss the Reformed Orthodox of the seventeenth century on the basis of their Aristotelianism: Aristotelian thought provided the dominant world view before the scientific revolution of the seventeenth century; thus, all significant thinkers in the years immediately prior to this were dependent upon Aristotelianism to some degree.[81] Bearing in mind the very close relationship that existed between Aristotelian logic, physics, and metaphysics, and the fuzziness of the boundary lines between where the Bible's sphere of authority ended and that of the human sciences began, the existence of a positive relationship between theology and philosophy in the seventeenth century is scarcely surprising. Indeed, when all this is borne in mind, it is tempting to ask the critics of Orthodoxy with what available alternative the seventeenth-century thinkers should have replaced the Aristotelian world view.[82] That of Plato? Those who adopted

---

[81]   Charles B. Schmitt makes a significant point in an essay on university education in the sixteenth century: 'The major point to keep in mind with regard to the influence of the Reformation on university philosophy is that, despite the enormous changes which were wrought, in the final analysis the end product in all universities, regardless of religious affiliation, was fundamentally Aristotelian. As much as Luther or others wanted to get away from the rather rigid intellectual structure which had grown up during the "Babylonian Captivity of the Church," when all was said and done the die had been cast centuries earlier and the appeal of Aristotelian Scholasticism remained too strong to be thrown aside easily.' 'Philosophy and Science in Sixteenth-Century Universities: Some Preliminary Comments', in *Studies in Renaissance Philosophy and Science*, pp. 485–530, p. 492. In light of this, the comment of Clifford with reference to the mid-seventeenth century that 'Aristotle had a few more years to reign in scholastic circles' (*Atonement and Justification*, p. 129) is incorrect. Even if we ignore the untenable equation of Scholasticism with Aristotelianism, it is still about as meaningful to criticize sixteenth- and seventeenth-century theologians for their use of Aristotle as it is, for example, to hold them responsible for being born before their logic could have the benefit of Frege's *Begriffsschrift* or their theology interact with Barth's *Church Dogmatics*.

[82]   Cf. the following comment of Schmitt on what he terms the problem of 'the escape from the Aristotelian predicament' in philosophy: '[T]hough dissatisfaction with various aspects of the Peripatetic system began to emerge during the late Middle Ages, it took several centuries for thinkers to escape the domination of the system. This was in part due to the fact that viable alternatives were lacking for a large number of specific Aristotelian doctrines. It is also in part because, even in cases where there were viable alternatives . . . they could not be readily absorbed into the existing Aristotelian world-structure. All too often to reject one Aristotelian doctrine meant only to place undue emphasis on other equally Aristotelian conceptions.', 'Towards a Reassessment of Renaissance Aristotelianism' in *Studies in Renaissance Philosophy and Science*, p. 175. If this was the case in philosophy, which then embraced natural science and logic as well as metaphysics, it was inevitable that Aristotelian elements within theology would prove equally resilient.

Platonic patterns of thought tended to be Arminian (at best) in their theology, as the great Reformed theologian William Twisse never tired of pointing out.[83] That of Ramus? Certainly some did, but Ramism is itself a revision, not a repudiation of Aristotelianism.[84] What about that of Descartes? Or that of Spinoza? History shows us that, when such substitution did take place, the resulting theologies were much further from the thought of the Reformers than were those of the Reformed Orthodox.[85]

---

[83]   For a contemporary seventeenth-century Orthodox assessment of the value of Platonism for Reformed theology, see William Twisse's 1631 treatise, *A Discovery of D. Jacksons vanitie* (London, 1631), where Twisse has no doubt that Jackson's Arminian understanding of the decrees is based upon his use of Plato and Plotinus. It is amusing to see on the frontispiece of Twisse's 1632 work, *Vindiciae Gratiae*, that Plato is depicted as the intellectual ancestor of Pelagius and Servetus, and as utterly opposed to True Religion. For a discussion of Twisse's conflict with Thomas Jackson, see S. Hutton, 'Thomas Jackson, Oxford Platonist, and William Twisse, Aristotelian', *JHI* 39 (1978), 635–52. In *A Display of Arminianism* Owen criticizes Jackson by name for rejecting the notion of God's decrees as determinate, a view which, later in the same work, he links explicitly with the Platonising of theology: see *Works* 10, pp. 17, 57. W. W. Bass, in his 'Platonic Influences on Seventeenth Century English Puritan Theology as expressed in the thinking of John Owen, Richard Baxter, and John Howe', unpubl. PhD diss. (University of Southern California, 1958), has argued for extensive Platonic influence on Owen. However, his arguments are inferential and unconvincing: for example, he argues that Owen's view of the intratrinitarian covenant is based on a neo-Platonic hierarchy, ignoring its origins in previous Christian tradition (pp. 108–9); he sees Owen's belief in the soul's immortality as 'Platonic' (p. 111); and he completely fails to notice the important role of Thomistic patterns within Owen's doctrine of God (pp. 108–9).

[84]   See D. Sinnema, 'Aristotle and Early Reformed Orthodoxy: Moments of Accommodation and Antithesis' in Wendy E. Helleman (ed.), *Christianity and the Classics: The Acceptance of a Heritage* (New York: University Press of America, 1990), pp. 119–48, p. 143; Schmitt, 'Towards a Reassessment of Renaissance Aristotelianism', in *Studies in Renaissance Philosophy and Science*, p. 175. For further discussion of Ramism, see P. Miller, *The New England Mind: The Seventeenth Century*, pp. 11–53; W. J. Ong, *Ramus, Method, and the Decay of Dialogue* (Cambridge: Harvard UP, 1958); K. L. Sprunger, 'Ames, Ramus and the Method of Puritan Theology', *HTR* 59 (1966), 133–51. Ramus' minor importance as mere modifier of the logic of Aristotle is brought out clearly in W. M. Kneale and J. Kneale, *The Development of Logic* (Oxford: Clarendon, 1962), pp. 301 ff.

[85]   While Reformed Orthodoxy remained remarkably resistant to new philosophical developments, it did ultimately come to absorb many of its ideas. In this regard, the work of Martin Klauber is particularly helpful: see his 'Reason, Revelation, and Cartesianism: Louis Tronchin and Enlightened Orthodoxy in Late Seventeenth-Century Geneva', *CH* 59 (1990), 326–39; 'Between Protestant Orthodoxy and Rationalism: Fundamental Articles in the Early Career of Jean LeClerc', *JHI* 54 (1993), 611–36; *Between Reformed Scholasticism and Pan-Protestantism: Jean-Alphonse Turretin (1671–1737) and Enlightened Orthodoxy at the Academy of Geneva* (Selinsgrove: Susquehanna University Press, 1994).

Furthermore, if not even the most advanced scientific thinkers of the sixteenth and seventeenth centuries, such as Galileo and Newton, were able to free themselves from using vocabulary that was remarkably Aristotelian in character, the persistence of this in theology is scarcely something at which to marvel.[86]

As works of their time, Owen's writings are no exception to the general tendency within Orthodoxy, both Reformed and Lutheran, to use Aristotelian language, logic, and metaphysics as useful tools both for polemical purposes and for positive theological construction.[87] While his library catalogue would seem to indicate his familiarity with other philosophical viewpoints, from his earliest work, *A Display of Arminianism* (1642), Owen put Aristotelian concepts and language to work in the service of Reformed theology, and this was to continue throughout his writings. For an Englishman of Owen's generation, this was scarcely surprising, as the England of his day stood in the aftermath of a significant renaissance of Aristotelian learning which had taken place in the latter decades of the sixteenth century, a revival indicated in part by the general increase in English publication of Aristotelian texts.[88] This revival was paralleled by the renewed interest in the scholastic theology of the Middle Ages which helped to reinforce the scholastic nature of university education, and, while opposition to such Scholasticism remained strong, many thinkers, including theologians,

---

[86] See Schmitt, 'Towards a Reassessment of Renaissance Aristotelianism' in *Studies in Renaissance Philosophy and Science*, pp. 163 ff. Schmitt regards Scholasticism as the dominant force within the universities of Europe up until the fifty years around 1700. Only then did it start to lose its grip on 'the more progressive and up-to-date universities'. *Ibid.*, p. 179.

[87] Of course, while the early Reformers tended to use less Aristotelian language than their successors, even they could not free themselves from their intellectual and cultural milieu, nor is there any sign that they wished to do so. Thus, we find Calvin himself deploying Aristotelian language when it is useful: see I. Backus, '"Aristotelianism" in some of Calvin's and Beza's Expository Exegetical Writings on the Doctrine of the Trinity' in *Histoire de l'exegese au XVIe siecle. Textes du Colloque International tenu a Geneve en 1976. Reunis par Olivier Fatio et Pierre Fraenkel* (Geneva: Droz, 1978), pp. 351–60; Schreiner, *The Theater of His Glory*.

[88] See C. B. Schmitt, *John Case and Aristotelianism in Renaissance England* (Kingston: McGill-Queen's UP, 1983), esp. pp. 13–76; also his Appendix One: Logic Books Printed in England before 1620.

found much in it that was of value without having to accept every jot and tittle.[89]

Given this general climate, it is not surprising to find evidence of significant appropriation of Aristotelian language in the writings of Owen. It seems certain that he was first exposed to the theological application of Aristotelian philosophy at Oxford, where he was a student of Thomas Barlow (1607–1691), the future Bishop of Lincoln. Barlow graduated as BA at Queen's in 1630, MA in 1633, and was made a Fellow of the College in the same year. In 1635 he became the 'metaphysical reader' in the University. Owen himself was a student at Queen's and studied under Barlow during his time there.[90] Barlow, a staunch Calvinist and opponent of the theological tendencies of leading churchmen such as Jeremy Taylor, wrote a book entitled *Exercitationes aliquot Metaphysicae* (1637, second edition 1658) which was apparently based upon his Oxford lectures. Owen himself possessed a copy of the 1658 edition,[91] but we can reasonably assume that he would have been familiar with the Aristotelian content from his days in Oxford. He also possessed sets of Aristotle's works, as well as those of Plato and other ancient philosophers.[92] In addition to these he also owned copies of numerous Christian scholastic thinkers, including Aquinas[93] and Suarez,[94] and also

---

[89] See Costello, *The Scholastic Curriculum,* pp. 9–10; Schmitt, *John Case,* pp. 61–8. Schmitt's comment on the appropriation of scholastic thought by English thinkers of the seventeenth century is particularly helpful: 'The medieval traditions that were revived were transformed in the process. As with all such revivals and renaissances the process of assimilation was partial and selective. Certain aspects of medieval doctrine were useful for seventeenth-century England; others were not. Consequently, the Thomism, Scotism, or nominalism that infused the works of Hooker or Boyle was partial, derivative, and selective, but in no way complete.' p. 67.

[90] Toon, *God's Statesman*, p. 6. Toon gives no primary source for this, nor does the *DNB* entry for Barlow, but in his 'Life of Dr Owen', Thomson quotes an epitaph on Owen, written by his friend, Thomas Gilbert, which refers to his studies under Barlow: see *Works* 1, p. xxiii.

[91] *Bibliotheca Oweniana: Libri Miscellanei in Quarto*, no. 68.

[92] Other ancient philosophical authors whose works were owned by Owen include Cicero, Seneca, Plotinus, and Boethius. These can be found scattered throughout the Latin section of *Bibliotheca Oweniana*, pp. 19–32.

[93] E.g. his 1632 edition of the *Summa Theologiae: Bibliotheca Oweniana: Libri Theologici in Folio*, no.60.

[94] E.g. his 1608 edition of *Metaphysicae Disputationes*, and his 1619 edition of *Tractatus de Legibus et Legislatore Amplissimus: Bibliotheca Oweniana: Libri Miscellanei in Folio*, nos. 45 and 46 respectively.

some Jewish scholastic texts such as those of Maimonides which the Oxford orientalist, Edward Pococke, published in 1655.[95] To these must also be added works by Descartes and Bacon.[96] The mere presence of particular books in his library does not necessarily mean that he read them, but the citations from many of these sources within his works indicate that he did read a significant number.

Of course, discussion of the details of Owen's use of Aristotelian vocabulary will form part of our subsequent study, but it is worthwhile noting here that, despite his methodological restrictions on the competence of human reason, Owen himself appears not to have regarded his use of Aristotle as either particularly remarkable or especially reprehensible. As we noted above, it was not something for which Baxter cared to criticize him, since Baxter's own use of such language shows his clear acceptance of the conventions of the day. Furthermore, in Owen's early works, all his explicit criticism of the use of philosophy in theology is aimed at Platonizing tendencies, doubtless a result of the association between Platonism and the Arminian elements within Anglicanism.[97] Alan Clifford correctly notes that the later Owen tends to be more critical of Aristotelian influence on theology,[98] but it is perhaps significant that these criticisms seem to start, and to be most pronounced, in the early 1660s; this was the time when Owen witnessed the obliteration of all that the Puritans had tried to achieve during the previous two decades, and the triumph of what he would have considered a Romish and Arminian party within the Anglican church. As such, Owen was enduring that

---

[95] *Porta Moris, sive Dissertationes aliquot Opera et Studio Eduardi Pocockii* (Oxford, 1655). This is listed in *Bibliotheca Oweniana: Libri Theologici in Quarto*, no. 106. For Owen's use of Maimonides, see Carl R. Trueman, 'Protestant Scholasticism, Jews, and Judaism: Some Notes on their Connection', *Journal of Progressive Judaism* 4 (1995), 61–76, esp. 70–5.

[96] *Bibliotheca Oweniana: Libri Miscellanei in Quarto*, nos. 72–3; *Miscellanies in Octavo*, no.125. Owen's interest in Descartes is further indicated by his possession of a biography of the philosopher: *Miscellanies in Octavo*, no. 52.

[97] Owen makes his belief in a positive connection between the use of Platonism in theology and Arminianism (and its ancient counterpart, Pelagianism) explicit at several points in *A Display of Arminianism*: see *Works* 10, pp. 57, 110, 111.

[98] *Atonement and Justification*, pp. 95–6, 106 n. 8.

'experience of defeat' which caused such soul-searching and despair among the Puritan intelligentsia.[99] Furthermore, even at this time, Owen could both criticize and praise Aristotelian philosophy within a few pages of text.[100] This, coupled with the fact that Owen himself continued to draw positively on Aristotelian language and concepts in his later works,[101] indicates that his apparent attacks on Aristotelianism should be read as a mixture of the rhetoric of a defeated man and of criticism of specific theological errors rather than a general repudiation of his earlier approach.

This leads to the second point which must be made if we are to be fair to Owen: not only should we remember to view his Aristotelian language in terms of its historical context, but we should also bear in mind some basic points about the way language itself works. Clifford's arguments against Owen's use of Aristotelian language and concepts seem at times to proceed on the assumption that demonstration of the mere presence of Aristotelian language is enough to prove that the content of his theology has been Aristotelianized, although he does not bring out Baxter's extensive use of such language as a basis for drawing parallel conclusions about the latter's theology.[102]

The close connection between scholastic and Aristotelian language, and the content of theology has been asserted many times. Interestingly enough, as Richard Muller has recently pointed out, the debate bears an uncanny resemblance to the arguments about the Hellenization of Christianity which were advanced by such as von Harnack at the start of this century, and which have

---

[99] On this subject, see the excellent study of Christopher Hill, *The Experience of Defeat: Milton and some contemporaries*, 2nd. edn. (London: Bookmarks, 1994).

[100] See *Works* 17, pp. 18, 20.

[101] E.g. *Works* 3, pp. 69, 436, 502–3.

[102] E.g. Clifford, *Atonement and Justification*. There is, of course, more to Dr Clifford's case than a simple equation of language with content, but his failure to deal with the implications which the arguments of Schmitt and others have for the relationship between form and content does tend to lead to arguments which bear an uncanny resemblance to such an equation: e.g. *Atonement and Justification*, pp. 96–8, 129. It is in fact arguable that Owen is using the language of essence and accidents which Dr Clifford criticizes here in a very similar way to that in which Dr Clifford himself uses the terms *qualitatively* and *quantitatively* a few paragraphs previously: see Ch. 5, note 50.

continued in various forms in neo-orthodoxy and the biblical theology movement of the mid-twentieth century.[103] The view of language reflected here was one which held that the attempt to express Hebraic thought-forms in the language of Greece destroyed or perverted the original Hebrew concepts simply because Greek was incapable of conveying their original import and also brought with it a metaphysical content of its own. It is the same with some of the arguments posed by the 'Calvin against the Calvinists' camp: Aristotelian language and concepts are assumed to be incapable of, or at the very least inappropriate for, conveying the content of the thoughts of the sixteenth-century Reformers. Such arguments with reference to biblical language have been brilliantly exploded by James Barr in his classic study, *The Semantics of Biblical Language*.[104] Barr has shown that the root of a word is no sound guide to its meaning in any given context, and has refuted the notion that a particular language contains a particular implicit metaphysics. It is how words are used in their context that supplies their meaning at any given point.

That this is the case with the language of Aristotle is easy to demonstrate. For example, if we examine the famous case of Aquinas's exposition of the doctrine of transubstantiation, we see him not developing a doctrine on the basis of Aristotelian metaphysics (the doctrine was defined in 1215 at the Fourth Lateran Council, a generation before Aristotle's metaphysics started to play a significant role in Western theological discourse), but attempting to explicate an established church dogma using the conceptual vocabulary of Aristotle: thus, transubstantiation is couched in terms of accidents and substance. This, of course, is nonsense in terms of Aristotle's own thought, where accidents had to be supported by a relevant substance, a criticism

---

[103]   Muller, 'Calvin and the "Calvinists"', 150–1; for neo-orthodox constructions of truth which utilize arguments reflecting the root fallacy, see, for example, E. Brunner, *Truth as Encounter*, trans. A. Loos and D. Cairns (Philadelphia: Westminster, 1964); T. F. Torrance, 'One Aspect of the Biblical Conception of Faith', *Expository Times* 68 (1956–57), 111–14.

[104]   Oxford: OUP, 1961.

which John Wyclif made in his own work on the Eucharist;[105] but this does not invalidate Aquinas's use of the terminology providing we are willing to allow that, in the light of the miraculous nature of his subject matter, Aquinas is using the terms 'substance' and 'accidents' in a way which involves a transformation of their original meanings. While there may be legitimate grounds for objecting to Aquinas's teaching at this point, it simply will not do to reject his position solely on the basis that his view is incoherent in terms of Aristotle's own original metaphysics: Aquinas's use of Aristotle's *language* in no way implies that he regards Aristotle's *system* as the ultimate arbiter of the truth or falsehood of his doctrine.

For the same reasons, we cannot place too much reliance upon the mere presence of Aristotelian language as a sound guide to the nature of the content of a particular theologian's thought. Scholars working on Renaissance and Reformation thought have demonstrated that the presence of Aristotelian language, logic, and thought-forms within a text does not allow for any significant prejudgment of the views expressed therein. The fact is that the word 'Aristotelian', when referred to Renaissance and post-Renaissance theology, can be used only as an umbrella term reflecting a broad methodology covering a variety of emphases, approaches, and content which no more allows us to assume belief in certain doctrines than positive use of, say, positive approval and commitment to the language of the Labour Party manifesto allows us to predict a particular person's view of socialism. Aristotelianism therefore cannot be treated as if it was an easily defined, monolithic entity whose presence in a thinker's work allows for a priori generalizations about content before any serious engagement with the relevant texts.[106] Lutheran and Reformed, Orthodox and Remonstrant: all used Aristotelian language and patterns to establish their respective, and radically different, theological viewpoints. Thus, Owen's positive use of Aristotelian thought does not allow us to prejudge his theology;

---

[105] See Anthony Kenny, *Wyclif* (Oxford: OUP, 1985), pp. 80–90.
[106] For a summary of the problems inherent in attempting to produce a precise definition of Aristotelianism, see Schmitt, *John Case*, pp. 217 ff.

cheap victories over Reformed Orthodoxy based on such philo-
sophically naive presuppositions are no substitute for careful and
dispassionate examination of the texts. Owen's Aristotelian language must be judged by how the words are used by him, not
what they meant to Aristotle, and his Aristotelian metaphysics
must be judged by its result, not simply by its presence. That can
be done only when it has been set within the intellectual context
outlined above, and within the structure of his theological
method as a whole.

Conclusion

From the above discussion, a number of points emerge which are
of significance for the detailed analysis of Owen's views on
certain topics which will occupy subsequent chapters. First, this
overview, though brief, has yet given some indication of the
intellectual flux of the seventeenth century, even in the comparatively conservative (from our later perspective) area of English
Reformed Orthodoxy. There can, therefore, be no real justification for marginalizing the world of seventeenth-century theology
as if its protagonists were merely concerned with systematizing,
expounding, or applying, the thought of their sixteenth-century
predecessors, while the theological world trod water, as it were,
awaiting the impact of the Enlightenment to shatter its cherished
certainties. New questions arose in the late-sixteenth and seventeenth centuries which required answers which the theology of
the Reformers was not, in its original form, capable of immediately answering. The growth of Arminianism and Socinianism
with their adherence to the Scripture principle, and the development of new theories and emphases in the matter of atonement
and justification within the broad boundaries of the Reformed
camp raised problems for Owen which simple recourse to the
Reformers or even to the patristic authors could not, by itself,
solve. Thus, when we come to see the answers which he did give
to these new questions, we should not be surprised to find that
his theology does exhibit significant development when compared to those of his sixteenth-century antecedents. Owen's task
as defender of orthodoxy required that he did not simply indulge

in sterile repetition of those same old formulations that were themselves now under question.

Secondly, it is quite obvious that the intellectual content of Owen's thought defies simplistic reduction to one or two key themes. His use of the various strands of the Western tradition, the need to develop new ways of expressing and defending Reformed theology in the light of novel heresies and attacks, and the sheer breadth of his own reading all suggest that we are dealing with a thinker whose thought can be reduced to a few simple 'big ideas' only at the cost of losing much of the subtlety of what he has to say, and indeed transforming his theology into a caricature which he himself would not have recognized.

The immediate agenda of Owen's theology is set by the specific times in which he lived, and therefore those times should themselves provide the basic context for any fair and historical analysis of his thought. This should be an obvious point, but failure to appreciate its significance has led, for example, to direct comparisons being drawn between Owen and Calvin and Owen and Wesley without regard to the radically different historical and intellectual contexts in which these three men worked.[107]

---

[107] See Clifford, *Atonement and Justification, passim*. Dr Clifford argues that such a comparison is historically and theologically legitimate because all the theologians he considers held to the axiom of *sola scriptura*: see pp. viii–ix. The problems with this view are enormous. The Protestant doctrine of *sola scriptura* is scarcely an isolated concept but must be seen as standing in relation to exegetical and doctrinal concerns: biblical exegesis developed significantly between Calvin and Owen, and between Owen and Wesley; the doctrinal conflicts in which Protestants were engaged changed between Calvin and Wesley; and the Enlightenment stands between the sixteenth and the eighteenth centuries. To make the point another way, using the language of modern hermeneutical theory, the personal 'horizons' of Calvin, Owen, and Wesley, shaped as they were by the social and intellectual contexts of three very different centuries, are so dissimilar as to make fruitless any straightforward and direct comparison between them without extensive reflection on these differences, even given their adherence to *sola scriptura*. They were historical figures and cannot be treated as existing in some kind of time vacuum, alone with their chosen authoritative text. On the 'two horizons' of text and of interpreter, see Anthony C. Thiselton, *The Two Horizons* (Carlisle: Paternoster, 1980), pp. 10 ff. For an interesting discussion of *sola scriptura* in relation to doctrinal concerns, etc. see A. N. S. Lane, 'Sola Scriptura? Making Sense of a Post-Reformation Slogan' in P. E. Satterthwaite and D. F. Wright (eds), *A Pathway into the Holy Scripture* (Grand Rapids: Eerdmans, 1994), pp. 297–327, p. 298. For the importance of the impact of the Enlightenment as a watershed in the development of evangelical theology in the eighteenth century, see D. W. Bebbington, *Evangelicalism in Modern Britain* (London: Unwin, 1989), pp. 20–74.

Owen was working at a point in time when the Reformed tradition was seeking to defend itself not just, or even principally, against the assaults of Rome but was rather faced with challenges which were much closer to its own stated principles and method and therefore that much more dangerous. In this task, Reformed Orthodoxy in general engaged in an intensive restatement of the orthodox, patristic roots of its theology while also pressing forward to an extensive reappropriation of the technical language of medieval and Renaissance Scholasticism in order to give its theological formulations the rigorous precision needed to distinguish itself from the tenets of Arminianism and Socinianism. To this general tendency, Owen was no exception, and in his writings we find the confluence of patristic, medieval, and Reformation thought in a synthesis designed to meet the needs of the hour. Once this is understood, the stage is set to understand the apparent regression to a pre-Reformation Scholasticism which is evident in parts of Owen's work not as a return to some alleged arid rationalistic approach to theology (a notion which, incidentally, itself betrays a rather unhistorical and generalized picture of medieval thought) but as a move forward towards a critical reappropriation of aspects of the Western tradition for the purpose of developing a systematic restatement of Reformed thought capable of withstanding the assaults of both the subtly heterodox and the openly heretical.

Two

The Principles of Theology

Introduction

One of the points which most clearly separates the Protestantism of the Reformation from its post-Reformation expressions is the increased attention which theologians came to give to discussion of the principles of theology. The development of elaborate prolegomena to Protestant theology is a distinctly post-Reformation phenomenon, marking a move within Protestantism towards a formal systematization of Reformation theology in terms of its own inner principles in order to provide clearer understandings of the nature and task of theology, better tools for teaching theology, and a firmer foundation for polemical engagement with opponents.[1] Thus, in the theological prolegomena of the period, one finds explicated and elaborated the basic methodological principles which arise out of, and in turn shape, the whole theological enterprise.

The significance of this development for the interpretation of Owen's theology is not hard to discern: accusations of rationalism and of an uncritical use of Aristotle are, at bottom, criticisms of certain methodological commitments to which Owen is alleged to adhere. Thus, a formal discussion of how he understands the theological task, of how he arranges theological topics, and of how he construes the relationship between revelation and reason, must form a primary part of any study of his theology which is

---

[1] For discussions of Lutheran and Reformed prolegomena respectively, see Preus, *Post-Reformation Lutheranism* 1 and Muller, *PRRD1*.

interested in either establishing or refuting the truth of such claims.

Fundamental Distinctions

The nature of theology

The tradition of English Puritanism to which Owen belonged was not renowned for its production of systematic syntheses of doctrine, the place where one normally expects to find sophisticated prolegomenal discussion. There were a number of exceptions, but even these are not on the same scale as their continental counterparts: for example, Ussher's *Body of Divinitie*, structured catechetically, does have some preliminary discussion of general revelation and then an extended treatment of the Scripture principle; Ames' *Marrow* starts by defining theology, with Scripture not being formally discussed until Chapter Thirty-Four; and Watson's *A Body of Practical Divinity* (London, 1692) follows the course of the Shorter Catechism and discusses humanity's purpose and the Scripture principle at the outset.[2] Such works, while demonstrating some explicit concern for matters of methodology, lack the elaborate prolegomena of, say, Turretin's *Institutio Theologicae Elencticae* (Geneva, 1679–85), where the whole of the first topic is devoted to defining theology, and the second to analysing the Scripture principle.[3]

Compared to the generality of English Puritans, Owen's writings exhibit a moderately high degree of prolegomenal discussion and yield significant insight into his understanding of the theological task. While he wrote no theological *summa* in the manner of Thomas Aquinas or, from his own era, Francis Turretin or Richard Baxter, he did write one work which attempted to embrace the whole of theology: *Theologoumena Pantodapa, sive,*

---

[2]   Ussher, *A Body of Divinitie*, pp. 3 ff.; Ames, *The Marrow of Theology*, trans. J. D. Eusden (Durham: Labyrinth, 1983), pp. 77–83, 185–9; Watson, *A Body of Divinity* (Edinburgh: Banner of Truth, 1983), pp. 6–38.

[3]   Francis Turretin, *Institutes of Elenctic Theology* 1, trans. G. M. Giger, ed. J. T. Dennison, Jr. (Phillipsburg: Presbyterian and Reformed, 1992), pp. 1–167.

De Natura, Ortu, Progressu, et Studio, Verae Theologiae (1661).[4] This work seems so far to have been largely neglected in the secondary literature, but, as Owen's most comprehensive statement of theology, it is of great importance to any understanding of his thought.

Perhaps the most striking thing about the work is its structure. Rather than choosing to express his theology using a synthetic arrangement whereby the order of topics follows the order of being, moving, for example, from God to Trinity to creation and so on,[5] Owen chooses a more historically focused approach, moving from a definition of theology to discussion of the history of theology framed by the various epochs of biblical history: before the Fall; after the Fall; within the Noahic, Abrahamic, and Mosaic covenants; and under the gospel.[6] The choice of this order is not without significance.

Underlying this choice of organization is Owen's fundamental belief that theology is relational; that is, it depends upon the nature of the relationship that exists between God the revealer and the one revealed, and humans, the recipients of that revelation.[7] In this context, the progressive nature of the covenant scheme serves to take account of the fact that theology requires a divine–human relationship, and that the biblical record shows that relationship has itself not been static but subject to historical movement, a movement which can be articulated by setting forth in order the key points at which God has explicitly defined his relationship with humanity: the various covenants which are found within the Bible.[8] As we shall see below, we also find this

---

[4] *Works* 17.

[5] For example, James Ussher's *A Body of Divinitie*.

[6] For further discussion of why this arrangement was chosen, see below.

[7] See below.

[8] For the concept of *historica series* in the Reformation, see P. Fraenkel, *Testimonia Patrum: The Function of the Patristic Argument in the Theology of Philip Melanchthon* (Geneva: Droz, 1961), pp. 52–109. As for his sources for this arrangement, it has to be confessed that no single source stands out. Internal evidence is weak: within the *Theologoumena Pantodapa*, Owen refers to writers as varied as Maimonides and Bellarmine, and cites no one as his authority for adopting this structure. Certainly, by the time he came to write, there were no shortage of models which took historical sequence as their basic organizational principle, and, in this context, it would appear that the work belongs to the growing tradition of federal theology which focused on

historical pattern in Baxter's *Methodus Theologiae* and in his
Catholick Theologie,[9] but in both cases this ordering is determined not specifically by a relational–historical understanding
of theology but by his doctrine of God and the order of God's
external operations. With Owen, the order is not formally determined by the doctrine of God, as the *Theologoumena Pantodapa*
contains no locus on this topic, but rather by biblical history.
This is confirmed by the fact that Owen devotes time to explicating the Noahic covenant, something which does not necessarily
need to be fitted into discussion of the history of salvation and
which is consequently omitted from Baxter's more synthetic

Footnote 8 (*continued*) the divine-human covenants as the basic context for theology.
The impact of Arminianism on the development of federal theology has been little
noticed until recently, but two essays by Richard Muller draw attention to the historical
focus of Arminius's critique of supralapsarianism and the role of covenant in remonstrant thinking: 'God, Predestination, and the Integrity of the Created Order: A Note
on Patterns in Arminius' Theology', in W. Fred Graham (ed.), *Later Calvinism:
International Perspectives* (Kirksville: Sixteenth Century Essays and Studies, 1994), pp.
431–50; 'The Federal Motif in Seventeenth Century Arminian Theology', *NAKG* 62
(1982), 102–22. Owen's emphasis upon the centrality of the Fall to any discussion of
Christology prevents his thought from being vulnerable to this particular Arminian
argument, and indicates a definite infralapsarian tendency within his soteriology. On
the development of federal theology, see J. W. Baker and C. S. McCoy, *Fountainhead
of Federalism: Heinrich Bullinger and the Covenantal Tradition* (Louisville: Westminster, 1991), pp. 11–79. The argument of this work is rendered problematic by its attempt
to see unilateral and bilateral covenant theologies as mutually exclusive in a manner
reminiscent of the tendencies of the work of Perry Miller: see Miller's 'The Marrow of
Puritan Divinity' in *Errand into the Wilderness* (New York: Harper and Row, 1956);
also, *The New England Mind: The Seventeenth Century*, pp. 365–97. For a critique of
Miller, see J. von Rohr, *The Covenant of Grace in Puritan Thought*. For a critique of
the 'two traditions' hypothesis, see L. D. Bierma, 'Federal Theology in the Sixteenth
Century: Two Traditions?', *WTJ* 45 (1983), 304–21.
[9]   *Catholick Theologie* 1, pp. 63–5. The existence of a clear awareness of the historical
development implicit in the biblical narrative which is demonstrated by the structure
of works by Baxter and Owen, and by the rise of federal theology, shows that the
following statement by George Eldon Ladd, echoing the sentiments of popular mythology about post-Reformation dogmatics, is, at best a massive overstatement, at worst
simply wrong: 'The gains in the historical study of the Bible made by the reformers
were soon lost in the post-Reformation period, and the Bible was once again used
uncritically and unhistorically to support orthodox doctrine. The Bible was viewed not
only as a book free from error and contradiction but also without development or
progress. The entire Bible was looked upon as possessing one level of theological value.
History was completely lost in dogma, and philology became a branch of dogmatics.'
A Theology of the New Testament, rev. edn. (Grand Rapids: Eerdmans, 1993), p. 2.

LIBRARY BOOK SUGGESTION

Date of request 16/3/98

Order No 1542977

(BLOCK CAPITALS ONLY)

AUTHOR (sumame first) TRUEMAN, CARL R

Date Ordered 7.4.98

TITLE The CLAIMS of TRUTH: JOHN OWEN'S TRINITARIAN THEOLOGY

	No of copies (2)	Supplier DAW

PUBLISHER PATERNOSTER

Date of Publication 1998

Recommended by C R TRUEMAN

Dept THEOLOGY

Details found

Reserve for

Libertas ✓
Card cat.

BF ✗
BRID ✗ ISIS
AYSEX ✗
CUSTI ✗

AY MAX 1998

Price		ISBN											Record bought
	HBK												(Y) N
£19.99	PBK	0	8	5	3	6	4	7	9	8	4		
	Branch 000	Loan 000	Fund THEOL										
	Branch 000	Loan 000	Fund Anterin										
	Branch 000	Loan	Fund										

Control No

USE REVERSE FOR NOTES

90039 revised 1/95

systems, where the Fall, the covenant with Abraham, the Mosaic legislation, and the coming of the Messiah are emphasized, being key elements of the one soteriological structure deriving from God.

A comparison with the structure of Baxter's *Methodus Theologiae* is here instructive. Unlike Owen, Baxter prefaces his work with an extensive discussion of theological method, which, in the typical seventeenth-century way, he understands in terms of systematic organization. In classic scholastic fashion he ask whether there is only one correct method or many, and affirms that there are indeed many, identifying by name the following: the *methodus synthetica*, which follows the order of being and of operation; the *methodus notificativa et probativa*, which follows the order of knowing and which works from things below to things above; the *methodus practica intentionis*, which starts from ends and works back to means; and the *methodus practica executiva*, which starts with means and works forward to ends. Of these, Baxter chooses the first, the synthetic method which starts from the doctrine of God and moves through the doctrine of creation to redemption.[10] Such a model has clear medieval precedents, most obviously in the great *Summae* of Thomas Aquinas. Baxter's resulting system moves as follows: in Part One from the doctrine of God, to the doctrine of creation, to the doctrine of humanity, including detailed analysis of faculty psychology; in Book Two, to a more historically ordered discussion of grace under the Old Testament; in Book Three to a discussion of Christology, soteriology, and New Testament faith; and in Book Four to eschatology. In his prolegomena, Baxter explicitly links this structure to his understanding of Aristotelian causality, modified in light of the Campanellan critique, where God, viewed as Creator, is the Efficient Cause, creatures are the Constitutive Cause, and God, viewed as the object of rational creatures, is the Final Cause.[11]

---

[10]   *Methodus Theologiae*, (London, 1681) Praefatio, p. 3 (not paginated in original).
[11]   Ibid. 1a.1, pp. 4 ff. Baxter gives no reason for his replacement of fourfold causality with threefold causality, other than that the standard distinctions 'haud accurate quaternarius statuitur'. One can perhaps detect here the influence of Baxter's penchant for finding 'trinaries' within nature as evidence for the Trinity, a suggestion which finds

Compared to this arrangement, Owen's approach in the *Theologoumena Pantodapa* clearly represents an attempt to organize theology much more closely around the historical structures of the Bible itself and is, in that respect, methodologically less speculative than the *Methodus Theologiae*. Owen has no separate locus on the doctrine of God, and his ordering is not built upon the order of being and operation, as it is in Baxter; even though Baxter's system embodies elements of historical order, the formal reason for this is not that it emulates the biblical structure but that it follows the order of God's external operations. In this, we can perhaps detect the impact of William Twisse's critique of overly-complex decretal systems: Twisse argued that there were only two decrees, of the end and of the means, and that the ordering of the means could be discussed only in terms of their historical execution.[12] Such an approach automatically brought the issue of the historical ordering of God's acts to the fore but did so more on the grounds of logic and metaphysics than commitment to the pattern of biblical history.

The comparison of Owen's *Theologoumena Pantodapa* with Baxter's *Methodus* has obvious implications for Alan Clifford's argument that Owen's theology is vitiated by an overarching commitment to Aristotelian teleology as opposed to Baxter's more biblically oriented, less speculative approach. It is indeed true, of course, that the technical language of causes, ends and means is derived from Aristotelian philosophy rather than the New Testament.[13] By implication, therefore, a comparison of the explicitly causal structure of the *Methodus* with the biblical-

---

Footnote 11 (*continued*) support in a passage of his autobiography which refers to his plans to write the *Methodus Theologiae*: 'Having long (upon the suspension of my *Aphorismes*) been purposing to draw up a method of theology, I now began it. I never yet saw a scheme or method of physics or theology which gave any satisfaction to my reason . . . I had been twenty-six years convinced that dichotomising will not do it, but that the Divine Trinity in Unity hath expressed itself in the whole frame of nature and morality.' *The Autobiography of Richard Baxter* (Mobile: RE Publications, n.d.), p. 212; cf. *Methodus Theologiae*, Praefatio, p. 6 (not paginated in original). The trinary structure is derived from Tommaso Campanella: see below.

[12] *Vindiciae Gratiae* 3, pp. 152–3; cf. Baxter, *Catholick Theologie* 1, p. 58.

[13] *Atonement and Justification*, p. 96.

historical federal structure of the *Theologoumena Pantodapa* has some unfortunate, if not utterly devastating consequences, for his attempt to characterize Owen as the scholastic Aristotelian and Baxter as the man of simple, biblical faith. Owen's 'Aristotelian method' may be evident in the opening lines of *The Death of Death*,[14] but at no point in his writings does he explicitly discuss 'method' as a formal prolegomenon in which causality, understood in the explicitly Campanellan–Aristotelian way we find in Baxter, is elevated to the level of a fundamental methodological principle as it is in the *Methodus*. Indeed, if it is true that 'the philosopher's conception of teleology governs [Owen's] understanding of the design of the atonement', how much more true is it that Baxter's methodological reflections indicate that this same basic teleology governs Baxter's whole view of theology? Baxter's own writings are, after all, absolutely emphatic on this point. Of course, if one accepts, in the light of the work of Schmitt, Muller and others, that form and content can be, to a large degree, separated, then this use of Aristotelian causality may be viewed simply as a heuristic device which articulates theological content built on other premises. It need not therefore have particularly damaging implications for one's view of either Owen's or Baxter's theology; unfortunately, as Dr Clifford clearly considers that Owen's use of Aristotle in itself vitiates his teaching on atonement, the avenue of escape offered by Schmitt and co. has already been closed with regards to Baxter, whose entire theological *summa*, and not just his theology of atonement, is structured by Aristotelian causality.[15] The simple fact is that both Owen and Baxter made positive, constructive use of Aristotelian causal categories.

While Owen does not develop his prolegomena in quite the same detail as Baxter, he does spend some time discussing the

---

[14] Ibid.

[15] Clifford expresses surprise at Owen's positive citations of Aristotle (*Atonement and Justification*, p. 98), but it is just as easy, if not more so, to find such statements of approbation in Baxter: see, for example, *Methodus Theologiae*, p. 6. The truth is that, as noted in Ch. 1, Aristotelianism of one form or another was the supremely dominant philosophical force of the time, and there was nothing that Owen or Baxter either could or indeed wanted to do about it.

nature of theology itself before proceeding to develop the main body of his argument in the *Theologoumena Pantodapa*, and this discussion is the only source we have for seeing clearly into some of the central aspects of his understanding of the theological task. Unlike Baxter and many other scholastic authors, he does not engage in extensive reflection upon the meaning of method/methodus, and any attempt to talk about Owen's theological method as such must take note of this fact. Instead, he starts by trying to define exactly what theology is. In this context, he rejects as frivolous and impiously speculative the medieval scholastic discussions about whether theology is a science, etc.[16] Such impatience with the medieval tradition on this point is not uncommon, and can also be found in Baxter.[17] While apparently rejecting the content of scholastic discussion, however, Owen nonetheless proceeds to build upon medieval ideas in order to establish his own view of revelation. In Chapter Three of the work, he argues that it belongs to God's infinite self-sufficiency that he alone knows himself perfectly, and he characterizes this self-knowledge of God as archetypal.[18] Baxter, while not using the term 'archetypal' also declares that theology is preeminently in the mind of God himself, and that this divine self-knowledge is the causal basis for human theology.[19] For Owen, this archetypal knowledge is not the knowledge that humans have of God: because humans are themselves finite, they are incapable of infinite knowledge; therefore human knowledge of God is not

---

[16] *Works* 17, pp. 31–5. On the history of the notion of theology as a science, see W. Pannenberg, *Theology and the Philosophy of Science*, trans. F. McDonagh (Philadelphia: Westminster, 1976), pp. 228–96; G. R. Evans, A. E. McGrath, A. D. Galloway, *The History of Christian Theology 1: The Science of Theology* (Grand Rapids: Eerdmans, 1986); for an analysis of this discussion in Protestant Scholasticism in general, see Muller, *PRRD1*, pp. 205–30.

[17] *Methodus Theologiae* 1a.1.6, p. 3.

[18] 'Ad infinitam Dei *autarkeian* pertinet, ut ipse solus se cognoscat perfecte . . . Itaque scientia illa, qua Deus se atque omnia sua attributa perfectissime novit, cum sit infinita et necessaria, non nisi ipse Deus infinite sciens et sapiens est. Haec ideo primae veritatis ipsam se perfectissime comprehendentis atque amantis cognitio, non nisi improprie a quibusdam theologia *archetypos* dicitur.' *Works* 17, p. 36. For a discussion of the use of the term 'archetype', and its corollary, 'ectype', see Muller, *PRRD1*, pp. 126–36.

[19] *Methodus Theologiae* 1.1. 2, p. 3.

infinite in nature, nor is it immediate, and it must therefore be considered as ectypal, and mediated. Furthermore, God cannot be grasped by human effort: revelation is an act of his will without which he would remain unknown and unknowable. Human theology is concerned with the revelation which God chooses to give us, and he does this supremely in Christ as exhibited in the gospel. In terms of its essential foundation, this depends upon God's knowledge of himself; in terms of its content, it reveals how he wishes us to relate to him.[20] For Owen, then, theology is relational: it is knowledge of God as he has revealed himself to be towards humans.[21]

Following the example of the medieval scholastics and of his Reformed contemporaries, Owen makes a further distinction within his understanding of theology, not this time in terms of the nature of theology in itself but in terms of the human recipients of revelation. Here he uses language borrowed from medieval Scholasticism to distinguish the theology of humans into two kinds, that of the *viator*, literally, 'the one on the way', and the *possessor*, 'the one who possesses'. The terms are medieval, and reflect a fundamental distinction between the knowledge of God available to those still on their earthly pilgrimage and those who have arrived in heaven.[22] The distinction between the two forms of knowledge is not in their object, which in both cases is God as he has revealed himself, but in their respective modes of knowl-

---

[20] 'Neque enim aut nostra Dei notitia infinitae illius scientiae divinae expressus est character (quod uni Filio naturae divinae proprium, Heb. 1:3), ita ut *ektypos* eius respectu dici possit; neque illius vi aut virtute quicquam de Deo cognoscere possumus, nisi intercedente libero voluntatis divinae consilio. Equidem sepculum nostrum non est immediate Deus ipse, sed verbum eius seu evangelium in quo *retecta facie*, per Christum *gloriam Domini* intuemur 2 Cor. 3:18. Aeternam in mente sua veritatis eius, quam a nobis cognosci velit *ideam*, seu conceptum Deus habet. Atque hinc omnis nostra theologia pendet; non immediate quidem, sed ab eo voluntatis divinae actu, quo ei placuerit veritatem istam nobis revelare . . . Revelatio ideo mentis et voluntatis divinae, hoc est Dei verbum, ea est doctrina de qua agimus, ad quam omnes mentis nostrae de Deo, eius cultu, atque obedientia ei debita, conceptus conformes esse debeant.' *Works* 17, p. 36.

[21] This is another aspect of Owen's thought which would commend the covenant scheme as an organizational structure for his theology, emphasizing as it does the fact that theology takes place only in terms of the divine–human covenant relation.

[22] *Works* 17, pp. 38–9.

edge: for the former, the *viatores*, the mode is faith, while the latter, the *possessores* see God face to face, and Owen, like other Puritans, drew on the medieval scholastic tradition in order to make this point clear.[23] The medieval vocabulary therefore allows him to preserve the fundamental continuity between the church on earth and the church in heaven, while not losing sight of the dynamic nature of the Christian's earthly pilgrimage.

The implications of what Owen has to say on the subject of theology in terms of the archetype and the ectype are clear: the possibility of human theology depends upon God's accommodation of himself to a form which finite beings are capable of grasping, and this is as much the result of the ontological distinction between the finite and the infinite as of the impact of sin upon human nature. Owen's use of scholastic distinctions between archetype and ectype, union, viator and possessor, all serve to clarify this point and to restate what is a basic presupposition of much Western theology from Augustine to the Reformed systems of the sixteenth and seventeenth centuries: finite human beings cannot grasp the infinite truth of God in its infinite nature. Furthermore, while Owen does not here use the precise terminology, it is quite clear that theology can be seen as having its *principium essendi*, its principle of being, in the being and action of God himself, and its *principium cognoscendi*, its principle of knowing, in God's ectypal revelation of himself. This is an obvious implication of his emphasis upon the connection between the archetypal and ectypal theology: human knowledge of God depends upon the ectype, while the ectype depends for its existence and reliability upon the archetype.

Theology before the Fall

In dealing with revelation in general, Owen makes a number of distinctions, some of which refer to revelation as it exists objectively, some as it is acquired subjectively. Of the former, Owen distinguishes three kinds: revelation in God's works of creation and providence; revelation through the innate sense of God's

---

[23] See Carl R. Trueman, 'Heaven and Hell (12): In Puritan Theology', *Epworth Review* 22.3 (1995), 75–85.

existence which humans possess; and revelation through God's word, meaning the Scriptures.[24] To bring out the practical, teleological thrust of revelation, he combines these with the historical distinction between theology before the Fall and theology after the Fall, a distinction which in this context has specific reference to the subjective appropriation of theology by humans, and which has a decisive impact upon the objective forms of revelation.[25]

According to Owen, at creation God endowed humans with an inner light which taught them that God was Creator, lawmaker, ruler, and rewarder. This knowledge was supplemented by God's sacramental command and by consideration of the world. This arrangement is characterized by Owen, in the manner typical of post-Reformation Reformed theology, as the covenant of works, and it served as the basis for humanity's pre-Fall knowledge of, and relationship with, God.[26] In terms of its appointed end, this revelation was fully adequate: if humans had obeyed God's command, they would ultimately have enjoyed eternal life.[27] This last point is of great importance, because throughout his discussions of theology, the underlying principle is that theology must be an adequate basis for the end it is to achieve. The language of *viator* and *possessor* pointed clearly to such a teleological understanding of theology, and the theology of the former must be continuous with, and able to lead to, the theology of the latter. This again reflects the basic presupposition behind Owen's thinking: theology is fundamentally relational, determined by and determinative of, the divine–human relationship.

Owen links the natural theology of pre-Fall humanity to his understanding of the image of God. In traditional fashion he locates this image in humanity's moral and intellectual qualities. These qualities were quite sufficient to enable humans to know God through his implanted law, his works in creation, and his

---

[24] *Works* 16, pp. 309–10.
[25] *Works* 17, p. 39.
[26] Ibid., p. 39; for a classic confessional statement of the covenant scheme, see *The Westminster Confession of Faith*, Chapter 7.
[27] Ibid., pp. 39–40.

sacramental law, and thus provided the subjective point of contact for the objective revelation, the personal cognitive basis for
the divine covenant of works. Pre-Fall humanity knew how to
worship God, and that eternal blessedness would be the reward
for so doing.[28] With the intrusion of sin at the Fall this image was
abolished, along with all that went with it: the intimate union
between God's teaching and the disposition of the human mind
was completely disrupted; the inner light was extinguished; and
the covenant was abolished.[29] Thus, natural theology as an
adequate means of achieving the end of eternal enjoyment of God
simply does not exist after the Fall. The covenant of works, no
longer adequate for leading to God, cannot provide humanity
with a means of reaching up to divine truths.

What is particularly interesting about Owen's discussion of the
inner light of natural theology is the way in which he makes quite
clear the connection between this and the second person of the
Trinity. The inner light is 'Verbum *endiathetos*', a term borrowed
from the Apologists and which Owen uses in his discussion of the
Trinity in his controversy with the Quakers.[30] In the *Theologoumena Pantodapa*, his use of the word *endiathetos*, coupled
with his insistence that the light is not *emphytos*, innate or
natural, serves to guarantee the special, gracious nature even of
the covenant of works, and points clearly to its positive relation-

---

[28] 'Cum itaque Deus hominem *rectum fecerit . . . in imagine sua . . .* quae in sapientia,
justitia, et sanctitate consistit . . . eique ut alias creaturas imperio teneret ad sui gloriam,
praeceperit; cui dominationi nisi earum naturae ei penitus perspectae fuissent, omnino
esset impar; atque ab eo obedientiam sub poena mortis aeternae, cumque praemii vitae
beatae pollicitatione, exegerit, ea sapientia et morali lumine, quo potuit et Deum
cognoscere, et legem *emphyton* et revelationem proprietatum Dei in omnium creatione,
et *nomothesia* sacramentali perfecte intelligere, instructum fuisse constat: Hac vero
theologia instructo nihil plane defuit ad Deum rite colendum, aut ad vitam bene
beateque agendam.' *Works* 17, p. 42. Owen refers to God's explicit statement to Adam
concerning the tree of knowledge as sacramental because it does not establish or reveal
the covenant of works to him – these are the natural results of his status as creature
and of his knowledge of that fact – but is a seal added to the covenant: 'praeceptum
autem sacramentale superadditum, foedus non revelavit, sed ad illud obsignandum
viam aperuit.' Works 17, p. 42.
[29] Ibid., pp. 43–4.
[30] See *Works* 16, pp. 429–33; for discussion of Owen's use of these terms in relation
to the Apologists, see below.

ship to God the Son.[31] Even natural theology is, for Owen, a theology of the Word.

Owen's rejection of natural theology after the Fall should not be seen in terms of the abolition of the objective revelation in itself, but of its subsequent insufficiency to lead sinful humanity to its appointed end in the eternal enjoyment of God. There still exists a general revelation, and humans can still know some things about God, such as the fact that he exists. Such knowledge is still part of human nature but is restricted to things that pertain to God as Creator.[32] The natural law that requires obedience to God retains its validity, and is subjectively reinforced by human conscience.[33] The problem is that humans now need to know God as Saviour, not simply as Creator, and (given humanity's sinfulness) general revelation and the natural theology of the unregenerate are incapable of providing this. Owen makes clear the point that God's works of creation and providence still speak of him, but are insufficient to lead to true knowledge and worship of God.[34]

This coupling of true knowledge with proper worship marks a clear point of continuity with the emphasis of both Calvin and the Reformed tradition upon the inseparability of true knowledge of God and true godliness.[35] As noted above, for Owen, as for Reformed theology in general, knowledge of God is relational in that it exists solely and entirely within the framework of a relationship which God established with humanity, for a

---

[31] *Works* 17, p. 39.

[32] 'Naturam ideo humanam tanta quamvis per peccatum clade confectam, et pene suae solum residuam, theologiae hujus reliquiis adhuc instructam esse dicimus. Deum esse, eumque talem, qualis ut sit exigit ipsa veritatis ratio, nempe *optimum* ob virtutem, ob beneficia *maximum*, eam non fugit. Hanc cognitionem, sub Deo Creatore, sibi ipsi acceptam fert. Viget adhuc in natura nostra ea lex et ratio quae veritatem hanc docet, clamat.' Ibid., p. 45.

[33] Ibid., pp. 46–7.

[34] 'Addit quidem Psaltes, doctrinam hanc operum creationis, et providentiae Dei, haud sufficientem esse, ut quis Deum rite cognoscat, et sancte colat.' Ibid., p. 51.

[35] See Calvin's classic statement, *Inst.* 1.2.1; cf. Ames, 'Theology is the doctrine of living to God.' *Marrow*, p. 77. For an excellent discussion of the practical thrust of Puritan divinity, see Schaefer, 'The Spiritual Brotherhood'; *idem*, 'Protestant "Scholasticism" at Elizabethan Cambridge: William Perkins and a Reformed Theology of the Heart', in Trueman and Clark, *Protestant Scholasticism*.

purpose: that humans might know and enjoy God. This basic presupposition is reinforced by the way in which the dynamics of the historical structure of Owen's work reflect his practical, teleological view of its purpose. In pre-Fall Eden, the covenant of works directed humans to the true knowledge of God and was normative for conduct. In the Garden, the end of theology was the enjoyment of God and the means was obedience to God. Sinless humanity was fully capable of this obedience: the revelation of God in creation, Adam's possession of the *logos endiathetos*, and the explicit precepts given to him were fully adequate to lead him to true worship and obedience. It is only after the intrusion of sin that these are no longer sufficient as means to bring humanity to the eternal enjoyment of God. By shattering this covenant relationship, sin destroyed the possibility of a proper natural theology viewed in terms of its adequacy to achieve its set purpose.[36] Thus, when talking of natural theology after the Fall, Owen regards the word 'theology' as being used only in an improper sense. After sin, therefore, there is need for further revelation and action on God's part.

Theology after the Fall

After the Fall, humans are no longer merely in need of a Creator: they need to know God as Saviour and Redeemer too. This points clearly to the epistemological inadequacy of general revelation/natural theology, as this can speak of God only as Creator. Such inadequacy leads directly to the need for the revelation of God in Christ, which is more than a mere repristination of what went before. For Owen, a vital part of the incarnation is that it reveals the saving love of God: Christ is the gracious God, manifest in the flesh, and it is only on this basis that fallen humanity can know the love of God as Saviour. There is thus a

---

[36] '[N]ulla doctrina theologia proprie dici potest, quae non foedere aliquo divino, cujus vi ipsi theologi Deo placere possint, atque ipso tandem frui, nititur. Etenim omnis viatorum theologia dirigit homines in cognitione Dei, et ad obedientiam secundum normam foederis quod cum iis inire Deo placuerit, debitam praestandam stimulat. Foedus autem illud, quod primigeniae istius theologiae fundamentum erat, ita, ut dixi, abolitum est.' *Works* 17, p. 44.

vital epistemological dimension to Owen's understanding of in-carnation, a dimension which reflects a need created by the Fall and which is emphasized by the structural importance of Christ's prophetic office in his discussion of the Mediator.[37] In the *Theologoumena Pantodapa*, Owen makes this explicit by emphasizing that Christ is the author of all true evangelical (i.e. gospel) theology by virtue of his consubstantiality with the Father.[38]

Christ's consubstantiality with the Father is of vital impor-tance to Owen's understanding of revelation, because the theol-ogy of union is the foundation of the objective reliability of special revelation: the personal union of the divine Logos with the human nature in the person of the Lord Jesus Christ is the basis for a gracious communication of knowledge of the Father to the person of the Mediator.[39] As the Mediator is, in turn, the revelation of the gracious God to humanity, the reliability of this revelation is directly dependent upon the identity of substance between Father and Son. This theology of union does not, of course, involve the communication of the archetype to Christ's humanity, as, in line with Augustinian and Reformed Christol-ogy, Owen considers that the finitude of the human nature means that it cannot comprehend the infinity of God. The knowledge available to the human Jesus is accommodated, limited, to that of which the human nature is capable, and this is reflected in the

---

[37] See Chapter Four.

[38] 'Auctor ideo theologiae evangelicae immediatus est ipse Jesus Christus, Filius Dei unigenitus.' *Works* 17, p. 411; 'Christum e sinu Patris missum, perfectissime Dei voluntatis cognitione instructum fuisse, ita ut nihil omnino novi iis relictum sit e veritatis fonte hauriendum, qui post regem venturi essent, Ecc. 2:12, inter se conveniunt Christiani pene omnes. Ipse quidem *ho logos*, aeternum Dei Verbum, infinitam rerum omnium scientiam, totius essentiae et voluntatis divinae intelligentiam absolutissimam habet sibi congenitam, hoc est, una cum *hypostasei* divina a Patre sibi ab aeterno communicatam. Qua vero ecclesiae Caput Mediator et *tes homologias hemon apostolos* a Patre delegatus exstitit, ea tantum novit (illa scilicet in natura, qua ipse totum munus mediatorium peregit), quae ei a Patre data et revelata sunt.' *Works* 17, p. 415. The role of the communication of properties will be discussed more fully in Ch. 4.

[39] 'Quae de Jesu Christi, "in quo absconditi sunt omnes thesauri sapientiae et scien-tiae," Col. 2:3, theologia deque scientia illa, quam per unionem personalem habuit, habetque, atque *revelationibus* ei a Patre datis' *Works* 17, p. 38. It is important to understand that Owen does not believe this communication takes place solely by virtue of the hypostatic union, as this has important christological implications: see Ch. 4 below.

fact that Owen, in standard Reformed fashion, does not regard the Logos as fully contained within the bounds of the incarnation.[40] The theology of union is therefore an ectypal theology, one which depends upon and reflects but does not fully reveal the archetype. It is this which forms the basis for the saving knowledge of God available to other humans, thus providing a Christological focus to Owen's teaching on revelation. Indeed, for Owen the resurrected humanity of Christ is the medium through which the saints will gaze upon God for eternity, even after the Day of Judgment.[41] Finite humans can never grasp God as he is in himself, and must always depend upon ectypal theology, as exhibited in Christ, even in glory. Christ's role as Mediator therefore has considerable epistemological significance which, as will be clear later, is reflected in Owen's doctrine of Scripture.

The Christological focus of the theological structure

It can now be seen that Owen's choice of a historical/covenantal scheme as the organizational principle for his most theologically comprehensive piece of work, the *Theologoumena Pantodapa*, has a significant advantage, given his distinctions between archetypal and ectypal theology, and his emphasis upon all theology as relational or covenantal: these factors all point towards a christologically focused system which the historical structure of the work is well-suited to provide. In terms of ontology, the radical distinction between archetypal and ectypal theology focuses attention on the ontological gap that exists between an infinite God and a finite creation, a gap that existed even before sin and which will continue after the Day of Judgment and for all eternity. Given Owen's insistence upon the continuing relevance of the incarnation after the Last Day as the

---

[40] See *Works* 1, p. 234 ff. For a full discussion of this, see the section on the prophetic office in Ch. 4 below.

[41] 'I do believe that the person of Christ, in and by his human nature, shall be forever the *immediate head of the whole glorified creation* . . . I do therefore also believe, that he shall be *the means and way of communication* between God and his glorified saints forever.' *Works* 1, p. 271. Cf. Trueman, 'Heaven and Hell'; also R. A. Muller, 'Christ in the Eschaton: Calvin and Moltmann on the Duration of the *Munus Regium*', *HTR* 74 (1981), 31–59.

only means by which knowledge of God will be mediated to humanity even after sin has been finally done away with, there is obviously within his thought the possibility of removing the need for incarnation from the context of soteriology to the context of creation itself, a move which could lead to a highly speculative doctrine of incarnation. In fact, this is never Owen's position, and he repeatedly emphasizes the fact that the necessity of incarnation is not to be considered except as logically subordinate to the Fall.[42] Nevertheless, his insistence on the special, gracious nature of the *logos endiathetos* as the basis for the natural theology of the covenant of the works points to the fundamental continuity between theology before and after the Fall as theology of the Word – theology which centres in the second person of the Trinity.

The ontological tension between God and creation might be great, but it is not to be regarded as the motivation for incarnation. This is where Owen's historical emphasis is so important. Owen, like Calvin, sees the problematic implications of the ontological aspects of the incarnation, but, also like Calvin, refuses to go down the more speculative route of divorcing incarnation from sin.[43] It is Owen's emphasis upon the historical order of theology, on the Fall as a decisive watershed for God's dealings with humanity and for the nature and content of his revelation, that enables him to bring this point out so clearly and to place the incarnation at the centre of the historical drama of sin and redemption as well as at the centre of the metaphysical problem of relating infinite to finite.

Given claims about the radical subordination of Bible to Aristotle in Owen's theology, it might appear surprising that in his most comprehensive treatment of theology he does not choose some form of causality as its organizational principle, as does Baxter, but rather a pattern which reflects as closely as possible the narrative flow of the Bible. If, however, we examine what Owen actually says about the teleological, relational, and covenantal nature of theology, and about the importance of the

---

[42] See Ch. 3 and Ch. 4.
[43] See Calvin *Inst*. 2.12.5.

Fall for the nature of revelation, the choice of such a historically structured approach is, if not inevitable, then clearly advantageous in the way in which it leads to a presentation of theology which focuses on the person of Christ.[44]

Scripture and Revelation

The Scriptures as revelation of God

If God in himself, and especially God in Christ provides the ultimate foundations for theology and for knowledge of God, then it is the Scriptures which, for Owen as for other Reformed Orthodox, provide the normative secondary source of such knowledge:

> Our belief of the Scriptures to be the Word of God, or a divine revelation, and our understanding of the mind and will of God as revealed in them, are the *two springs* of all our interest in Christian religion.[45]

These, the opening lines of Owen's treatise, *The Causes, Ways, and Means of Understanding the Mind of God* (1678), point directly to the heart of his theology in terms of its principle of knowing: the Scriptures.[46]

Owen's approach to the nature of the Scriptures arises primarily from his understanding of the nature and purpose of theology

---

[44] It is perhaps worth noting that Owen's *Theologoumena* also exhibits structural similarities to theological systems organized around the principle of the twofold knowledge of God. Such a structure is evident in Calvin's *Institutes* and was adopted with considerable success by the Reformed tradition which developed from the mid-sixteenth century onwards. While the systematic flow of Owen's argument can be seen as controlled by the historical movement from creation to Fall to redemption, an underlying move can be discerned from knowledge of God the Creator to knowledge of God the Redeemer. This movement derives from Owen's adherence to the federal structure of the history he is outlining, where the historical development itself embodies epistemological concerns. On these issues, see E. A. Dowey, *The Knowledge of God in Calvin's Theology* (Grand Rapids: Eerdmans, 1994); R. A. Muller, '"*Duplex cognitio dei*" in the Theology of Early Reformed Orthodoxy', *SCJ* 10 (1979), 51–61.

[45] *Works* 4, p. 121.

[46] For discussions of Owen on Scripture, see Stanley N. Gundry, 'John Owen on Authority and Scripture' in John D. Hannah (ed), *Inerrancy and the Church* (Chicago: Moody Press, 1984), 189–221; also D. McKim, 'John Owen's Doctrine of Scripture', 195–207. Gundry's article is a sound guide, although its polemical context, a response to the so-called 'Rogers–McKim proposal', means that it is fairly narrowly focused upon the issue of the truth of Scripture and not on the broader theological context.

after the Fall. It is also true, however, that his arguments are not developed in some kind of intellectual vacuum. Instead, specific polemical concerns exert a decisive impact upon the form and emphases of his teaching on Scripture – concerns which by their very novelty effectively prevent him from merely reiterating the position of his sixteenth-century antecedents. This is not to say that his teaching, and that of mid-seventeenth-century Reformed Orthodoxy necessarily represents a fundamental break with the past – such a conclusion could be drawn only if the doctrine of Scripture was to be isolated from its broader theological context – but rather a development of that position in order to safeguard the central scriptural principle of the Reformation. In fact, as will become clear, Owen's teaching on Scripture should be understood as an attempt to work out the implications of a number of other doctrines, such as Trinity, Christology, and providence, for the cognitive foundations of the Christian faith.

In terms of the actual nature of Scripture as revelation and as the normative cognitive foundation for the Christian faith, Owen had little, if any, dispute with his two most frequent foes, the Arminians and the Socinians. Both professed to hold to the Scripture principle, and Owen's conflict with them focused not on the principle itself but on the principles of interpretation, the relationship of reason to revelation and other such methodological foundations.[47] So, instead of a pointless engagement with

---

Footnote 46 (*continued*) McKim's article suffers from its assumption of a basic opposition between the alleged dynamic view of the Reformers and the Westminster divines, and the more static approach of later Orthodoxy. Again, it is not hard to detect the subtle working of a modern theological agenda, this time set more by the preoccupations of American Presbyterians in the debates over revising the Westminster Confession than by the historical and doctrinal concerns of the seventeenth century. For the full Rogers–McKim proposal, which includes a discussion of Owen, see *The Authority and Interpretation of the Bible: An Historical Approach* (San Francisco: Harper and Row, 1979).

[47] See Arminius, *Private Disputations* 5–10 in *The Works of James Arminius*, trans. J. and W. Nichols, 3 vols. (Grand Rapids, Baker, 1986) 2, pp. 322–31. While it is not primarily a discussion of the Scripture principle in Remonstrant theology, John Platt's analysis of nature, grace, and inexcusability provides many interesting insights of relevance, and indicates that it was not the Scripture principle itself, but differences over the epistemological capacity of human beings which was the foundation for much of the conflict between Remonstrants and Calvinists in the early-seventeenth century: see his *Reformed Thought*, pp. 179–201. For the classic Socinian statement of the Scripture principle, see *The Racovian Catechism*, trans. T. Rees (London: Longman, 1818), pp. 1–19.

these two groups on the issue of Scripture, Owen chose to frame his position in opposition, on the one hand, to those who opposed the sufficiency of the Scriptures as a source for theological reflection, and, on the other hand, to those who argued for their irrelevance, or, at least, for giving them a diminished role. The major representatives of the former viewpoint were, of course, the Catholics, who had been criticized by Protestants since the Reformation for adding their own traditions to the teachings laid out in Scripture.[48] When he came to attack the Catholics, therefore, Owen stood within a well-established tradition, with an armoury of well-rehearsed arguments at his disposal.

In Owen's day, however, the polemical situation had become somewhat more subtle than had previously been the case with the publication, in 1657, of the London Polyglot Bible by Brian Walton, representing as it did the development of a more critical approach to the Bible.[49] This work, a landmark in philological and textual study of the Bible, raised a number of crucial questions for Orthodoxy concerning the integrity of the biblical text. Owen was particularly perturbed by the implications which the variant readings contained in the appendix had for his arguments concerning the divine preservation and integrity of the Scriptures.[50] While Owen argued for a very high view of the biblical text, we must, however, beware of reading back into his treatise attacking Walton the concerns of certain nineteenth- and twentieth-century debates about the authority of Scripture: first, Owen's work represents not a crude attempt which demands, as logical consequence of some presupposed a priori considerations, a pure text whatever the evidence, but a learned engagement with textual and historical issues designed to establish by empirical

---

[48]   E.g. Calvin, *Inst*. 4.8.14.

[49]   For a full discussion of the issues raised by the Polyglot Bible, see R. A. Muller, 'The Debate over the Vowel Points and the Crisis in Orthodox Hermeneutics', *JMRS* 10 (1980), 53–72.

[50]   Owen outlined his view of this in his treatise of 1659, *Of the Divine Original, Authority, Self-Evidencing Light, and Power of the Scriptures* (*Works* 16, pp. 283–343). Owen relates how, on completion of this work, he came into possession of a copy of the Polyglot Bible and was so disturbed by it that he had to go into print again in 1659 with a second treatise, *Of the Integrity and Purity of the Hebrew and Greek Text of the Scripture* (*Works* 16, pp. 347–421).

methods the integrity of the biblical documents; and, second, the subtext to Owen's treatise really concerns not the implications for Scripture's reliability if Walton's case on, say, the late dating of the vowel points is conceded, but the implications for Scripture's sufficiency. For, if the vowel points, a central tool for biblical interpretation, are an uninspired, human addition, then the implication is that the original, inspired texts are utterly ambiguous and thus not in themselves sufficient for the theological task.[51] A defence of the verbal inspiration of the entire text, coupled with a defence of its providential preservation is thus crucial to Owen's attempts at maintaining the doctrine of Scripture's sufficiency in the face of certain mid-seventeenth-century scholarly trends.

The second group with which Owen engaged were the Quakers who, in their emphasis upon the direct leading of the Spirit and the 'inner light' tended to downgrade the role of Scripture, or even to discount Scripture as a source of knowledge of God and his leading.[52] Given their similarity in this respect to the various spiritualist sects of the sixteenth century, the points which Owen makes against them are very similar to the strictures made by such as Calvin against some of the more radical groups of his own day.[53] Following in the Reformed tradition, Owen stresses that word and Spirit belong inseparably together, and uses the Trinitarian and Christological underpinnings of his thought to articulate and defend this position.

Given the normative value of the Scriptures for Owen, it is obvious that understanding that they are the revelation of God and knowing how they should be interpreted are thus crucial to the well-being of every Christian.[54] In light of what has been said

---

[51] See *Works* 16, pp. 370 ff.

[52] For a good discussion of Quaker views of the Spirit in relation to the Bible, see Nuttall, *Holy Spirit*.

[53] E.g. *Inst.* 1.9; 4.8.13.

[54] Owen wrote three treatises which contain significant reflection upon the Scriptures as they stand in relation to the theological task: *The Divine Original of the Scriptures* (1659), a defence of the divine nature of the Bible; *Exercitationes adversos Fanaticos* (1659), a polemical work directed against the Quakers; and *The Causes, Ways, and Means of Understanding the Mind of God* (1678), part of his massive work on the work of the Holy Spirit.

above concerning the role of the intratrinitarian relationships and the incarnation in revelation, it comes as no surprise to find that Owen's articulation of the Scripture principle does not disrupt the Christological focus of his understanding of revelation but, as will become clear, rather reflects and reinforces the basic Christocentricity and Trinitarianism of his theology as a whole. In order to make this clear, Owen makes a distinction between Christ as the *essential* Word of God and Scripture as the *written* Word of God, thus allowing for a twofold application of the phrase 'Word of God' in his theology, a position entirely consistent with that of Calvin and the earlier Reformed tradition.[55] This parallels another distinction Owen makes in his anti-Quaker work, *Exercitationes adversos Fanaticos*, between the Word *hypostatikos*, *endiathetos*, and *prophorikos*. In this context, the first term refers to Christ personally, the second to manifestations of God's power (and not specifically to the Word implanted in human nature), and the third to Scripture.[56] In terms of the history of Christian theology, the terms *endiathetos* and *prophorikos*, while Hellenistic in origin, are of patristic vintage, being found, for example, in Theophilus of Antioch's *Ad Autolycum*.[57] Owen's use, however, represents a distinct modification of that of Theophilus: for the latter, the *logos endiathetos* is God's internal word, while the *logos prophorikos* is the word generated and externalized by the Father. As such, the terminology refers to intratrinitarian relations and represents one element of Theophilus' attempt to explain the

---

[55]   *Works* 16, pp. 435–36. Cf. R. S. Wallace, *Calvin's Doctrine of Word and Sacrament* (Edinburgh: Oliver and Boyd, 1953), pp. 96–114 with B. A. Gerrish, 'Biblical Authority and the Continental Reformation', *SJT* 10 (1957), 337–60, esp. 353 ff; also J. Murray, 'Calvin and the Authority of Scripture' in *The Collected Writings of John Murray* 4 (Edinburgh: Banner of Truth, 1982), pp. 176–90; and Dowey, *The Knowledge of God*, pp. 99 ff., 117 ff. Again, modern theological agendas often seem to have played an unhealthy role in this question. Even in 1994, it was claimed by at least one eminent scholar at the International Congress for Calvin Research that Calvin never identifies the Word of God with Scripture. In response, one can only comment that it is difficult to make sense of a passage such as *Inst.* 1.6.3 without allowing that such an identification can be found in Calvin.

[56]   *Works* 16, pp. 429–33.

[57]   For a detailed discussion of the two terms, see M. Muhl, 'Der *logos endiathetos* und *prophorikos* von der alteren Stoa bis zur Synode von Sirmium 351', *Archiv für Begriffsgeschichte* 7 (1962), 7–56.

generation of the Son by the Father.[58] Owen's application of the term *logos prophorikos* to Scripture, however, is clearly discontinuous with the patristic usage; indeed, its only similarity to the patristic usage appears to be that it is used by Owen to describe something which originates in God, i.e. Scripture is called the word of God because it originates in God, because it is an external revelation of the divine will, and because it was written down under the guidance and control of the Holy Spirit.[59] Therefore, *logos prophorikos* serves to emphasize the divine origin of Scripture, a use which Theophilus would not have recognized.

As Owen cites no source for his own use of the terms, we cannot be certain from where he borrowed them, although Theophilus, along with other patristic authors, is referred to by name a few paragraphs further on, and heavily criticized for importing the content, and not just the language, of Greek philosophy into Christian thought.[60] The origins of Owen's own use of these terms are therefore impossible to establish with any degree of certainty. The usage does not appear to be typical of Reformed Orthodoxy, and the only precedent in the literature which springs immediately to mind is that of Arminius in his fifth *Private Disputation*.[61] Owen makes no explicit reference to this text, where Arminius uses both *endiathetos* and *prophorikos* with reference to the Word, understood as revelation: he applies the former to the *semen religionis* and the latter to the written Scriptures. Thus, his use of *endiathetos* is identical to the use we noted in Owen earlier, while his application of *prophorikos* is identical to that we find here. Whether Owen is dependent upon Arminius at this point cannot be proved, but, given the apparent lack of other precedents, the similarity is at least suggestive.

---

[58]   *Ad Autolycum* 2:10 (*ANF* 2.98).
[59]   *Works* 16, p. 434.
[60]   Ibid., p. 431. The others named are Clement of Alexandria, Tatian, Eusebius, Cyril, and Theodoret.
[61]   Arminius, *Works* 2, pp. 322–4. Cf. Junius, *De vera Theologia* in *Opera Theologica* (Geneva, 1613) I, 1798–1801. I am grateful to Dr Sebastian Rehnman for bringing Junius' use of the terms to my attention: see his 'Theologia Tradita: a study in the prolegomenous discourse of John Owen', unpubl. DPhil Diss. (Oxford University, 1997), p.128. Given this distinctive use by both Arminius and Junius, it could well be that Owen is drawing on a specific terminological tradition of the Leiden faculty at this point.

In Owen's thought, it is the aspect of the *logos prophorikos* as
the revelation of the divine will which serves to make the point
of connection between Christ, the Word *agraphon*, and Scripture,
the Word *engraphon*. Both Christ and Scripture reveal the will of
God and thus both have the same formal content, the former
because of Christ's consubstantiality with the Father, the latter
because of the purpose of revelation, to reveal the grace of God
in Christ, and because of the Trinitarian structure of inspiration.
This is a connection which is standard in Reformed Orthodoxy.[62]
The distinction had a number of uses in Reformed Orthodoxy in
general, but for Owen it also had a very specific relevance for the
English theological world of the mid-seventeenth century. First,
the positive connection of Christ and Scripture must be maintained in order to allow that Scripture has authority: Christ is the
revelation of God the Father's gracious will, and the Scriptures
are the place where the believer finds Christ.[63] Second, this
connection is consequently of great importance in his conflict
with the Quakers, since Scripture's status as the revelation of
God's will allows him to draw it up into a Trinitarian understanding of revelation that avoids the Quaker divorce between
Word and Spirit. Since Owen held firmly to the Western order
of procession, where the Spirit proceeds from Father and Son,
the Spirit cannot be in any way divorced from the Son.[64]

It is this Trinitarianism which undergirds the authority of the
gospel. Part of this, the relationship between Father, Son, and
inscripturated gospel, is made clear in the following passage:

> The person of the Father is the eternal fountain of infinitely divine
> glorious perfections; and they are all communicated unto the Son by
> eternal generation. In his person *absolutely*, as the Son of God, they are
> all of them *essentially*; in his person as God-man, as vested with his
> offices, they are *substantially*, in opposition unto all types and shadows;
> and in the glass of the gospel they are *accidentally*, by revelation, – *really*
> but not *substantially*, for Christ himself is the body, the substance of all.
> As the *image of God*, so is he represented unto us in the glass of the gospel;
> and therein are we called to behold the glory of God in him, 2 Cor. 3:18.
> The meaning is, that the truth and doctrine concerning Jesus Christ, his

---

[62] On the twofold Word in Reformed Orthodoxy, see Muller, *PRRD2*, pp. 182 ff.
[63] E.g. *Works* 4, pp. 168–9; *Works* 17, pp. 415–17.
[64] See *Works* 4, pp. 158–9.

person and mediation, is so delivered and taught in the gospel as that the glory of God is eminently represented thereby; or therein is revealed what we are to know of God, his mind and his will, as he is declared by and in Jesus Christ.[65]

The role of Father and Son in revelation is thus clear. This, in turn, points clearly to the role of the Spirit: because the Spirit is the Spirit of the Father and of the Son, his task is to bear witness to Christ, the revelation of the Father.[66] Part of this witness-bearing consists in his role in the inspiration of the Scriptures.

Scripture and inspiration

While the Scripture's status as revelation points clearly to its positive relation to Christ, it is also *theopneustos*, Spirit-breathed, not only in terms of its content but also in terms of its written form.[67] This inspiration came about through God immediately moving the various authors, whether in the Old Testament by dreams, visions, voices, internal inspiration, and even face-to-face encounter, or in the New Testament through Jesus Christ, although Owen does not care to speculate in detail about individual cases.[68] In discussing the manner in which the writers were moved, Owen's language comes very close to advocating a mechanistic view of inspiration whereby the authors were purely passive tools in the hands of God, 'as an instrument of music, giving a sound according to the hand, intention, and skill of him that strikes it'.[69] He does allow that authors chose individual words and wrote in their individual styles, but this is in no way allowed to detract from the full inspiration of the Scriptures in every detail.[70] His position in fact helps him to maintain the inspiration of the Masoretic vowel points, necessary if he is to defend the full integrity and sufficiency of the biblical text.[71]

---

[65] Ibid., p. 169.
[66] Ibid., pp. 195 ff.
[67] Ibid., p. 300.
[68] Ibid., p. 298.
[69] Ibid., p. 299.
[70] Ibid., p. 305.
[71] See his *Of the Integrity and Purity of the Hebrew and Greek Text of the Scripture* in *Works* 16, pp. 347–421; on the controversy over vowel points in the seventeenth century, see Muller, 'The Debate over the Vowel Points'.

In his article on Owen's view of Scripture, Donald McKim has picked up on this mechanistic language and criticized the Puritan for allowing the human authors to be overwhelmed by the divine and regarding the authors 'as passive instruments for the recording of God's Word'.[72] This is not an entirely fair characterization, as it fails to set Owen's doctrine of inspiration within the larger theological context. Vital to this context is Owen's understanding of providence, which has direct bearing upon the inspiration of Scripture because this takes place within the created realm and therefore occurs within a framework determined by God's providential dealings with his creatures. What Owen is doing in his discussion of inspiration is, from one angle, simply applying the standard Reformed doctrine of providence to the specific issue of the composition of the Scriptures, whereby the sovereignty and decisive role of God, the First Cause, is maintained, while, at the level of human agency, the contingency of secondary causality is also allowed, thus safeguarding the freedom of the creature.[73] Thus, the passivity of the human authors in the process of inspiration must be seen as analogous to the passivity of the creature in providence: God's will will be done; ultimately not in an external–mechanical way, but in an internal–dynamic fashion. This is reflected in the fact that revelation is given via, and thus accommodated to, human rational faculties.[74] The humanity of the authors, and, indeed, of the writing of the text of Scripture is no more negated by the fact of such divine inspiration than is the humanity of any other human agent or act which depends upon God as its ultimate cause.

Owen's emphasis upon accommodation is one example of his attempt to articulate this. In accommodating himself to human capacity, God actually accommodated himself to the very jots and tittles of the specific languages used.[75] Thus, Scripture is a

---

[72] 'John Owen's Doctrine of Scripture', 202–3.
[73] Owen makes the connection between providence and inspiration explicit: see *Works* 16, p. 300; for detailed discussion of Owen on providence, see Ch. 3 below.
[74] *Works* 16, p. 198. The corollary of this is that the subsequent appropriation of revelation by the believing subject involves the supernatural exaltation of the rational faculties: see below.
[75] 'The whole course of speech, especially in the New Testament, is accommodated unto the nature, use, and propriety of that language, as expressed in other authors who wrote therein, and had a perfect understanding of it.' *Works* 4, p. 214.

quintessentially human document but is also an infallible revelation of God. The divine nature of the Scriptures is made possible
by God's condescension in his act of accommodation; the human
nature is guaranteed because God has accommodated himself to
language, the most human of conventions. Unlike modern neo-
orthodox theologians, such as Barth and Berkouwer, Owen sees
no antithesis between the humanity of the Bible and a doctrine
of verbal inspiration, a position which he can maintain because
of his commitment to the Reformed (or, perhaps better,
Augustinian) doctrine of accommodation combined with his
view of primary and secondary causality.[76]

The fact that inspiration is, for Owen, a providential act of the
Spirit also points once again towards the Trinitarian foundations
of his understanding of Scripture as revelation. Providence is
understood by Owen in a thoroughly Trinitarian way: the Father
acts in creation by the Son through the Holy Spirit.[77] Thus, the
act of inspiration, while consistently referred to the agency of the
Spirit in Owen's writings, is quite clearly the act of the whole
Trinity. This in turn guarantees the reliability of scriptural revelation: the Western understanding of the Trinity to which Owen
adheres binds Father, Son, and Holy Spirit together in one
Christ-centred plan of salvation. Such reliability is essential if
Scripture is to achieve its purpose.[78]

Scripture and Christ: some observations

In light of the above it is clear that Owen regards Scripture as
dependent upon Christ for its content. This is clear not simply
from his understanding of the necessarily Trinitarian nature of
revelation, but also from the doctrinal and historical distinctions
which he makes within the theological task which we noted
earlier. When he distinguishes archetypal and ectypal theology,
and stresses the need to know God as Redeemer, he points
unmistakeably to the revelation of God in Christ. It is Christ,
after all, who through his consubstantiality with the Father is the
very embodiment of the Father's revelation.

---

[76] See Barth, *CD* 2.2, pp. 532 ff.; Berkouwer, *Holy Scripture*, trans. Jack B.
Rogers (Grand Rapids: Eerdmans, 1975), pp. 18 ff.
[77] See Ch. 3 below.
[78] See *Works* 16, p. 300.

Then, while he regards all of the Bible as true in the sense that it is a proper and reliable revelation of God, he also clearly allows that revelation is progressive over time and finds its culmination in the incarnation: this is obvious from the distinctions he makes between the various covenants described in the biblical record. For example, the fundamental difference for Owen between the two testaments, and the thing which makes the New superior to the Old is that in the New God spoke directly in the historical person of his Son rather than through types and shadows.[79] There is thus a distinct historical progression involved in the content of revelation in the movement from the Garden of Eden to the culmination of God's revelation in the incarnation. This was in part determined by God's accommodation to the needs of the church in each particular age.[80] Such a historical development is epitomized in the federal structure of *Theologoumena Pantodapa* where God progressively reveals himself to his people through a series of covenants which have their goal, and reach their fulfilment, in the person of the Lord Jesus Christ. Thus, Jesus of Nazareth stands as the historical culmination of the history of the people of Israel.

There are then two lines, one vertical and one horizontal, in Owen's understanding of Scripture as revelation. First, there is the vertical line of God's gracious will to save, which, thanks to the Son's consubstantiality with the Father and his participation in the covenant of redemption, is revealed in the person of Jesus Christ through the Holy Spirit whose task is to bear witness to the will of the Father revealed in the Son. Second, there is the horizontal line of the gradual revelation of God's salvific will in history which starts in the Garden of Eden and culminates in the birth, life, and death of Christ. Both lines, the vertical and the horizontal intersect in the person of Jesus of Nazareth who is the

---

[79] Ibid., p. 305.

[80] 'In the writing of the holy Scripture, the Spirit of God had respect unto the *various states and conditions of the church*. It was not given for the use of one age or season only, but for all generations, – for a guide in faith and obedience from the beginning of the world to the end of it. And the state of the church was not always to be the same, neither in light, knowledge, nor worship. God had so disposed of things in the eternal counsel of his will that it should be carried on by various *degrees of divine revelation* unto its perfect estate.' *Works* 4, p. 189.

historical manifestation of God's eternal decision concerning salvation. This twofold significance of Christ serves to give Owen's theology of revelation a firmly christocentric focus.

In light of the above, Owen's solution to the problems with which Catholicism and the Polyglot Bible confronted him, along with the different challenges presented by the Quakers, is clear: Scripture is sufficient and central because of its relationship to Christ; Scripture is the foundation for knowledge about Christ because it is the Holy Spirit, the Spirit of Christ, the Spirit whose task is to bear witness to Christ, who controlled its composition. In terms of Scripture's content it is related to Christ as Word, *engraphon*, to Word, *agraphon*; and, as Christ is sufficient for salvation, so too are the Scriptures because only in them can one find the revelation of Christ. Nowhere else can this revelation of God's salvific will be found. In terms of its form, Scripture is sufficient because of the way in which it was inscripturated under the guidance of the Holy Spirit who, as proceeding from the Father and the Son, does not disrupt the christological focus and also, *pace* the Quakers, cannot act on individuals in isolation from the Word.

Nevertheless, Rome, the rise of textual criticism, and the emergence of the Quakers were only part of the problem for Owen. In asserting the objectivity of Christian revelation, he was able to engage and refute, at least to his own satisfaction, the challenges these raised. Nevertheless, he was also concerned about the subjective aspects of the Scripture principle, the way in which the individual was able to appropriate true doctrine from the biblical text. It was here that he clashed with his perennial foes, the Arminians and the Socinians.

Interpreting Revelation

The work of the Spirit

In line with his basically Augustinian anthropology, Owen considers human beings to be subject to two conditions which render their appropriation of God's revelation impossible: their essential finiteness; and their sinful depravity. The first cuts them off from God because God is an infinite object beyond the grasp of finite beings. As noted above, even in the state of integrity, Owen argues, the finiteness of the human mind renders it incapable, in itself, of understanding the mysteries of God.[81] Human minds are simply not capable of comprehending God, and this is why people are not only dependent upon ectypal theology, but also require God's assistance in order to grasp this theology for themselves.

The second condition, that of innate sinful depravity, serves to blind people to that revelation.[82] Owen regards this depravity as having two effects. First, it plunges human minds into darkness and blinds them to God's revelation; and, second, it implants corrupt affections which lead people to reject Scripture.[83] As a result, a person can only come to grasp God's revelation once this darkness and these corrupt affections have been overcome. In other words, objective revelation is not enough; there must also be a subjective transformation within human beings to make the grasping of revelation a reality. This is where the work of the Holy Spirit becomes vitally important.

As noted above, Owen regards the Spirit as proceeding from Father and Son and as the only one of the divine persons who acts directly within the created realm.[84] As such, all actions of God towards human beings, including the personal application of salvation, must be the direct work of the Holy Spirit, although dual procession guarantees the overall Trinitarian nature of such actions. In transforming human beings into beings capable of receiving and understanding revelation, the Spirit fulfils a double function: he removes the darkness from the human rational faculties; and he raises those faculties to a level far above any which they could achieve by themselves.[85] This latter point is very important for Owen, as he frames his position on this issue in opposition to twin perils: a Socinian reduction of divine truth to

---

[81] *Works* 4, pp. 137–8.
[82] Ibid., p. 130.
[83] Ibid., pp. 176, 178.
[84] *Works* 3, p. 92. The one exception to this is the assumption of human flesh by the Logos: see Ch. 4.
[85] *Works* 4, p. 126.

that which is compatible with, and available to, unaided human reason; and enthusiastic notions that truth can be appropriated without use of the reason.[86] Faith involves knowledge; knowledge presupposes an act of cognition; and so faith must involve an act of the intellect. It is thus very important for Owen that this action of the Spirit is understood not as standing over against human rationality, but as being fundamentally continuous with it. The gospel is not *irrational* but *suprarational* in that it does not involve the cancelling out of God's image in humanity (which involves, as we have seen, the rational faculties) but the perfection of that image.[87]

One result of the Spirit's work in elevating human rational powers beyond their usual capabilities is a certain knowledge of the gospel:

> The certainty and assurance that we may have and ought to have of our right understanding of the mind of God in the Scripture, either in general or as to any especial doctrine, doth not depend upon, is not resolved into, any *immediate inspiration or enthusiasm*; it doth not depend upon nor is it the *result of our reason and understanding* merely in their natural actings, but as they are elevated, enlightened, guided, conducted, by an internal efficacious work of the Spirit of God upon them.[88]

Such a position also delimits the usefulness of the so-called external arguments for the Scripture's truth and reliability: these are helps to those who believe but can never bring the unbeliever to faith.[89] Indeed, his presupposed Aristotelian understanding of physics, where effects are considered to be in proportion to their causes, is a help in radically restricting reason here: the finite nature of arguments based purely on human reason renders them

---

[86]   Ibid., pp. 124–6.

[87]   It is in this context that Owen's use of reason in theology must be understood. Theology is, for Owen, always 'reasonable' or 'rational' when set within the context of faith, and he is critical of those who would deny this: 'Those who would prohibit us the use of our reason in the things of religion would deal with us as the Philistines did with Samson – first put out our eyes, and then make us grind in their mill.' *Works* 3, p. 125. As Father Brown said to the master criminal, Flambeau, theology that is not rational is bad theology.

[88]   *Works* 4, p. 126.

[89]   Ibid., pp. 20 ff.

incapable of achieving a supernatural end, that of faith.[90] For Owen, then, the logic of Aristotelian physics, when applied to Christian theology, precludes rationalism.

The above quotation indicates a further aspect of the work of the Spirit within the believer, namely its connection with the Scriptures. The Spirit, Owen emphasizes, does not work on his own account, but operates only in relation to the written Word of God. This is indicated in the distinction he makes between objective and subjective revelation:

> [T]here is [in salvation] an *internal subjective revelation*, whereby no *new things* are revealed unto our minds, or are not outwardly revealed *anew*, but our minds are enabled to discern the things that are revealed already. All the things here mentioned by the apostle, which he desires they might *understand*, were already revealed in the Scriptures of the Old Testament, and the New that were then written, and the infallible declaration of the gospel in the preaching of the apostles. But there was a new work of revelation required in and unto every person that would understand and comprehend these things in a due manner; for *apokalypsis*, or 'revelation,' is the *discovery* of any thing, whether by the *proposal* of it unto us, or the *enabling* of us to discern it when it is so proposed.[91]

Here, in opposition to Quaker subjectivism, we find the objective and subjective poles of theology brought together: objectively, God has revealed himself in his Word, both Christ and Scripture; subjectively, God reveals himself to individuals by using his Holy Spirit to enable humans to grasp that objective revelation for themselves. It is also here that the full Trinitarianism of Owen's doctrine of revelation comes to the fore. The Son reveals the Father, and that revelation is appropriated by human beings through the work of the Holy Spirit. Because of the close connection between the Word *agraphon* and the Word *engraphon*, the Scriptures can act as a cognitive substitute in this arrangement for the second person of the Trinity and thus stand as the

---

[90] 'Our assent can be of no other nature than the arguments and motives whereon it is built, or by which it is wrought in us, as in *degree* it cannot exceed their *evidence*. Now these arguments [external arguments for Scripture's truth] are all human and fallible. Exalt them unto the greatest esteem possible . . . they produce an opinion only, though in the highest kind of probability, and firm against objections . . . But this exclusive of all divine faith.' *Works* 4, p. 50; cf. *Works* 4, pp. 7 ff.

[91] Ibid., p. 134.

revelation of the Father witnessed to by the Spirit. The position is undergirded by Owen's adherence to the Western Trinitarian formulation that stresses the *filioque*: the Spirit proceeds from the Father and the Son, and therefore has a necessary, indeed essential, Christological orientation. For Owen, the Holy Spirit is preeminently the Spirit *of Christ* and is thus to be understood as working within the framework established by the person and work of Christ.[92] Those like the Quakers, who in their emphasis upon the Spirit as inner light try to place a wedge between God's Word and the Spirit, are inevitably going to end up with a theology that is mere ungodly subjectivism. Owen's Trinitarianism means that Spirit and Word, subjective and objective, must be held together.[93]

Owen expounds his understanding of how the Spirit forges the relationship between the Word and the human subject using the categories of Aristotelian faculty psychology. We have seen that he regarded God's image in humans as residing in their rational faculties, and that the Spirit restores these and exalts them as part of the process of enabling humans to grasp truths of revelation which surpass normal human powers. These rational faculties consist primarily of the intellect, which can itself be divided into two parts, the theoretical and the practical, both of which are closely related to the will and affections.[94] In line with traditional Aristotelian thought, Owen regards the object of the theoretical intellect as being the true, and the object of the practical intellect as being the good. In fact, both the true and the good are the same object viewed from differing perspectives: the theoretical intellect recognizes the true, and the practical intellect then moves the will towards it.[95] The Fall, however, has thoroughly corrupted the mind so that it is incapable either of recognizing the

---

[92]   Ibid., pp. 158–60. The Christ-centredness of the Spirit in Owen's theology is made absolutely clear by his careful formulation of a Spirit-Christology: see the discussion in Ch. 4.

[93]   Nuttall has an excellent discussion of Spirit and Word in Puritan theology, but does not relate it to the Western Trinitarian tradition: see *Holy Spirit*, pp. 20–33.

[94]   *Works* 3, pp. 280–1.

[95]   Owen's intellectualism is a major subtheme throughout his work on the Holy Spirit: see *Works* 3, pp. 281, 303 ff., 330ff., 350 ff., 493 f., 498 ff., 503, 529 f., 551 ff., 641.

true or, as a consequence, of moving the will towards the good. Indeed, Owen argues for a twofold distinction with reference to the cause of humanity's ignorance: innate depravity, whereby the intellect is deprived of light; and the depravation of the will and affections, whereby they direct themselves naturally towards evil.[96] There can, therefore, be no true or saving theology within the unregenerate.

Given the argument that attempts to divide Owen and Baxter on the issue of the former's indebtedness to Scholasticism and metaphysics over against the latter's generally more 'biblical' approach, a comparison with Baxter is instructive here. In his *Methodus Theologiae*, faculty psychology is given a structural importance which is absent from the work of Owen. We have already noted the overall causal framework of Baxter's system, which places God as the Final Cause when viewed as the object of rational humanity. Human rationality is therefore of central importance to the shape of theology, and this is reflected in the massive explication of rational psychology which Baxter undertakes in Book One of the work. Opting for his typical threefold division, as opposed to the more normal bifurcation, he divides the topic into power [*potentia*], intellect, and will which are, respectively, the human centres of spiritual power, spiritual wisdom, and spiritual love.[97] Baxter argues that the image of God in human beings directly parallels God's own threefold nature of omnipotence, wisdom, and goodness.[98] In fact, he goes even further, and states that the order of the psychological faculties in humans directly mirrors the order of procession within the Trinity: as the Father begets the Son, and the Spirit proceeds from them both, so the power activates the intellect, and then the two of them move the will.[99] This move is not as harmless as it may seem, having decisive implications for the relationship between reason and revelation.

What the theological advantages of this threefold division are

---

96 Ibid., p. 244.
97 *Methodus Theologiae* 1a.5.8, p. 157.
98 Ibid. 1a.5.1 ff., p. 156.
99 Ibid. 1a.6.6, p. 177.

for Baxter are not immediately apparent, although by defining power as having a specific moral quality, he does avoid making the intellect and will into morally arbitrary phenomena and thus precludes the possibility of radical voluntarism 'in either the divine or human sphere;[100] however, this was scarcely a danger even within the straightforward twofold division of intellect and will, providing that the intellect was given priority. What is significant is that Baxter is using a distinctly philosophical source, the metaphysics of Tommaso Campanella, to shape and inform his theology. Campanella is mentioned by Baxter in the preface to the *Methodus Theologiae* as the one who first persuaded him of the propriety of the threefold, as opposed to the twofold, division of topics.[101] The change is more than a mere methodological modification, as Campanella's logic is built directly upon a metaphysics whereby *ens* (being), is understood as consisting of three primalities: power, wisdom, and love.[102] These categories are precisely those which Baxter sees as existing in God and which, as we noted above, parallel the human psychology of power, intellect, and will. In addition, there are profound similarities between Baxter and Campanella on the order of the primalities' operation, with Campanella also stressing the primacy of power, then wisdom, and then love.[103] This Campanellan metaphysics is more significant for Baxter's doctrine of God than a merely methodological move: it leads him to a rejection also of the standard scholastic twofold distinction of God's knowledge into that of simple intelligence and that of vision. To these two

---

[100]   Ibid. 1a.6.12, p. 177.

[101]   Ibid., Praefatio, p. 5 (not paginated in original). For the impact of Campanella on Baxter, see Trueman, 'A Small Step Towards Rationalism'.

[102]   Tommaso Campanella, *Metaphysica*, ed. L. Firpo (Turin: Bottega d'Erasmo, 1961), 1.3.3, p. 32; see also B. M. Bonansea, *Tommaso Campanella: Renaissance Pioneer of Modern Thought* (Washington: Catholic University of America Press, 1969), pp. 138–64; also J. Kvacala, *Thomas Campanella: Ein Reformer der Ausgehenden Renaissance* (Berlin: Trowitzsch, 1973); J. M. Headley, 'Tommaso Campanella and the end of the Renaissance', *JMRS* 20 (1990), 157–74; *idem*, 'Tommaso Campanella and Jean de Launoy: The Controversy over Aristotle and his Reception in the West', *Renaissance Quarterly* 43 (1990), 529–50; M-P. Lerner, 'Campanella, Juge d'Aristote', in *Platon et Aristote à la Renaissance, XVI Colloque International de Tours*, ed. M. Gandillac (Paris: Librairie Philosopique J Vrin, 1976), pp. 335–57.

[103]   Ibid., *Metaphysica* 2.6.12.7, pp. 90–1.

categories he adds a third, that of God's knowledge of what is fitting which gives a positive place in his doctrine of God to the connotations of the word 'wisdom' (*sapientia*).[104] The agenda at this point is aimed at avoiding any kind of moral voluntarism in the Godhead, but the metaphysical basis for so doing is provided by Campanella's revision of Aristotle.

There is not space here to establish in detail the extent to which Baxter's break with the more traditional faculty psychology of Owen, both in reference to humans and to God, represents a fundamental difference in basic metaphysics. What is clear is that the difference between the two of them is not determined by the fact that one of them uses a scholastic or metaphysical methodology while the other does not, but that each uses a different scholastic model based upon different readings of Aristotle. It is, however, worth pointing out that Campanella appears to have given Baxter the metaphysical framework he needed to speak of finding the 'vestiges of the Trinity' in the fabric of the natural world.[105] While it is arguable that in this context Campanella's understanding of being acted only as a heuristic device which enabled Baxter to express what was, after all, a position similar to that of the very unAristotelian Augustine, Campanella's influence will be significant later in that it will become clear that Baxter allows general revelation more scope than Owen and can thus be seen as moving towards a position which can potentially allow human reason a greater role in theological construction than is permissible on Owen's premises.[106]

To return to Owen, the twofold depravity for which he argues requires a twofold work of the Spirit to restore the marred image of God. First, in restoring the intellect, the Spirit gives light,

---

[104]   *Catholick Theologie* 1, p. 7.

[105]   See Trueman, 'A Small Step Towards Rationalism'.

[106]   The classic statement of the 'vestiges of the Trinity' argument is Augustine, *On the Trinity*, Book 9. Baxter does not cite Augustine as his authority in the *Methodus Theologiae*, and it is quite possible that he reached his conclusions independently. Certainly, his own divisions of power, intellect and will are clearly an appropriation of the Campanellan modification of the Aristotelian notion of being rather than of the Augustinian ideas of mind, love and memory. For Augustine, see *On the Holy Trinity*, *NPNF* (First Series) 3, pp. 125–33.

which is defined as the ability 'to discern and know spiritual things';[107] understanding, which is a comprehension of spiritual truths;[108] and wisdom, which is the ability to understand God's will as revealed in his word.[109] Thus, the theoretical intellect is repaired and brought to perfection, reflecting the intellectualist thrust of Owen's anthropology. But the Spirit does more than this: he also purges corrupt affections and implants spiritual habits which progressively fight against the innate depravity which pervades the human mind.[110]

What Owen does in analysing human psychology in this way is to create a detailed framework within which to understand both the act of human knowing involved in the knowledge of God and the role of the Spirit in this act. In line with the Reformed emphasis upon the inseparability of knowledge of God and true piety, Owen's view of human cognition has a vital practical direction. As the mind is enabled to grasp God in his revelation, so it inclines the will and affections to be obedient to him. Faith, then, can never be construed as *mere* intellectual assent, because intellectual assent is always more than that, leading as it does to an act of the will. In this context, Owen is clearly developing a notion of theology as a habit which stands in significant continuity with medieval discussions of this issue.[111] The advantage of this for Owen is that it allows him to draw attention to the need for human effort in the theological task without allowing that this can be divorced from God's sovereign action in salvation.

What emerges, then, from Owen's teaching on anthropology in relation to revelation is a clear theological structure which serves to delimit the use of reason. Particularly in his emphasis upon the effects of humanity's innate depravity and upon the

---

107   *Works* 4, p. 171.
108   Ibid., p. 172.
109   Ibid., p. 173.
110   Ibid., pp. 184–5.
111   E.g. Peter Aureole, *Scriptum super primum sententiarum* (New York: Franciscan Institute, 1952), 3.5., pp. 218 ff. For Owen on spiritual habits, see *Works* 3, pp. 502–3, where he draws explicitly upon Aristotle's teaching. On the issue in Reformed Orthodoxy in general, see Muller, *PRRD1*, pp. 226–30.

necessity for the Spirit's action in renewing and elevating the rational faculties, Owen's thought precludes the kind of quasi-Cartesian rationalism which some have sought to impute to Orthodoxy in general and to Owen in particular.[112] Indeed, as I have argued elsewhere, it is Baxter, with his concession that human psychology and the generalized Campanellan metaphysics upon which it is based provide insight, outside of the framework of special revelation, into the nature of the Trinity, who moves away from the radical distrust which we find in Owen of all attempts to find anything more than vestiges of the Creator God in the extra-scriptural natural revelation of the unregenerate.[113] This will become yet clearer as we move to analyse Owen's principles of biblical interpretation.

The principles of biblical interpretation

For Owen, the role of the Holy Spirit in perfecting human faculties and in revealing the truths of revelation to the individual is in no sense a replacement for human effort in the interpretation of Scripture. This is the obvious implication of his statements concerning the link between salvation and the renewal of human faculties: God has chosen to work out his salvific purposes through human nature. The meaning of Scripture is, he argues, plain and perspicuous, but this perspicuity does not prevent it from being incomprehensible to the unregenerate who may be able to understand the words of the Bible but have no insight into the real content which faith finds there.[114] Furthermore, perspicuity does not mean that the meaning of every passage is immediately obvious even to the regenerate: the movement from reading the text of Scripture to understanding what it means can be a difficult one which requires significant effort.[115]

A recent writer has disparaged Owen's belief that the Bible's meaning was not always self-evident on a straightforward reading:

---

[112] See O. Weber, *Foundations* 1, pp. 119–20; Clifford, *Atonement and Justification*, p. 96.

[113] See Trueman, 'A Small Step Towards Rationalism'.

[114] *Works* 4, p. 156.

[115] Ibid., pp. 192–4.

In keeping with this [scholastic] mentality, John Owen despised those who appealed to the 'bare word' of Scripture, and whose only hermeneutic was 'away with the gloss and interpretation; give us leave to believe what the word expressly saith'.[116]

In fact, as Owen himself proceeds to say in the sentences after the passage quoted, such a simple hermeneutic leaves the individual with no safeguard against heretical opinions. Indeed, in the light of the radical Scripture principle of the Socinians, there was a pressing need for theologians such as Owen to counterbalance the Reformation emphasis upon Scripture's perspicuity with an emphasis upon the need for responsible exegesis set in the context of broader theological concerns. Only in this way could such basic orthodox doctrines such as the Trinity be safeguarded. The naive anti-intellectualism which was the alternative could provide no realistic defence against the Socinian's radical onslaught.

Given the need for human effort and responsibility in interpretation, Owen breaks down the elements of the interpretative task into three basic categories: spiritual, disciplinarian (technical skills), and ecclesiastical. The order is itself highly significant. In view of the popular view of scholastic theology as excessively cerebral and rationalist in the worst sense of the word, it might be surprising to some to find that the primary emphasis in Owen's discussion of interpretation is on the spiritual life of the individual. In fact, of course, this parallels his understanding of human psychology, where it is the action of the Spirit on the intellect and will, and the infusion of spiritual habits, with all its practical/moral implications, which forms the bedrock of Owen's understanding of Christian cognition. In this context, the scholastic

---

[116] Clifford, *Atonement and Justification5, p. 142*. The quotation from Owen is from *The Death of Death* in *Works* 10, p. 303. Dr Clifford continues by saying that '[h]is impatience was understandable, for, as Wesley himself was to point out, there were no texts in which it is said in "express terms" that Christ did not die for all'. Regardless of whether Owen's exegesis of the passages referring to Christ's death are at all plausible, it is clear that the same criticism Wesley makes could also be applied to other doctrines, such as the Trinity, a point which Socinians never tired of pointing out. In fact, there is no such thing as exegesis based simply upon a plain reading of the text: a whole complex of theological and hermeneutical issues underlie and inform every move from the text of Scripture to the formulation of doctrine. For further discussion see Carl R. Trueman, 'Faith Seeking Understanding: Some Neglected Aspects of John Owen's Understanding of Scriptural Interpretation' in A.N.S. Lane (ed.), *Interpreting the Bible* (Leicester: Apollos, 1997), pp. 147–62.

categories of intellect and will scarcely block the path of piety: they merely serve to allow a clearer understanding of the origins of that piety in the sovereign work of God.

The believer's spiritual life is vital in allowing for a correct interpretation of Scripture. For a start, everyone should read the Bible frequently, as this has a number of helpful consequences: a general acquaintance with the Bible, a knowledge of the content of particular books, regular thoughts of heavenly things, proper conceptions of God, practical exhortations and reproofs from the Word, and a general instinct for good and bad interpretations of the Word.[117]

The believer should not rest content in such regular, but intellectually superficial, reading of the Bible but combine this with a more concerted study of the word. The most important aspect of this more concerted reading is prayer: above all, readers must pray earnestly that the Spirit will aid their understanding of what Scripture teaches. Without the Spirit's assistance, there can be no real understanding of the mind of God.[118] This is, of course, partly the result of human depravity and partly the result of the fact that many truths of the faith transcend reason.[119] While understanding is therefore only possible with the Spirit's assistance, Owen is nonetheless so confident in the power of the Spirit that he claims that no one who prays earnestly for understanding will ultimately be left in error or ignorance of any fundamental truth. Such error must be construed as much as a sign of moral and spiritual failure as of intellectual weakness.[120]

---

[117]　*Works* 4, pp. 200–1.

[118]　'[T]his may be fixed on as a *common principle of Christianity*, namely, that constant and fervent prayer for the divine assistance of the Holy Spirit is such an indispensable means for the attaining the knowledge of the mind of God in the Scripture as that without it all others will not be available.' Ibid., pp. 202–03.

[119]　Examples of truths inaccessible to reason given by Owen include the Trinity, the incarnation, the decrees, the resurrection of the dead, and the new birth: Ibid., pp. 194–5.

[120]　'Nor do I believe that any one who doth and can thus pray as he ought, in a conscientious study of the word, shall ever be left unto the *final prevalency* of any pernicious error or the ignorance of any fundamental truth. None utterly miscarry in the seeking after the mind of God but those who are perverted by their own corrupt minds.' Ibid., p. 203. This reflects Owen's basic conviction that, in matters of fundamental importance, the Bible's teaching is plain and clear: Ibid., p. 195.

True prayer in the context of Scripture reading renders one humble and teachable.[121]

In this argument, we see the close connection that exists between understanding and piety which the scholastic formulation of intellect and will, as it features in Owen's intellectualist understanding of the psychology of the regenerate, serves to reinforce. As God's image is progressively restored in the individual believer, and as the believer struggles daily against sin, this not simply results in practical sanctification in terms of an increased ability to do the good but will also lead to intellectual sanctification in terms of knowing exactly what the good is. This is directly relevant to the understanding of the Scriptures: the more sanctified believers' intellects are, the more they will understand the truth of the Scriptures.[122]

In addition to prayer, there are a number of other basic spiritual disciplines which help facilitate correct interpretation of Scripture. The mind must be ready to be transformed by the power of what is read, not simply by its form.[123] The believer must also walk obediently before God: theology is, among other things, a practical science and wisdom, and thus requires application to daily life; it is only as its precepts are put into practice that it can be truly said to be known by the individual.[124] Believers must also love God's truth so that they are never satisfied with the level of understanding attained but strive for more, desiring always to grow in the knowledge of Christ.[125] And finally, believers must be diligent in their attendance at religious ordinances. This last point gives a corporate dimension to Owen's otherwise individualistic view of the spiritual means available for understanding the Scriptures.[126]

These, then, are the essential foundations of Owen's approach to the interpretation of Scripture, an act which is primarily spiritual and which must therefore be performed within the

[121] Ibid., pp. 203–5.
[122] Ibid., p. 203.
[123] Ibid., p. 205.
[124] Ibid., p. 206.
[125] Ibid., pp. 206–07.
[126] Ibid., p. 207.

context of faith. However, while spiritual disciplines are the most important aspect of interpretation, ecclesiastical helps are the least important.

These ecclesiastical helps take three possible forms: universal tradition, the consent of the Fathers, and the endeavours of any holy and learned person.[127] Of these three, only the third has any real validity for Owen. As to the first, to the extent that there is a universal tradition about any one doctrine, to that extent the church has merely reflected the clear teaching of Scripture. Tradition itself therefore has no intrinsic authority.[128] This is simply the standard Protestant objection to the Roman principle of traditions. Regarding the second, Owen points to the fact that there is no doctrinal consensus among the early church Fathers.[129] This leaves only the third option: the endeavours of individual godly and learned people.

Individual godly and learned people are singled out by Owen as those who have most earnestly struggled to understand the mind of God from the Scriptures. Thus, the Scripture principle comes into play as the norm for theology, and for judging what works from the past are useful for the theological task of Owen's day. If he opposes Quakers for divorcing Spirit from Word, he must also oppose Catholics for supplementing the normative role of Scripture with an unscriptural notion of the authority of tradition. To Owen's precritical mind, works from the past have authority to the extent that they faithfully explicate Scripture on its own terms. In this context he names, amongst others, Chrysostom, Theodoret, Jerome, Ambrose, and Augustine from the Fathers, and Bucer, Calvin, Peter Martyr, and Beza from the Reformers.[130] This is scarcely revolutionary coming from someone who is self-consciously standing in the Reformation tradition with its emphasis upon Scripture alone as the cognitive ground of theology. What is interesting, however, is the insight which this passage gives into Owen's own understanding of the Refor-

---

[127] Ibid., *p. 226*.
[128] Ibid., pp. 226–7.
[129] Ibid., p. 227.
[130] Ibid., pp. 228–9.

mation, of its theological significance, and of the position which he sees it occupying in the ongoing history of the church:

> Especially since the Reformation hath the work [of biblical exposition] been carried on with general success, and to the great advantage of the church; yet hath it not proceeded so far but that the best, most useful, and profitable labour in the Lord's vineyard, which any holy and learned man can engage himself in, is to endeavour the contribution of farther light in the opening and exposition of Scripture, or any part thereof.[131]

It is quite clear here that Owen in no way regards the Reformation as the end-point of biblical exposition and doctrinal reflection. On the contrary, while it marks a major contribution, the Reformation's work must be continued and developed, not simply preserved as some final authority.

This view is, of course, consistent with Owen's Scripture principle: it is Scripture, not any human theologian, which is to be the final authority in matters of the faith. Furthermore, it is scriptural exposition that is to be the foundation of all theology. While a myth of popular theology tends to see an antithesis between seventeenth-century Protestant Scholasticism, with its alleged emphasis on systematizing, and the sixteenth-century Reformation, with its fundamental concern for biblical exposition, this is not how the Protestant scholastics viewed themselves. They simply saw their own task as part of an on-going tradition of biblical exposition, derived from their common adherence to the principle of Scripture alone, and demonstrated by their large output of Scripture commentaries. Owen's own single largest work was his massive *Commentary on Hebrews*, which occupies seven volumes in the nineteenth-century edition.

It is, then, the believer's spiritual life, combined with the principle of Scripture alone, which provides the basic foundation of scriptural interpretation. Having established this, however, Owen does allow a role, albeit subordinate, to human technical skills and knowledge, which he characterizes with the broad adjective 'disciplinarian'. These skills fall into three basic categories: linguistic, historical and geographical, and methodo-

---

[131] Ibid., p. 228.

logical.[132] The usefulness of these broad areas of learning had been understood by the Reformers and became a commonplace amongst the Puritans, helped no doubt by the influence of Perkins, whose *Art of Prophesying* had the status of a classic instruction manual on preaching.[133] The first two categories of skills are straightforward and self-explanatory. The knowledge of the original languages of Scripture is helpful because Owen's high view of inspiration means that he regards the very words of the original Scriptures as inspired and thus as an essential part of God's accommodation of himself to human capacity.[134] As for geography and chronology, these are useful for a number of reasons: a knowledge of the Bible as history allows for an understanding of the progression of God's revelation to Israel over time up until the coming of Christ, thus leading to an appreciation of the historical dimension of theology which we noted as one of Owen's concerns;[135] it also encourages believers to see how many prophecies have been fulfilled, although Owen advises caution over excessive interest in chronologies and the like.[136]

These two kinds of human aids for the interpretation of Scripture are fairly uncontroversial. More important, especially in light of current criticism of Owen's rationalism, is the third category, namely the way in which he relates human reason to the theological task. We have already noted that theology is a rational discipline for Owen, in that it reflects the rational nature of human psychology. Owen, however, is no rationalist in the mould of a Descartes, and there are clear limits placed upon reason's competence by his understanding of the theological task.

The theological limits-of reason

In *The Causes, Ways, and Means of Understanding the Mind of God*, Owen briefly outlines what he regards as the appropriate

132 Ibid., pp. 209 ff.
133 See *The Workes of . . . William Perkins* (Cambridge, 1609) 2, pp. 731–62 (hereafter, *Workes*); cf. Ames, *Marrow*, p. 188.
134 *Works* 4, pp. 213–16.
135 Ibid., p. 220.
136 Ibid., p. 221–3.

role of human reason in theology: it is to be restricted to the spheres of logic and inference. This position was typical of Puritan theologians.[137] In light of the argument that Owen's theology is vitiated by Aristotelianism and rationalism, what may at first seem surprising about this discussion of the use of human reasoning is not simply its position and length (coming as a brief note after the long discussion of the role of prayer and the spiritual life), but the radical way in which the usefulness of human reasoning is limited to logic, in strict subordination to revelation.[138] In fact, when set in the context of the educational background of the sixteenth and seventeenth centuries, it is not at all surprising. At that time the use of logic, like that of grammar and rhetoric, was regarded simply as a tool for opening up the meaning of a text, and thus was considered as no more innovative, nor, one may add, sinister, than the use of an appropriate Hebrew lexicon would have been considered in the same context.[139] Nor is such subordination of the tools of reason surprising given Owen's specific theological perspective: use of human reason in theology is necessary, given the essential rational nature of humanity; but, when set against the background of Owen's understanding of revelation, the impact of the Fall, and of theology as something supernatural which, by the canons of Aristotelian logic and physics, cannot be caused by the merely natural, it is obvious that human finitude and depravity inevitably render human reason useless outside the context of the internal work of the Holy Spirit and of personal faith. It is quite clear that there can be no 'rationalism' in some quasi-Cartesian sense within Owen's theology. Rationality, yes – in that doctrines are above reason, not contrary to it, and can therefore have their internal content and their relationship to each other subject to rigorous explication on the presupposition that they are true;

---

[137] Ibid., pp. 223–4.

[138] For a general discussion of the relation of reason to faith in Reformed Orthodoxy, and the need for care in defining 'rationalism' in a pre-Enlightenment context, see Muller, *PRRD1*, pp. 231–49.

[139] See, for example, Perkins' advice that the preacher should use 'gramaticall, rhetoricall, and logicall [mg., Opening of the text] analysis, and the helpe of the rest of the arts' to read the Bible: *Workes* 2, p. 736.

rationalism, no – in that doctrines cannot be subordinated to the criteria of autonomous human reason, and thereby be judged as true or false, a position which is absolutely basic to Owen's whole dispute with the Socinians. Indeed, it is his Socinian opponents, if anyone, who deserve the epithet of rationalists.[140] As in regeneration the Holy Spirit does not oppose human rational powers, but rather restores and perfects them, and as the truths of faith are not irrational but rather suprarational, so the tools of reason and logic have their role to play, but only within the framework of faith, not as parallel and independent sources for saving knowledge.

The same sentiments are found in Owen's only detailed treatment of the relationship between theology and philosophy, *Digressio de philosophia cum theologia mistura* [*Digression on the mixing of philosophy and theology*] which is found in the *Theologoumena Pantodapa*.[141] Here Owen protests at the contamination of theology by philosophy, a problem which he sees becoming serious in the attempts of the Apologists to meet their philosophical adversaries on common ground. In opposition to abstruse philosophical speculations, Owen argues, in line with the practical thrust of much Puritan divinity, that the primary purpose of theology is that of living to please God. Keeping this point in mind provides a practical, non-speculative orientation to the

---

[140]   In this context Owen makes the following comment, which is worth quoting in full: 'But this [i.e., reason] also must be admitted with its limitations; for whatever perfection there seems to be in our art of reasoning, it is to be subject to the wisdom of the Holy Ghost in the Scripture. His way of reasoning is always his own, sometimes *sublime* and *heavenly*, so as not to be reduced unto the common rules of our arts and sciences without a derogation from its *instructive*, *convictive*, and *persuasive* efficacy. For us to frame unto ourselves *rules of ratiocination*, or to have our minds embondaged unto those of other men's invention and observation, if we think thereon absolutely to reduce all the reasonings in the Scripture unto them, we may fall into a presumptuous mistake. In the consideration of all the effects of infinite wisdom, there must be an allowance for the deficiency of our comprehension; when humble subjection of conscience, and the captivating of our understandings to the obedience of faith, is the best means of learning what is proposed unto us. And there is nothing more contemptible than the *arrogancy* of such persons as think, by the shallow measures and short lines of their own weak, dark, imperfect reasoning, to fathom the depths of Scripture senses.' *Works* 4, p. 224.

[141]   *Works* 17, pp. 458–68.

theological enterprise.[142] In the context of true theology, philosophy is a Trojan horse.[143]

It is clear from this that Owen's theology is not rationalistic, and this should come as no surprise if only because there is no positive pathway between Reformed Orthodoxy and the truly rationalistic theology which was to take hold in the late seventeenth and early eighteenth centuries.[144] In fact, truly rationalistic theology arose within Reformed ranks only as the traditional scholastic and Aristotelian frameworks of Reformed Orthodoxy were shed in favour of approaches which were indebted to Enlightenment ideas. It has been shown in exhaustive detail that the development of 'Enlightened Orthodoxy', which ultimately bore fruit that was distinctly rationalist, in the true sense of the word, was in part a specific repudiation of the older scholastic form of Protestantism and not a continuous development thereof.[145] Indeed, there are suggestive points of interesting similarity between the later rationalist theology of, say, a Jean-Alphonse Turretin and tendencies present at the Academy of Saumur, amongst the Remonstrants, and even the Socinians.[146] In the context of England in the mid-seventeenth century, it was not Owen's traditional Aristotelianism but Baxter's adoption of the Campanellan revision of Aristotelian metaphysics which pointed towards a more rationalistic theology;[147] in light of this, Owen's thought

---

[142] 'Finem hic omnis scientiae primarium, nempe Deo vivendi, solum consideramus; de nudis speculationibus, quibus exercet se innata mentis humanae curiositas, quaeque intellectum rationalem in ordine ad Deum non dirigunt, neque perficiunt, parum soliciti.' Ibid., p. 459.

[143] Owen uses this very image: Ibid., p. 466.

[144] On the rise of rationalism, scepticism, etc. see R. H. Popkin, *The History of Scepticism from Erasmus to Spinoza* (Berkeley: University of California Press, 1979).

[145] See M. Heyd, 'From Rationalist Theology to Cartesian Voluntarism', *JHI* 40 (1979), 527–42; M. I. Klauber, 'Reason, Revelation, and Cartesianism'; *idem*, 'The Drive Toward Protestant Union in Early Eighteenth-Century Geneva: Jean-Alphonse Turretin on the "Fundamental Articles" of the Faith', *CH* 61 (1992), 334–49; *Idem*, 'Reformed Orthodoxy in Transition: Benedict Pictet (1655–1724) and Enlightened Orthodoxy in Post-Reformation Geneva' in *Later Calvinism*, pp. 93–113; *idem*, *Between Reformed Scholasticism and Pan-Protestantism*.

[146] See Klauber and G. S. Sunshine, 'Jean-Alphonse Turretin on Biblical Accommodation: Calvinist or Socinian?', *CTJ* 25 (1990), 7–27. On rationalistic tendencies in Remonstrant thought, see J. Platt, *Reformed Thought and Scholasticism*.

[147] See Trueman, 'A Small Step Towards Rationalism'.

should be interpreted not as pointing towards a rationalist theology but as fighting against it. We noted in Ch. 1 that he owned books by and about Descartes, and so a truly rationalist model was available to him; and yet he apparently chose to continue operating within the framework provided for him by medieval and Renaissance Aristotelianism and Scholasticism, a framework which he presumably considered more conducive to the maintenance of Orthodoxy in the face of Socinian and Remonstrant onslaughts.

The analogy of faith

The problem of the relationship of revelation and reason is at its most acute in the context of biblical interpretation. In the early Reformation, a simple appeal to the principle of Scripture's perspicuity had been considered enough in itself to provide a framework for sound doctrine. For example, as J. P. Donnelly has commented, Jerome Zanchi's loyalty to *sola scriptura* was sufficient to delimit the role of reason and, even when he appears to use rationalistic argumentation, he is simply supplying philosophical confirmation of what he takes to be revealed in the Scriptures.[148] By the mid-seventeenth century, however, mere adherence to the shibboleth of Scripture alone was no safeguard against rationalism. In the development of Socinian thought, the Scripture principle was vigorously asserted, but within an interpretative framework which stressed human rationality as the criteria for interpretation. In this context, the Reformed Orthodox such as Owen had to clarify the theological framework of interpretation in a way which delimited human reason and allowed them to preserve the central tenets of Reformed faith without surrendering the Scripture principle.

For Owen, the basic principle that regulates the use of philosophy and human reason within the framework of faith, and which also happens to control his biblical interpretation, is the analogy

---

[148] J. P. Donnelly, 'Italian Influences on Calvinist Scholasticism', *SCJ* 7 (1976), 81–101, 92; also, John Farthing, 'Patristics, Exegesis, and the Eucharist in the Theology of Girolamo Zanchi', in Trueman and Clark, *Protestant Scholasticism*.

of faith. He uses this principle to relate exegesis of particular passages to the overall doctrinal content of the Christian faith, and as such it also supplies limits to the competence of human reason:

> [W]hat sense soever any man supposeth or judgeth this or that particular place of Scripture to yield and give out to the best of his rational intelligence is immediately to give place unto the *analogy of faith* – that is, the Scripture's own declaration of its sense in other places to another purpose, or contrary thereunto.[149]

The analogy of faith, then, embodies on one level the Reformation principle of *Scripture alone*, along with the rule that obscure passages are to be understood in the light of passages where the meaning is clear.

The principle itself had proved problematic almost from the very start of the Reformation, as demonstrated by the differences between Luther and Zwingli over the understanding of the words, 'This is my body'.[150] The difficulty was in deciding which passages were obscure and which clear, a judgment often based upon prior theological commitments. By Owen's time, the problem had been accentuated by the radical biblicism of the Socinian movement, which pushed the principle of Scripture to radical extremes, and thus excluded doctrines such as the Trinity from the content of Christian faith on the basis that they were not explicitly taught in the Bible but were the product of logical and philosophical inferences.[151] One of the most dramatic examples of this radical biblicism is provided by Owen's opponent, John Biddle, in his *A Twofold Catechism* (London, 1654). In this work, Biddle's theology is expressed catechetically, through a series of leading questions followed by a list of biblical proof texts. The

---

[149]   *Works* 4, p. 224.
[150]   See the helpful discussion in W. P. Stephens, *The Theology of Huldrych Zwingli* (Oxford: Clarewood Press, 1986), pp. 66–9.
[151]   In the light of much of the scholarship of the 'Calvin against the Calvinists' ilk, it is both ironic and amusing that the most radical seventeenth-century critics of the intrusion of philosophical patterns and reasoning into Christian theology, the Socinians, were also the least orthodox by any contemporary standards, sixteenth- or seventeenth-century.

point is clear: the Bible's meaning is plain to all who will read it without prejudice – but the very questions asked determine the interpretation of the texts subsequently cited.[152]

That Owen felt the pressure of Socinian criticisms in this area is evident from the fact that in his major anti-Socinian polemic, *Vindiciae Evangelicae*, he finds himself in substantial agreement with his opponent, John Biddle, on the matter of Scripture.[153] This pressure, however, was not apparently great enough to lead him to an extensive elaboration of the analogy of faith. Indeed, it seems on the whole that his confidence in the power of prayerful reading of the Scriptures was sufficient to guarantee ultimate correct understanding.

There is, however, one passage in his work *On the Divine Original of the Scripture* which would appear to reveal the fundamental content of the analogy of faith, the foundation of all interpretation, and the limit of reason's competence. The point of departure for this discussion is the doctrine of the Trinity: that God is one and that God is also three persons is a nonsense to reason and human philosophy.[154] Yet, Owen argues, if the doctrine of the Trinity is rejected, then the whole of Christian theology collapses.[155] Communion between God and humans involves two things: God's communication of his love to humans; and human obedience to God by way of grateful response – but these two elements, which summarize the whole of theology, are so intimately bound up with the doctrine of the Trinity that rejection of Trinitarianism precludes any true understanding of theology.[156] The former, God's communication to humans, is rooted in the Trinitarian doctrine of predestination and the eternal covenant between the Father and the Son. The latter depends both upon the Son's incarnation through the power of

---

[152] See, for example, the question referring to God's mutability: *Twofold Catechism*, pp. 43–4.
[153] 'The first chapter, then, concerning the Scriptures, both in the Greater and Less Catechisms, without farther trouble I shall pass over, seeing that the stating of the questions and answers in them may be sound, and according to the common faith of the saints.' *Works* 12, p. 85. For Biddle's arguments, see *Twofold Catechism*, pp. 1–6.
[154] *Works* 16, p. 340.
[155] Ibid.
[156] Ibid.

the Holy Spirit, and upon the Holy Spirit's subjective work within believers. As the Spirit is the Spirit of the Father *and* the Son (again, we see the *filioque* coming into play), these acts too must be seen as Trinitarian.[157]

Two consequences flow from what Owen has to say here. The first is that biblical interpretation, by the very fact that its content is theology, is thus to be conducted with reference to the Trinity, especially in terms of the eternal intratrinitarian relations respecting salvation (i.e., the covenants), and the temporal outworking of these in terms of incarnation and individual salvation. Owen does not use the term 'analogy of faith' here, but it is obvious that this is what his statement amounts to. His message is clear: if the Trinity is rejected, it will quickly become apparent that nothing of value can be derived from the Scriptures.[158] The Trinitarian economy of salvation thus provides the hermeneutical key for unlocking the meaning of the Scriptures, a key which gives due weight to both the eternal and historical dimensions of scriptural teaching which we noted earlier.

This basic foundation of revelation in a Trinitarian understanding of God is evident from the way in which, time and again, Owen stresses a correct understanding of the Trinity and the intratrinitarian relations as the basis for other doctrines. The reasons for this lie in what he had to say about Christ and Scripture as the Word of God. There, the whole argument reflected his understanding of the Trinity: in the ontological order, the Father begets the Son, and the Spirit proceeds from both; in the voluntary, soteriological order the Father covenants with the Son which provides the basis for the saving activity of the Spirit. As the Word *engraphon* stands as the revelation of the Father's saving purposes which are embodied and revealed in the Son through the Spirit, it is inevitable that the basic principle underlying how to interpret the Scriptures should reflect the basic theology underlying what the Scriptures contain: the Trinitarian economy of salvation.

---

[157] Ibid., p. 341.

[158] 'Here reason is entangled; yet, after a while, finds evidently, that unless this be embraced, all other things wherein it hath to do with God will not be of value to the soul.' Ibid., p. 340.

This Trinitarian interpretative device is no abstract doctrine but helps to maintain the link which Owen has argued exists between doctrine and piety, as is shown in his understanding of personal piety, which he expresses through the notion of the believer's communion with God as Trinity.[159] Also, his defence of the perseverance of the saints is an argument remarkable for the way in which the life of the individual believer on earth is shown to be rooted in the eternity of God's life as Trinity. The basic axiom of *The Doctrine of the Saints' Perseverance Explained and Confirmed* is that God is immutable and so his purposes of salvation in election cannot be frustrated. Yet this is no abstract 'blind watchmaker' doctrine of immutability, but immutability understood as God's unchanging commitment to the intratrinitarian covenants of salvation. Using the classic scholastic distinction of *principium essendi* and *principium cognoscendi*, Owen argues that it is God's free and loving commitment in his own voluntary covenanting with himself, and with the elect through Christ, that provides the absolutely unchanging and utterly reliable basis for his revelation of himself in the covenant promise as one who will love and keep believers to the end.[160] Thus, the Trinity is again stressed as providing the essential context within which revelation must be interpreted and understood. In short, the importance of the Trinity for Owen's writings on salvation cannot be underestimated, and it is a theme to which we will have cause to return on numerous occasions in the future.

The second, and methodologically crucial, consequence of this Trinitarian analogy of faith is that it once again indicates the structural limitation of the powers of human reason and of philosophy within Owen's theology. As he himself declares, reason can give no insight into the Trinity, and so, by implication, reason on its own can give no real insight into the meaning of Scripture. There can therefore be no truly rationalistic theology on Owen's premises precisely because of the explicitly Trinitarian nature of theology and revelation. This is not to deny that human methods of reasoning and philosophical language cannot be used

---

[159] See his *Of Communion with God* in *Works* 2, pp. 3–274.
[160] *Works* 11, p. 205.

within theology, but it is to say that the use of these is to be subordinated to, and controlled by, God's Trinitarian revelation. This is absolutely continuous with all that Owen has said elsewhere about the limitations on human reason imposed by its own finiteness and depravity, and represents a crucial methodological insight against the background of which the rest of Owen's theology must be understood.

In contrast, the approach of Baxter, with its explicit appropriation of Campanellan metaphysics as providing the basis of the vestiges of the Trinity in nature, represents a clear move away from the radical delimitation of general revelation to insights about God as unity towards a position where it even gives insights into God's Trinitarian nature. Baxter himself does not care to make the move to arguing that the Trinity can be proved on the basis of a natural theology, but he is putting into place a doctrinal concept which clearly points in such a direction and, as such, represents both a break with the general Reformed tradition of the sixteenth and seventeenth centuries and a small, but significant, step in the direction, of a truly rationalist approach to theology.[161] If the Trinity is available to unaided natural reason, then the very thing which in Owen's theology delimits the role of autonomous human rationality in the theological enterprise and guarantees its special, supernatural nature, is surrendered; and, in theory, the truths of Scripture can now be appropriated without the need for the subjective action of the Holy Spirit. By opening the way to making the Trinity part of natural theology, Baxter's approach exhibits tendencies which place it much closer to the Socinian emphasis upon the Bible as rational in a human sense than the more cautious, and traditionally Reformed, approach of John Owen.

Conclusion

What is clear from the above survey is that while Owen wrote no formal prolegomena to his theology, there is sufficient relevant

---

[161]   See Trueman, 'A Small Step Towards Rationalism'.

discussion in his writings to construct a coherent picture of the principles of his theological method. For those who are committed to the caricature of Reformed Orthodoxy as a corrupt synthesis of Jerusalem and Athens, what will be most surprising is not what Owen does discuss at length but what he virtually ignores: the use of Aristotle as a methodological tool and (some would claim) as the criterion for theological formulation.[162] As we have seen, the fact that Owen does, on occasion, use Aristotle's language is only to be expected of someone who was educated and working within a pre-Enlightenment world. Furthermore, the sheer variety of views expressed by pre-Enlightenment thinkers using Aristotle precludes a priori generalizations about the necessary effects of such use. In fact, while Owen allows a legitimate role for human reasoning within theology, it is only a subordinate part of a larger methodological approach which is itself defined and controlled by a theological structure which explicitly transcends, and therefore radically limits, its sphere of competence.

Close examination of Owen's various reflections upon the principles of theology reveals a basic Trinitarian orientation to his approach, which he builds in part on the radical distinction which he sees as existing between the infinite and the finite. This, a theological and philosophical commonplace of the Western tradition from the patristic era onwards, is crucial for Owen. It determines that the knowledge humans have of God cannot be qualitatively or quantitatively the same as that which God has of himself. Human theology is thus ectypal, not archetypal, and needs to be mediated to humanity in a comprehensible form.

This points to the incarnation: it is through the Logos's consubstantiality with the Father, his hypostatic union with human flesh, and the communication of properties *via* the Holy Spirit, that knowledge of God as Saviour is mediated to fallen

---

[162] Cf. Clifford's comment (*Atonement and Justification*, p. 97): 'In other words, it was Aristotle rather than Paul who prevented Owen from saying, with Calvin, "Although Christ suffered for the sins of the world, and is offered by the goodness of God without distinction to all men, yet not all receive him"'. In fact, as we shall see, it is Owen's Trinitarianism, not Aristotle, which is the methodological principle underlying his view of atonement.

humanity. The incarnate Christ is then the focus of Scripture: as consubstantial with the Father, he embodies God's eternal will to save, which is the causal ground and the theological content of the Bible; and as incarnate, he manifests God on earth, and is thus the historical focus of the biblical narratives. The incarnation is the point at which the eternal will of God and the historical economy of salvation intersect.

The Trinitarian structure of objective revelation in the Son is paralleled by a similar structure in the subjective appropriation of revelation by humans. As both finite and sinful they need to have their sin dealt with and their rational faculties perfected if they are to grasp even ectypal theology. This is done by the Spirit. But because the Spirit is the Spirit of both the Father *and* the Son, there can be no divorce between Word and Spirit as the Quakers attempted, and the Trinitarian structure is maintained: the Spirit shows believers the Son, who is himself the revelation of the Father.

This Trinitarianism is thus determinative of the whole theological task: objectively, it defines the content of revelation, and thus is the hermeneutical key to understanding Scripture; subjectively, it defines the way in which human beings are themselves brought to understand revelation, thus pointing in practical terms to the need for a close spiritual walk with God while at the same time radically subordinating reason to revelation within theology.

What is impressive about Owen's methodology is the way in which he draws so heavily on the doctrinal concepts of patristic theology and Scholasticism to establish his case: his use of the archetypal/ectypal distinction, the importance of the Son's consubstantiality with the Father, and the crucial significance of the *filioque* clause show him utilizing the catholic tradition as a means of developing an understanding of the principles and task of theology which is determined not by the criteria of human rationality, but which arises from the content of his theology. His method is not predogmatic; it is, in fact, determined by his doctrine of God. It is to this doctrine that we turn in the next chapter.

Three

The Doctrine of God

Introduction

In the discussion of Owen's reflections on the principles of theology it soon became clear that his whole approach was shaped and controlled by his doctrine of God, from the fundamental distinction between the infinite God and a finite creation to the Trinitarian structure of divine revelation. It is worth noting in this context that, despite the obvious importance of the doctrine of God for Owen's understanding of the nature of theology, his writings are on the whole thematic in their approach, and he wrote no comprehensive system of theology in which he discussed the doctrine of God as a separate locus. Nevertheless, as the Trinitarian God is quite clearly the underlying principle behind all theology, the doctrine of God pervades his writings and it is not difficult to piece together a coherent picture of his views in this area.

Owen's statements on the doctrine of God can be divided into three basic groups: those dealing specifically with God's attributes, those dealing with the relationship of God to creation and providence, and those dealing with predestination and the economy of salvation.[1] In light of what emerged in the previous chapter it will come as no surprise that in each of these areas there will again be evident the emphasis upon God as Trinity which was so typical of Owen's reflections upon the principles of

---

[1] The boundaries between the groups are, of course, somewhat fluid, each having implications for the others.

theology, and which underlines the intimate connection between theology's principle of knowing and its principle of being.

The Attributes of God

Absolute and relative attributes

The fundamental distinction which Owen makes within the attributes of God is between absolute and relative attributes rather than between incommunicable and communicable ones.[2] The latter was the more common Reformed distinction, while the former was more traditionally Lutheran. This is not as historically or theologically significant as might appear at first glance, since neither pair of terms was exclusively linked with one party at this point in time, and Owen himself is at times happy to use the more common Reformed distinction.[3] Absolute attributes are those which God possesses simply by virtue of his own act of self-existence, while relative attributes are those which are predicated of him in terms of his dealings with his creatures.[4]

One criticism of this distinction is that it seems to allow that human beings may be able to have some knowledge of God as he is in himself apart from the relations in which he stands to his creation.[5] It might also be appropriate to ask whether this distinction leads Owen to a radical separation of God in himself from God as he acts in history, which fails to do justice to the

---

[2] While Owen never provides a single exhaustive list of God's absolute attributes, those which he does categorize this way include God's omniscience, infinity, perfection, wisdom, power, eternity, and immutability. Works 11, p. 508; 12, pp. 93, 104–05; cf. 10, p. 508.

[3] For Lutheran views of God's attributes, see H. Schmid, *The Doctrinal Theology of the Evangelical Lutheran Church*, trans. C. A. Hay and H. E. Jacobs (Minneapolis: Augsburg, 1961), pp. 117–29; J. T. Mueller, *Christian Dogmatics* (St Louis: Concordia, 1934), p. 162; Preus, *Post-Reformation Lutheranism* 2, pp. 53–111. The Lutherans also used the terms absolute and operative to describe this distinction. In the context of Christology, Owen himself does assume the validity of the incommunicable/communicable distinction: see *Works* 1, p. 93.

[4] See the references in note 2 above.

[5] L. Berkhof, *Systematic Theology* (Grand Rapids: Eerdmans, 1949), p. 55.

biblical, and Reformation, emphasis upon God as the one who reveals himself *to us*. Even a scholar as generally sympathetic to Protestant Scholasticism as Robert Preus feels it necessary to raise this as a point of criticism with reference to later Lutheran Orthodoxy.[6] As regards Owen, however, a number of points can be made in this context which serve to rob this criticism of its power. First, Owen's purpose is not to create the separation of God and creation which these criticisms fear but, in fact, to effect the exact opposite: to stress the intimate connection between God in himself and God as he acts in the world, and thus to make impossible an abstract and speculative doctrine of God. Secondly, and following on from the first point, the kind of separation which Preus rightly regards as a danger is actually precluded by the issue which underlies Owen's use of the distinction. The absolute/relative distinction is not developed by Owen in a purely systematic context as a way of categorizing God's attributes, but is being deployed in a controversy where the real issue is the relationship between God as he is in himself and God as he has revealed himself to be. The question at issue is: Does God's revelation, general and special, of his decretive will, bear only an arbitrary (from a human perspective) relationship to his essence, or does it have some positive relationship to God's inner being? Owen's position means that issues of epistemology and ontology cannot be separated in the manner which is required if Preus's criticisms of Lutheran Orthodoxy are also to hold good for Owen. As will become clear, the importance of this distinction in Owen's theology is not that it allows him to construct an abstract doctrine of God in himself, as opposed to God *for us*, but that it serves to underline the causal connection between God's eternal self-existence, his will to save, and the execution of that will in history; and it defines the nature of the relationship between the eternal and the historical economies – two foundational aspects of his understanding of the principles of theology.

---

[6]   *Post-Reformation Lutheranism* 2, p. 63.

The relationship of God's attributes to the nature of salvation

The context in which Owen makes his clearest and most sophisticated statement and application of this distinction between divine attributes is his *A Dissertation on Divine Justice* (1653), which both reveals his firm grasp of highly complex theological distinctions and represents a significant development in his understanding of the doctrine of God.[7] The idea that God could, if he had wished, have forgiven sin merely by an act of his will without recourse to incarnation, etc. was a view advocated by many Reformed Orthodox, including such leading lights as the brilliant and influential scholastic theologian William Twisse (*c.*1575–1646), first prolocutor of the Westminster Assembly;[8] the Scottish divine Samuel Rutherford (1600–61);[9] and even John Owen himself in his early treatise, *The Death of Death* (1648), where he argued that attempts to deny this represented Arminian error.[10] Thus, his early thought regarded incarnation and atonement as deriving their necessity purely from God's decision that it should be so. By 1653, in contrast, Owen had come to regard this as a halfway house to the Socinians' complete denial of incarnation and atonement.[11] In *A Dissertation on Divine Justice*, he argues that, given God's will to save sinful humanity, incarnation and atonement became a consequent necessity because God's righteousness needed to be satisfied. God's freedom is

---

[7] For a full discussion of this treatise, see Trueman, 'Owen's *Dissertation on Divine Justice*', *CTJ* forthcoming.

[8] See his *Vindiciae Gratiae* (Amsterdam, 1632).

[9] See his *Disputatio Scholastica de Providentia*; *Christ Dying and Drawing Sinners to Himselfe*.

[10] *Works* 10, p. 205.

[11] Owen's mature position also represents a break with the teaching of Calvin as expressed in his comment on John 15:13: 'Poterat nos Deus verbo aut nutu redimere, nisi aliter nostra causa visum esset, ut proprio et unigenito filio non parcens, testatum faceret in eius persona quantam habeat salutis nostrae curam.' *OC* 75:343–44. The Orthodox assertion of the contingency of atonement is reminiscent of the medieval distinction between *potentia absoluta/potentia ordinata*, although Calvin rejected it because of the apparent arbitrariness which it injected into the doctrine of God: see D. C. Steinmetz's *Calvin in Context*, (New York: OUP, 1995) pp. 40–52. For a discussion of the distinction, see Oberman, *Harvest*, pp. 30–8; also, Francis Oakley, *Omnipotence, Covenant, and Order: an Excursion in the History of Ideas from Abelard to Leibniz* (Ithaca: Cornell UP, 1984).

preserved, because the decision to save is an act of his will; but the necessity of atonement is asserted because the nature of God's being requires such satisfaction.[12]

This change in the understanding of atonement rests upon an implicit change in Owen's theology towards a more intellectualist understanding of God. This becomes clear when the discussion of the necessity of atonement is set against the background of debates over the doctrine of God which extended back into the Middle Ages, where theologians debated whether God's intellect or will had logical priority in the divine psychology.[13] Voluntarist doctrines of God, which stressed the primacy of God's will over his intellect, were in fact never intended by the medievals to mean that God's actions were purely arbitrary but were, rather, an attempt to underline the fact that God's ways are not human ways. They thus represented a statement more about the limitation on human epistemology than about the being of God.[14] These medieval roots of the seventeenth-century controversy are evident throughout Twisse's discussion, which freely utilizes the

---

[12] '[T]hese attributes of the divine nature are either for the purpose of preserving or continuing to God what belongs to him of right, supposing that state of things which he hath freely appointed, or for bestowing on his creatures some farther good. Of the former kind is *vindicatory justice*; which, as it cannot be exercised but upon the supposition of the existence of a rational being and of its sin, so, these being supposed, the supreme right and dominion of the Deity could not be preserved entire unless it were exercised. Of the latter kind is *sparing mercy*, by which God bestows an undeserved good on miserable creatures; for, setting aside the consideration of their misery, this attribute cannot be exercised, but that being supposed, if he be inclined to bestow any undeserved good on creatures wretched through their own transgression, he may exercise this mercy if he will. But again; in the exercise of that justice, although, if it were not to be exercised, according to our former hypothesis, God would cease from his right and dominion, and so would not be God, still he is a free and also an absolutely necessary agent; for he acts from will and understanding, and not from an impetus of nature only, as fire burns. And he freely willed that state and condition of things; which being supposed, that justice must necessarily be exercised. Therefore, in the exercise of it, he is not less free than in speaking; for supposing . . . that his will were to speak any thing, it is necessary that he speak the *truth*.' *Works* 10, p. 511.

[13] On intellectualism/voluntarism, see F. Copleston, *A History of Philosophy*, 9 vols. (London: Burns, Oates and Washbourne, 1946–75) 2, pp. 382–3, 538–41; on Scotus and voluntarism, see B. M. Bonansea, 'Duns Scotus' Voluntarism' in Bonansea and J. K. Ryan (eds.), *John Duns Scotus, 1265–1965* (Washington: Catholic University of America Press, 1965), pp. 83–121.

[14] See Oberman, *Harvest*, p. 98.

language of medieval Scholasticism to clarify the points at issue.[15] Twisse's argument was built upon his rejection of a number of arguments against his position. It is arguable, he says, that if God could not forgive sin without satisfaction, it was because of either a limitation in his power or a specific demand of his justice.[16] The former Twisse rejects by arguing that God's power is answerable to nothing higher than itself, and what God can will is, by definition, therefore just. He supports this with a quotation taken directly from Duns Scotus which Twisse criticizes only for its restraint.[17] The necessity of atonement must therefore derive from God's inner being which demands that he punish with an absolute necessity.[18] Among the unacceptable consequences to which this would lead, Twisse points out, would be the need for God totally to annihilate the creature. In support of this observation, he quotes from Durandus, Gerson, and Bradwardine.[19] However, if God is able to lessen the punishment

---

[15]   The relevant section in Twisse occurs in his *Vindiciae Gratiae* 1.25, digr. 8 (pp. 198–207). Twisse's use of medieval categories is evident from the start: both the title and first sentence of the digression on this topic (Bk. 1, digr. 8) refer to God's ability to forgive sins without satisfaction through his *potentia absoluta*: see *Vindiciae Gratiae*, p. 198.

[16]   'Si Deus non possit peccata sine satisfactione remittere, tum vel quia non potest per potentiam, vel quia non potest per justitiam.' *Vindiciae Gratiae* 1, p. 199.

[17]   'Videat Lector, an non multo magis accurate et sobrie in hoc apice philosophetur Iohannes Scotus: *Ad nullum objectum secundarium ita determinate inclinatur voluntas divina, per aliquid in̄ ipsa, quod sibi repugnet juste inclinari ad oppositum illius: quia sicut sine contradictione potest oppositum velle, ita potest juste velle; alioquin posset absolut velle, et non juste, quod est inconveniens* (Mg., In 4, d. 46, q. 1, paragr. Non improbando). Ego vero hoc non modo inconveniens esse judico, sed etiam non procul abesse a blasphemia.' Ibid.

[18]   'Si Deus non potest peccatum impunitum dimittere: tum necesse est ut puniat, necessitate absoluta.' Ibid.

[19]   'Denique si Deus teneretur per justitiam punire peccatum quantum meretur; necesse foret, ut Deus creaturam suam prorsus annihilaret, quemadmodum arguit Durandus: *Secundum rigorem justitiae propter vitium ingratitudinis meretur aliquis privati omnibus beneficiis gratis acceptis. Sed quicquid sumus, et quicquid habemus, totum a Deo accepimus secundum illud Apostoli. 1 Cor. 4. Ergo per ingratitudinem, quae committitur in omni peccato mortali, meretur peccator amittere, secundum rigorem justitiae, quicquid a Deo accepit, hoc est, quicquid est in se, et quicquid habet in se, quo facto esset homo annihilatus* (Mg., In 5 dist. 46, q.3). Quare concludo multo sanius meo judicio philosophatum esse Iohannem Gersonem, de vita spirituali animae lect. 1 Coroll. 8. *Implicat* (inquit) *Deum punire ad condignum, si per hoc intelligamus sic eum punire, quod juste non possit amplius: Si autem dicamus punire ad condignum, quia punit,*

demanded for sin, as the continued existence of creatures obviously indicates that he can, then he is able to abolish it altogether by his absolute power and is thus under no absolute necessity to resort to the incarnation. Again, to support this position he refers the reader to Duns Scotus.[20] The choice of medievals is hardly random but in fact reflects Twisse's realization that the separation between *potentia absoluta* and *potentia ordinata*, which he needs to establish for his case to hold, is exactly the same as that for which such medieval voluntarists argued.[21]

Against such a background Owen's arguments for the absolute

Footnote 19 (*continued*) *quantum recta ratio, et justitia exigunt, et taxant tale peccatum esse puniendum; tunc omne peccatum punitur, aut punietur ad condignum, quia scilicet tantum punitur quantum puniri Deus vult et ordinat rectissima juris ratione.* Et ante Gersonem, Thomas de Bradwardina, de causa Dei contra Pelag. l.1.c.39. *Actualiter mereri, est facere aliquid praemiandum, scilicet cui praemium actualiter debeatur, et sic nullus peccans meretur poenam aliam, quam habebit; Non enim est dignum aut debitum, quod aliter puniatur, quam Deus ipsum statuit puniendum: Mereri autem potentialiter, est facere aliquid praemiabile, scilicet cui praemium posset reddi: sicque omnis peccans mortaliter, tam damnanus quam salvandus, meretur majorem poenam quam habebit et forsan poenam aeternam quantam libet intensive. . . .' Vindiciae Gratiae,* p. 200.

[20] 'Potest Deus mitiorem poenam inferre quam peccatum meretur; ergo potest pro absoluta sua potentia poenam universam suspendere. Nam ponantur, si placet, tres gradus poenae promeritae: huic si possit Deus subtrahere gradum unum, cur non et alterum; et si duos possit, cur non simul etiam et reliquum tertium? Nam si potest poenam debitam mitigare, potest permittere unum gradum in peccato esse impunitum; ergo pari ratione potest et gradum alium impunitum relinquere; et consequenter etiam omnem gradum, et peccatum universum. Ad hanc objectionem jubet nos quaerere responsionem Iohannes Scotus in 4, dist. 46, q. 4.' *Vindiciae Gratiae*, p. 200.

[21] Rutherford, while not making the same direct references to the medievals as Twisse, is in substantial agreement with him: 'Nunquam est judex mundi, si non in puniendis vel absolvendis hominibus judex est; nam *justus mundi judex* iniqui nihil potest facere, neque fontem absolvere, neque innocentem condemnare . . . Nec sola voluntas hic absoluta ex mero absoluto dominio agens est norma judicii, se voluntas justa et determinata, nos autem Deum, si spectemus absolutum ejus dominium, posse absolvere vel non punire peccatorem, et necessitate naturae ad actum non facere quae facit ut est absolutus Dominus, docemus.' *Disputatio Scholastica de Providentia*, pp. 580–81. It should perhaps be noted that even such vigorous intellectualists as Thomas Aquinas did allow that it was hypothetically possible for God, *de potentia absoluta*, to pardon sin without satisfaction, and so this was not a voluntarist distinctive. What is different about the position of Aquinas is that, unlike the voluntarists, he thought one could provide good rational reasons as to why God should choose to act in this way: see *ST* 3a.46.2, where he argues that humanity *could* have been freed without Christ's satisfaction, and then 3a.46.3, where he immediately proceeds to argue that no *better* way could have been found than by Christ's passion.

necessity of incarnation and satisfaction, given God's desire to save, represents a move towards a more intellectualist doctrine of God in the interest of closing the gap between rational human expectations of how God can and should act, and the way in which he does in fact do so, with obvious implications which are much broader than the narrow focus on atonement would at first imply. Indeed, Owen's intellectualism is at points absolutely explicit.[22] In the mature Owen, the analogy between God's justice and human conceptions of justice, and between God's mercy and human conceptions of mercy, is so close that, given the reality of both human sin and God's will to save, Owen is quite certain that God can only harmonize the two through the incarnation in a manner reminiscent of the Anselmic argument.[23] Parallel to this is Owen's understanding of God's revelation in Scripture as giving real insights not simply into how he has willed to be towards his creatures, but how, in effect, he must be towards them.[24]

Some might be tempted to see here the potential for just the kind of rationalistic metaphysical speculation in Owen's thought that his explicit understanding of the relationship between re-vealed theology and human reason purports to exclude. After all, is Owen not smuggling into his view of God an anthropomorphic principle which then enables him to dictate how God must act? Such a claim, while perhaps appealing in an age still struggling to free itself from the Barth–Brunner debate in the 1930s over natural theology, is nevertheless entirely misplaced. Owen's care-ful defence of the freedom of God in his assertion that the decision to save is an act of God's will, not an essential part of his being, automatically delimits the scope of natural theology in

---

[22] '[God's] intellectual will is carried towards happiness by an essential inclination antecedent to liberty, and notwithstanding it wills happiness with a concomitant liberty.' *Works* 10, p. 510.

[23] See Ibid., pp. 495 ff.

[24] Owen's argument from Scripture is as follows: some Scriptures speak of God as being in himself holy (e.g., Hab. 1:13); some refer to God as a judge who judges justly (e.g., Gn. 18:25); and some speak of the infliction of sin as the result of God's justice (e.g., Rom. 1:32): see *Works* 10, pp. 512–17. The movement from God as he is in himself to God as he must act, given certain conditions, is clear. The crucial step in the argu-ment is the first, that Scripture gives real insight into God's absolute being.

this context.[25] The heathen described by Owen in *A Dissertation*, know by natural insight that God needs to be propitiated, but they have no knowledge of his desire to be merciful or of the economy of salvation.[26] Given Owen's understanding of the principles of theology, this is hardly surprising: the incarnation is the act of the Trinitarian God and can only be understood in that context; and the Trinity is a doctrine into which unaided natural reason can give no insight. Furthermore, the incarnation is also an act which reveals God as Redeemer, not merely Creator – another aspect of the divine into which natural theology and general revelation can, in Owen's scheme, give no insight whatsoever. It is only after believers have knowledge of the Trinitarian economy of salvation by revelation that they can then use their reason, in conjunction with the intellectualist doctrine of God, to explore the Christian doctrine of atonement.

A further point to make in this context is that Owen's metaphysical understanding of God in terms of these attributes of being which effectively regulate his acts *ad extra* does not open the door to unbounded theological speculation but actually closes it. There can be, for Owen, only a very limited discussion of God *de potentia absoluta*, because that concept is itself more radically limited in Owen's theology by his essentially Thomist metaphysics than in the more Scotistic theology of William Twisse: Owen's God is subject far more to restrictions as a result of his own being than restrictions imposed by the principle of non-contradiction.[27] In this, Owen's metaphysical interest can be seen as allied to the infralapsarian tendencies and historical focus of his theology, a pattern which is not untypical within the Reformed tradition.[28]

There are then two foundational points concerning Owen's doctrine of God which emerge sometime between 1647 and 1653,

---

[25] *Works* 10, pp. 509–11.
[26] Ibid., pp. 525–41.
[27] On the difference between Thomas and Scotus, see Copleston, *History* 2.
[28] For a more detailed discussion of this, see L. C. Boughton, 'Supralapsarianism and the Role of Metaphysics in Sixteenth Century Reformed Theology', *WTJ* 48 (1986), 63–96. On the issue as it relates specifically to Owen, see Trueman, 'Owen's *Dissertation on Divine Justice*'.

as a result of his increasing concern about Socinian theology: first, God's freedom does not mean that he is subject in his actions only to the logical restrictions demanded by the principle of non-contradiction but refers simply to the fact that all of his external acts derive from his will, uncoerced by external factors; and, second, God's essence, his absolute attributes, determine the nature of these external acts. Thus, God is the causal ground of created being, and it is therefore in God as he exists in himself that we can find the framework within which his external acts must be understood.

God, Creation and Providence

The general framework

In Owen's early theology his debt to the language of philosophical metaphysics is most evident in his treatment of the nature of God's sovereignty in providence. His most detailed discussion of this issue occurs in his earliest published work, *A Display of Arminianism* (1642). Throughout this treatise Owen's arguments exhibit a considerable amount of continuity not only with the anti-Pelagian thrust of Reformation Protestant thought but also with the doctrinal patterns and vocabulary of the medieval scholastics, whose philosophical insights inform Owen's arguments concerning God's sovereignty at almost every turn.

The foundation of Owen's view of God's sovereignty is his understanding of God's being, and the implications which this has for the realm of creation. For Owen, God can be described using the scholastic notion of pure or simple act.[29] This means that God is fully actualized being, with no potential to change, and no cause either logically or ontologically anterior to himself. This concept lies at the heart of scholastic formulations of the doctrine of divine immutability, and has obvious implications

---

[29]   On act/potency and pure act, see Copleston, *History* 2, pp. 329–35. For Owen's use of the idea, see *Works* 10, pp. 19–20. This terminology was not unusual for either continental scholastics or English Puritans: e.g., Turretin, *Institutes* 1.3.7; Goodwin, *Works* 5, p. 16.

for, among other things, the nature of eternity, the relationship of God to time, God's simplicity, and thus also for the nature of language about God.[30] While such a definition of God might appear very abstract and impersonal, we shall see below that the attributes which are implied by God's being as pure act are employed by Owen primarily to provide the necessary metaphysical basis for the reliability of God's saving purposes. Owen hints at this in his early definition of God's simplicity as determinative for the nature of the decrees:

> The decrees of God, being conformable to his nature and essence, do require eternity and immutability as their inseparable properties. God, and he only, never was, nor ever can be, what now he is not. Passive possibility to anything, which is the fountain of all change, can have no place in him who is 'actus simplex,' and purely free from all composition . . . The eternal acts of his will not really differing from his unchangeable essence, must needs be immutable.[31]

As God, therefore, is fully actualized being, with no potential to change whatsoever, one obvious inference is that, if creation is to stand in any relation to God at all, it must be in a position of strict ontological and causal subordination. If this were not the case, then God would be mutable and thus not pure act. It is this thought, combined with the rejection of the possibility of an infinite chain of causal regression, which lies at the heart of Aquinas's famous 'Five Ways' to prove God's existence. Owen, however, does not use the argument here as a way of proving that God exists but applies it instead to the problem of providence and, in a more strictly soteriological sphere, to the relation between human acts and God's grace.

While the doctrine of God's simplicity serves to point to the radical limitation of human language about God, it does not prevent Owen from making a series of scholastic distinctions which serve to clarify and define God's relationship to the created realm. We have already noted that, from at least the early 1650s, Owen's theology takes on a distinctively intellectualist hue,

---

[30] For a classic scholastic statement of these issues in relation to God as pure act, see Aquinas, *ST* 1a.3 ff.
[31] *Works* 10, pp. 19–20.

reflecting his general predilection for a Thomist orientation to theology, a predilection which actually makes him more intellectualist than Thomas himself on certain issues.[32] In *A Display of Arminianism*, his position on the issue of intellectualism is less clear, although it has to be said that the language of intellect predominates, and, as we shall see, Owen follows Thomas, both explicitly and implicitly, at a number of important points. To begin with, he adopts the distinction between God's intellective or intuitive knowledge, and his so-called knowledge of vision.[33] Intellective knowledge is God's knowledge of all possibles, while knowledge of vision is his knowledge of all actual existents. Between the two comes God's free decree, whereby he determines which of the possibles he will actualize, along with when and how he will do it. As such, the distinction is the corollary of the classic division of God's power into *potentia absoluta*, whereby God can do anything not involving logical contradiction, and *potentia ordinata*, whereby God wills to actualize a subset of all possibles. While the latter distinction safeguards God's infinite omnipotence in the face of questions raised by a finite creation, the former safeguards God's omniscience in the same context.

Of crucial importance in Owen's discussion is the logical priority over the knowledge of vision that he gives to God's decrees:

> Out of this large and boundless territory of things possible [i.e., the realm of intellective knowledge], God by his decrees freely determines what shall come to pass, and makes them future which before were but possible. After this decree, as they commonly speak, followeth, or together with it, as others more exactly, taketh place, that prescience of God which they call 'visionis,' 'of vision,' whereby he infallibly sees all things in their proper causes, and how and when they shall come to pass.[34]

This passage is important for a number of reasons. First, it gives

---

[32] E.g. on the necessity of the death of Christ: cf. Owen's *A Dissertation of Divine Justice* (*Works* 10) with Aquinas, *ST* 3a.46.1–4; see also Trueman, 'Owen's *Dissertation on Divine Justice*'.

[33] *Works* 10, p. 23; also 12, pp. 127–8. Cf. Aquinas, *ST* 1a.14.9.

[34] *Works* 10, p. 23.

clear logical, and therefore causal, priority to the decrees over the knowledge of vision and thus precludes any notion in the soteriological sphere that election can be on the basis of foreseen merits. Secondly, it shows that Owen himself is clearly aware of the logical and linguistic tightrope upon which he is walking at this point. His evident unease about the use of language of temporal priority with reference to God's inner acts reveals his acute sensitivity to the philosophical problems that the doctrine of divine simplicity creates for any talk of God which makes logical distinctions within God's essence.[35] There is no temporal priority of decree over knowledge of vision because there is no change or procession within God: he is pure act, and thus his decrees and his knowledge of vision are simultaneous and coextensive, a fact which leads him to adopt the Boethian view of eternity as an infinite present:

> By one most pure act of his own essence he discerneth all things . . . So that those things concerning which we treat he knoweth three ways: First, In himself and his own decree, as the first cause; in which respect they may be said to be necessary, in respect of the certainty of their event. Secondly, In their immediate causes, wherein their contingency doth properly consist. Thirdly, In their own nature as future, but to his infinite knowledge ever present.[36]

It is highly significant that in this passage he sets his Boethian view of time within a Thomist framework whereby the simultaneity of knowledge is grounded primarily in God's knowledge of himself as cause. Thus, while he is cautious about the use of the language of temporal procession with regards to God, Owen does not allow this to jeopardize the causal priority of God's knowledge over all aspects of creation. Indeed, such an assertion is

---

[35] Sensitivity to the logical problems created by the inadequacy of human language to express divine truths is something which the Reformed inherited from the rich tradition of logical reflection in the Middle Ages and is another aspect of the scholastic heritage which should caution scholars against too hasty an equation of the scholastic with the rationalistic. Perhaps one of the most acute Puritan discussions of linguistic/logical problems relating to futurity, which interacts explicitly with the medieval nominalist tradition, occurs in Richard Baxter's *Catholick Theologie*, Bk.1, pp. 8 ff.

[36] *Works* 10, p. 28. Cf. Aquinas, *ST* 1a.14.7, 1a.14.13. For Boethius on eternity, see *De Consolatione Philosophiae* 5.

crucial if he is to avoid compromising the Reformed emphasis upon God's absolute sovereignty over everything.[37]

In the mid-sixteenth century the problem of the causal relationship between God's knowledge and future events had been made more complex by the development of the notion of middle knowledge as a possible solution to the problem of relating God's sovereignty to human freedom. This doctrine had originated in the thinking of Jesuits, such as Luis de Molina and Francisco Suarez, and had then been imported into Protestant theology by Jacob Arminius who had used it in his modification of the Reformed understanding of predestination.[38] The issue was thus of great significance in both the Jansenist–Molinist controversy within the Roman Church and the Orthodox–Remonstrant conflict within the Reformed churches. As noted earlier, Owen was himself not only involved in the latter but was also very well-read in the literature of the former, where his sympathies inevitably lay with the Jansenists. It is therefore perhaps a little surprising that in his discussions of providence he makes little reference to middle knowledge as an issue. In his early work, *A Display of Arminianism*, he refers to Arminians and Socinians as both giving God only a conjectural foreknowledge. In so doing, he perhaps misses the subtlety of the middle knowledge doctrine and is a little harsh on the Remonstrants.[39] Then, in *Vindiciae Evangelicae*, he makes a passing reference to the idea as a 'late figment' with which he does not intend to deal in that particular

---

[37]   Indeed, it is Arminius's modification of the Thomist position on the causal priority of God's knowledge over creation which forms a significant part of his deviation from Reformed Orthodoxy on the issues of providence and predestination: see Muller, *Arminius*, pp. 167–207.

[38]   Owen, *Works* 12, p. 128. On the development of the idea of middle knowledge by Suarez and Molina, see Copleston, *History* 3, pp. 342 ff. For more detailed discussion of Molina's thought on this and related issues, along with a translation of the relevant section of his *Concordia*, see *On Divine Foreknowledge*, trans. and intro. A. J. Freddoso (Ithaca: Cornell UP, 1988). On Arminius on middle knowledge, see Muller, *God, Creation, and Providence*, pp. 163 ff. For an examination of one Reformed response see J. A. van Ruler, 'New Philosophy to Old Standards: Voetius' Vindication of Divine Concurrence and Secondary Causality', *NAKG* 71 (1991), 58–91. For a discussion of Arminius's positive relationship to Molinism, see Eef Dekker, 'Was Arminius a Molinist?' *SCJ* 27 (1996), 337–52.

[39]   *Works* 10, p.27.

work.[40] Owen's silence on this issue is not theologically significant, however. A number of classic works on this subject were produced by Orthodox theologians in the seventeenth century,[41] and we know that Owen was well acquainted with some of these, such as Rutherford's *Disputatio Scholastica de Providentia*, and that he owned copies of others.[42] In addition, his explicit theological statements show that his system embodied all the elements which featured in the standard Reformed attack on the notion. While both Orthodox and Arminians were superficially agreed in allowing that God had a knowledge of all possibles, the crucial difference was that the former never allowed that these possibles could be conceived, even hypothetically, as lying outside the divine willing, while such a conception was absolutely fundamental to the latter's case.[43] It is this metaphysical issue which lies at the core of the Orthodox–Arminian debate on this point, and it is precisely this that Owen's overarching emphasis upon the necessity of the causal priority of God's will precludes.[44] He may

---

[40]   *Works* 12, p. 128.

[41]   For example, Twisse's *Dissertatio de scientia media* (Arnhem, 1639).

[42]   His library contained works by Twisse, Ames, Voetius, and Baxter, all of whom spent varying amounts of time refuting the middle knowledge doctrine: see *Bibliotheca Oweniana, passim.*

[43]   'Actus nostri liberi pendebunt causative a divinae providentiae libero decreto, sed ii actus, omniaque quae eveniunt contingenter imo vel necessario (est enim omnium par ratio) futura sunt citra et ante omnem divinae voluntatis aut praescientiae actum, quod ipsa fortuna est antevertens Deum, ejusque voluntatem, curam, providentiam, sapientiam, et omnipotentiam.' Rutherford, *Disputatio Scholastica*, p. 13; 'A middle knowledge by which God is imagined by some to know by a hypothesis before the decree of his will that certain things will be, if such and such free causes meet such and such conditions – knowledge of this kind cannot stand with the absolute perfection of God. For it both supposes that events will happen independently of the will of God and also makes some knowledge of God depend on the object.' Ames, *Marrow*, p. 96; cf. van Ruler, 69 ff. For a provocative discussion of this issue in the wider context of the historic Reformed–Arminian debate, see R. A. Muller, 'Grace, Election, and Contingent Choice: Arminius's Gambit and the Reformed Response' in T. R. Schreiner and B. A. Ware. (eds.), *The Grace of God and the Bondage of the Will* (Grand Rapids: Baker, 1995), pp. 251–78.

[44]   In light of recent attempts to propose middle knowledge as a basis for Reformed–Arminian rapprochement, Richard Muller has made the following astute observation: 'For *scientia media* to become the basis for such rapprochement, however, the Reformed would need to concede virtually all of the issues in debate and adopt an Arminian perspective, because, in terms of the metaphysical foundations of the historical debate between Reformed and Arminian, the idea of a divine *scientia media*, or middle knowledge, is the heart and soul of the original Arminian position. Middle knowledge is not a middle ground.' 'Grace, Election, and Contingent Choice', pp. 265–6.

not deal with the issue at length, but then it is ruled out of his system a priori, and he may well have felt that others had sufficiently exposed the problem.

Another important point to make about Owen's understanding of God's providence is that he does not regard God's causal priority and his decrees as in any way precluding contingency within the realm of creation. Contingency for Owen is rooted in the notion of secondary causality: things happen contingently with reference to their immediate causes. Thus, contingency in the realm of secondary causes does not imply freedom from necessity with regards to the First Cause, and, indeed, given the basic metaphysical structure of Owen's world, cannot do so.[45] There is nothing innovative in what Owen says here, as his argument parallels the basic position worked out by Thomas Aquinas in the Middle Ages which is in turn reflected in the Westminster Confession's statement on the issue.[46]

This argument has a twofold significance for Owen. First, it allows him to safeguard human freedom within a deterministic framework. Depending once again on faculty psychology, Owen argues that the human will is radically free and self-determined with respect to its internal principle of operation, i.e. its own desires and ambitions. Thus, if a human being chooses to act in a particular manner it is because that individual's own intellect and will lead in that direction. Second, this does not negate God's purpose or his control over human action: God uses humans to fulfil his purposes by moving them in a manner consistent with their own internal principle of operation. Thus there is, from a human perspective, a happy coincidence of God's plan and human willing which preserves the former's sovereignty and the latter's freedom.[47]

---

[45] 'Now, we call that contingent which, in regard of its next and immediate cause, before it come to pass, may be done or may not be done; as, that a man shall do such a thing tomorrow, or any time hereafter, which he may choose whether he will do or no. Such things as these are free and changeable, in respect of men, their immediate and second causes; but if we, as we ought to do, look up unto Him who foreseeth and hath ordained the event of them or their omission, they may be said necessarily to come to pass or to be omitted. It could not but be as it was.' *Works* 10, p. 22.

[46] Cf. *ST* 1a.14.13 with WCF 5.2; also, The Irish Articles 11.

[47] *Works* 10, pp. 35–6.

Of course, the danger here for Owen is parallel to that created by the close identification of God's decree and his knowledge of vision: the causal priority of God might easily become lost and leave the way open for that role to be taken over by the creature. Such a notion is precluded by what Owen has already said about the logical order of God's internal acts which effectively requires his commitment to a premotionist understanding of the relationship between God and creature.[48] This latter point is what underlies his more philosophical objection based upon the order of being:

> This opinion, that God hath nothing but a general influence into the actions of men, not effectually moving their wills to this or that in particular . . . [g]ranteth a goodness of *entity*, or being, unto divers things, whereof God is not the author, as those special actions which men perform without his special concurrence; which is blasphemous. The apostle affirms that 'of him are all things'.[49]

The point which Owen is making is that if there is any action or thing which is only in a general sense caused by God and dependent upon him for its existence and its motion, and which does not therefore involve him as a specific, individual cause, then the chain of being which derives from God is disrupted because there would be need of another First Cause and another chain of being to provide specific existence to the phenomenon in question. In other words, there is something else which stands as the First Cause of another chain, and thus, for want of a better description, there is another God. Such a thing would stand outside the causal will of God and would therefore possess some kind of being in and of itself, which would be metaphysical and theological nonsense within the framework of Owen's thought. This is why the philosophical implications of Arminianism, as much as its heterodox theology, are so utterly unacceptable to Owen: they effectively deny that God is the sole source of being for, and the only sustainer of, the universe. The significance of this point can be made clearer by making sure that we avoid the common

---

[48] On premotionism, see W. L. Craig, *The Problem of Divine Knowledge and Future Contingents from Aristotle to Suarez* (Leiden: Brill, 1988), pp. 201–2.
[49] *Works* 10, p. 42.

misconstruction of God being understood as First Cause by virtue of the fact that he stands at that start of a chronological succession of events. In fact, this is not how Thomistic theology understood the notion: God as First Cause means that God stands at the start of every logical succession of events. Thus, any event which takes place without God being here and now its First Cause in a specific sense is, quite literally, free of God, part of another order of being, and dependent upon another First Cause which is, as a Thomist would argue, another God.[50]

This then is the basic framework within which the early Owen develops his general theory of providence. Using scholastic concepts and argumentation which, at significant points, reveal obvious debts to Thomas Aquinas and the later Thomist tradition,[51]

---

[50] See Aquinas's arguments, based on Aristotle, *Physics* 8:7, in *Summa contra Gentiles* 1.42; also, Robert L. Patterson, *The Conception of God in the Philosophy of Aquinas* (London: George Allen and Unwin, 1933), pp. 265–76. Owen himself makes this point quite clear in *A Display of Arminianism*: 119–20. 'First, Every thing that is independent of any else in operation is purely active, and so consequently a god; for nothing but a divine will can be a pure act, possessing such a liberty by virtue of its own essence. Every created will must have a liberty by participation, which includeth such an imperfect potentiality as cannot be brought into act without some premotion (as I may say so) of a superior agent. Neither doth this motion, being extrinsical, at all prejudice the true liberty of the will, which requireth, indeed, that the internal principle of operation be active and free, but not that that principle be not moved to that operation by an outward superior agent. Nothing in this sense can have an independent principle of operation which hath not an independent being. It is no more necessary to the nature of a free cause, from whence a free action must proceed, that it be the first beginning of it, than it is necessary to the nature of a cause that it be the first cause. Secondly, If the free acts of our wills are so subservient to the providence of God as that he useth them to what end he will, and by them effecteth many of his purposes, then they cannot of themselves be so absolutely independent as to have in their own power every necessary circumstance and condition, that they may use or not use at their pleasure. Now the former is proved by all those reasons and texts of Scripture I before produced to show that the providence of God overruleth the actions and determineth the wills of men freely to do that which he hath appointed. And, truly, were it otherwise, God's dominion over the most things that are in the world were quite excluded; he had not power to determine that any one thing should ever come to pass which hath any reference to the wills of men. Thirdly, All the acts of the will being positive entities, were it not previously moved by God himself, "in whom we live, move, and have our being," must needs have their essence and existence solely from the will itself; which is thereby made *auto on* a first and supreme cause, endued with an underived being.' *Works* 10, pp. 119–20.

[51] In *A Display of Arminianism*, Owen not only uses Thomas, but also refers with approval to Diego Alvarez (d. 1631), Bishop of Trani, a significant defender of anti-Pelagian views of grace from within a Thomist framework: see *Works* 10, pp. 52, 73, 131.

Owen argues for a notion of providence which is rooted in his understanding of God as pure act. He expounds this in the traditional scholastic language of faculty psychology which he uses to safeguard God's causal priority over creation, while preserving the reality of creaturely contingency. Owen's position on the relationship between the divine will and human agency is therefore what modern philosophers would characterize as 'soft' determinism.[52] What is interesting is that Scholasticism, with its wealth of psychological and ontological distinctions, provides him with the vocabulary necessary to avoid having his position misunderstood as 'hard' determinism or as some form of incipient Pelagianism. The kind of subtlety needed would scarcely be possible without recourse to such language.

Providence and Trinitarianism

One issue that has not yet been made clear is how this view of creation and providence relates to Owen's specifically Trinitarian understanding of God which was so important for his theological prolegomena. One does not have to dig very deep in Owen's writings, however, to rectify this deficiency.

Fundamental to Owen's doctrine of God is the traditional idea that all acts of God are acts of the whole God. This is an obvious implication of belief in the consubstantiality of the three persons of the Godhead, and in a marginal note Owen cites Athanasius, Basil, and Ambrose as his authorities for this.[53] Within each act so considered, there exists a specific economy in which each person of the Godhead plays a particular part. In creation and in providence the Trinity is absolutely foundational: the Father creates and governs through the Son by the Holy Spirit.[54] Again, the Western order of procession is integral to the whole scheme. It is true that Owen does not spend a great deal of time in his writings as a whole explicating this idea in detail, but that is no doubt because his major opponents on the issue of providence are the Arminians, whose error in this area he did not regard as

---

52   Anthony Kenny, *Aquinas on Mind* (London: Routledge, 1993) pp. 77–8.
53   *Works* 3, p. 93.
54   Ibid.

lying in their understanding of the Trinity as such but in the causal relationship of God's knowledge to his creatures. It is different when Owen debates with the Socinians who, consistent with their anti-trinitarianism, ascribe the act of creation to the Father alone; in this context, Owen vigorously asserts the Trinitarian nature of the work, largely in the context of establishing the preexistence of Christ which is so central in his conflict with Socinianism.[55] God's external acts may, in one sense, be acts of God in unity, but they presuppose the nature of God as Trinity.

God and Predestination

Predestination and providence

When Owen comes to deal with predestination, he chooses to consider it as a subset of providence, a position common among scholastic theologians but apparently rejected by Calvin.[56] Owen,

---

[55] *Works* 12, pp. 142–3; cf. Johannes Crellius, *De Uno Deo Patre, Libri Duo* (Cracow, 1631), pp. 88–9. On the role of Christ and the Holy Spirit in providence, see *Works* 12, pp. 278–83 and 3, pp. 95–105. For further discussion of Christ, creation, and providence, see Ch. 4.

[56] Much has been made of the Calvin's placement of predestination under soteriology and Christology rather than under the doctrine of God. The latter is seen as helping to make the decree one of the key foundations for theological reflection: see, for example, P. C. Holtrop, 'Decree(s) of God', in Donald K. McKim (ed.), *Encyclopedia of the Reformed Faith* (Edinburgh: Saint Andrew Press, 1992), pp. 97–9. As regards the notion of the decrees as a foundation for theological reflection, Richard Muller's extensive study of Reformed Orthodox prolegomena has found no evidence to support such a thesis: see *PRRD1*. Furthermore, as regards the significance of the systematic placement of the decree, Muller has pointed out that the following words of Herman Bavinck seem to contain a central (and, one would think, logically obvious) insight: 'Whether predestination is made a part of the doctrine of God (the a priori order) or is treated at the beginning or in the middle of the doctrine of salvation (the a posteriori order) does not necessarily imply an essential difference in principle. Nevertheless, it is a significant fact that the a priori order is usually followed by Reformed theologians . . . The reason for this . . . is not that the Reformed in a speculative manner derive predestination from an a priori, philosophical, deterministic conception of the Deity . . . but that for the Reformed the doctrine of predestination has not merely an anthropological and soteriological but especially a theological significance. God's glory, not man's salvation, is considered the chief purpose of predestination.' *The Doctrine of God*, trans. W. Hendriksen (Edinburgh: Banner of Truth, 1977), pp. 358–9.

following the medieval paradigm, sees predestination as being a restricted form of providence: while providence covers all works of creation, predestination has reference only to rational creatures, i.e. humans and angels; furthermore, while providence respects only natural ends, predestination respects supernatural ends, in other words, the ultimate destiny, heaven or hell, of the rational creature.[57] While allowing that predestination has this broad meaning, Owen actually expresses his intention in *A Display of Arminianism* to use the word to refer to God's predestination of individuals to salvation, and thus, he says, predestination and election can be regarded as synonyms. In important respects Owen's discussion here parallels that of Thomas Aquinas in the *Summa Theologiae*: predestination is part of providence; it involves the predestining of rational creatures (humans and angels) to a supernatural end, within a presupposed nature–grace framework; and it is virtually synonymous with election. A comparison with Aquinas at this point brings out the clear parallels between the structure of Owen's argument and that of his medieval antecedents.[58]

Owen's major point of disagreement on this issue with the Arminians is that he regards predestination as originating solely in the being of God and not as the result of God's foreknowledge or of any human act of faith. From what has been said concerning Owen's understanding of the metaphysical structure of creation, it is obvious that the Arminian notion of election, allowing as it does for a realm of action outside the direct will of God, is incompatible with Owen's basic philosophical presuppositions, whereby the source of any action or events being cannot ultimately derive from anywhere other than God. Within such a framework, conjectural foreknowledge of particular events that may happen, without that knowledge also involving knowledge of God's causation of those particular events, is obviously logically impossible and metaphysically nonsensical. To reinforce this position, Owen uses two further strands of argumentation: one is based upon philosophical concerns; the other on theologi-

---

[57] *Works* 10, pp. 53–4.
[58] Cf. Ibid. with *ST* 1a.23.

cal ones. The first strand of argumentation, from cause to effect is based upon Aristotelian concepts and parallels the argument noted in Ch. 2 regarding the limits of reason: no given effect can be greater than its cause; salvation is something which transcends the natural realm, and is thus beyond the causal potential of anything within the natural realm; therefore, no human acts are sufficient to cause any eternal act of God, and this includes election.[59] The argument here parallels that of Thomas Aquinas in the *Summa Theologiae*, where the nature of eternal life as a supernatural end is used to show that its cause cannot lie within the power of the creature but must reside in God alone.[60]

The point of the Thomist argument as it is appropriated by Owen is that it stresses the radical difference in the order of being between the Creator and the creature, between supernatural ends and natural ends, and between eternity and time, in the interest of safeguarding the anti-Pelagian structure of salvation. Such a clear distinction leaves no room for the kind of correlation of the two which one finds, for example, in the covenantal structure of late-medieval patterns of salvation in the *via moderna* or the Arminian insistence on the reality of middle knowledge.[61] Any form of semi-Pelagianism is ruled out by the metaphysical framework of reality which it reflects. Nevertheless, we must not overplay the wider significance of this philosophical argument for Owen's theology. This causal framework provides the basis for only one of the six arguments Owen uses at this point in *A Display of Arminianism* in order to establish the priority of God's

---

[59] 'Operation in every kind is a second act, flowing from the essence of a thing which is the first. But all our graces and works, our faith, obedience, piety, and charity, are all temporal, of yesterday, the same standing with ourselves, and no longer; and therefore cannot be the cause of, no, nor so much as a condition necessarily required for, the accomplishment of an eternal act of God irrevocably established before we are.' *Works* 10, p. 64.

[60] 'Finis autem, ad quem res creatae ordinantur a Deo, est duplex. Unus, qui excedit proportionem naturae creatae, et facultatem; et hic finis est vita aeterna, quae in divina visione consistit, quae res supra naturam cujuslibet creaturae . . . Ad illud autem, ad quod non potest aliquid virtute suae naturae pervenire, oportet, quod ab alio transmittatur; sicut sagitta a sagittante mittitur ad signum: unde proprie loquendo, rationalis creatura, quae est capax vitae aeternae, perducitur in ipsam, quasi a Deo transmissa.' *ST* 1a.23.1.

[61] See Oberman, *Harvest*, pp. 169–78; Muller, *Arminius*, pp. 155 ff.

action in individual salvation. As such, it stands as an auxiliary
to more biblical and theological arguments, and its function is to
undergird biblical teaching on God as a sovereign, personal
Saviour, rather than to emphasize God as an abstract, impersonal First Cause. It thus represents only one part of Owen's
attempt to construct a Reformed soteriology and should not be
abstracted from context and used as evidence of an agenda aimed
at building a God out of the raw material of metaphysics with no
reference to biblical teaching.

This last point is reflected in a similar argument to that based
on causal priority which Owen uses in *The Death of Death*. Here,
Owen points out that God's saving love towards humanity does
not negate the need for the intervention of God's saving grace in
history.[62] It is probable that he is implicitly countering the doctrine of eternal justification at this point, a conjecture which his
comments later on the same page seem to support.[63] Nevertheless, the importance of this passage also lies in the fact that it
shows that Owen's theology, for all its emphasis upon God's
sovereignty, eternity, and immutability, does not lead to a swal-
lowing-up of history in eternity. The economy of salvation may
be rooted in eternity, but it is also firmly tied to history, and this
aspect of Owen's theology becomes more pronounced as he
develops his intellectualist doctrine of God along with the Aristotelian and Thomist elements of his theology, and uses them to
stress the need for incarnation and atonement. The priority of
eternity over time is not emphasized to undermine the importance of time in itself but to underscore the reliability and consistency of God's eternal saving purposes *in* time. Thus, to the
extent that the basic distinction and balance between the eternal
and the historical which we noted in his reflections upon the
principles of theology are supported, rather than obscured, by
his use of metaphysical language and concepts, to that extent the
same metaphysical language and concepts help to support and
clarify the reality and constancy of God's grace towards those
being saved.

---

[62]   *Works* 10, p. 276.
[63]   Ibid., pp. 276–7. On eternal justification in Puritan theology, along with a discussion of various seventeenth-century responses, see Boersma, *A Hot Peppercorn*; also
Ch. 5 below.

The second broad strand of argumentation is based more closely upon biblical texts and categories.[64] It is here that Owen points to a second, and very important, element in his doctrine of predestination: the role of theological anthropology. By contrast, the argument from cause and effect, based upon a broadly Thomist model of reality, can perhaps be described as an argument for predestination 'from above', whereby the metaphysical implications of God's sovereignty are worked out in the realm of creation. But we must be careful not to overemphasize the importance of this approach: all that definitions of God as pure act or First Cause *per se* tells us is that creation is subordinate to the Creator and dependent upon him for its being and its movement. As such, these definitions simply point to a framework for creation which is broadly deterministic; they tell us nothing about any of the central elements of the Christian notion of predestination. For Owen these central elements are provided by his understanding of the Trinity and his understanding of humanity, both in terms of biblical categories.

Owen's doctrine of predestination is predicated upon two ideas: in the eternal realm, the decrees; and in the historical, the sinfulness of humanity.[65] The point of intersection between these two ideas is the person of Jesus Christ, incarnate God and Mediator. As God he is a partner to the eternal covenant, and as incarnate being he is the one who deals with humanity's sin.[66] In the order of logical priorities Owen is careful to stress that the covenant and subsequent incarnation are predicated upon the existence of sin. He will have nothing to do with the kind of speculative theology which would allow for incarnation even if sin had never happened.[67] Thus, logically speaking, sin comes first, with the incarnation following as God's response. In

---

[64] *Works* 10, pp. 63–6.

[65] Ibid., pp. 53 ff.

[66] Ibid., pp. 168–75.

[67] Ibid., p. 69. While the incarnation must not be considered in isolation from humanity's sin, Owen does have an ontological and epistemological relevance in that it overcomes the gap between infinite and finite, a gap which existed even before the Fall. This comes out most clearly in Owen's eschatology: see Trueman, 'Heaven and Hell'.

between the two comes the covenant of redemption, with its corollary, the covenant of grace.

The importance of sin

For Owen, humanity before the Fall was not only designed for a supernatural end, but also possessed the means to achieve that end in the form of habitual grace and original righteousness. These were lost at the Fall and thus the supernatural end was placed beyond human reach.[68] Furthermore, post-Fall humanity is not simply the 'nature' part of the 'nature–grace' model: humans as they now exist are utterly corrupted, turned away from God, and committed to lives of ungodliness. This sinfulness derives from Adam, both by direct imputation and natural propagation.[69]

A number of significant points arise from these considerations. First, it is obvious that the arrangement within the Garden of Eden between God and humanity, known as the covenant of works, was itself essentially gracious. Sinclair Ferguson makes this point with great clarity when he indicates that the rewards attached to obedience in the Garden went far beyond anything that human obedience could intrinsically merit. There is, even in this covenant, a strong promissory element which provides the context within which the conditions must be understood.[70] One can add at this point that it is Owen's adoption of the scholastic nature-grace model of humanity that enables him to bring this point out so clearly: ability to fulfil the covenant conditions is predicated on human beings' possessing supernatural grace, by its very nature a gracious gift of God. We must be careful, therefore, of misunderstanding the covenant of works as nothing more than a conditional contract based upon straightforward commercial considerations. For Owen, it has God's gracious love at its heart.

The second point flows from his emphasis on human sinfulness and impotence in matters of salvation. Such considerations de-

---

[68] *Works* 10, p. 85.
[69] Ibid., pp. 70–72.
[70] *John Owen on the Christian Life*, pp. 22–4.

mand that, if salvation is to be actualized, then God must take
the initiative. By closely correlating sin and incarnation, and
insisting on the logical priority of the former, Owen points to the
need for seeing God's graciousness and love as the foundation of
the decrees. For Owen, election and reprobation should be discussed only in the context of God's saving purpose.[71] This is given
a strongly Christocentric and antispeculative twist when Owen
argues that Christ must become incarnate and die if sin is to be
forgiven.[72] The result is that the doctrine of predestination must
be explicitly Christocentric, as no economy of salvation can be
envisaged in even a theoretical manner without reference to the
incarnation.[73]

Such emphasis on the centrality of Christ for predestination
is, of course, a Reformed commonplace, but it is important to
note that Owen's development of this theme, particularly in his
understanding of the relation between sin and incarnation, does
not lead him to adopt a supralapsarian position. This is clear
when a comparison is made with his friend and contemporary
Thomas Goodwin. For Goodwin, God's acts in election can be
considered under two heads: the ordination of the end; and the
ordination of the means.[74] The idea is not unique to Goodwin,
but reflects the accepted understanding of causality at that time:
that which is first in intention, the end, is last in execution but
determines what steps or means intervene. Among English Puritans, the most significant application of this idea is found in the
work of William Twisse, who used the notion to simplify the
growing complexity of Reformed decretal structures in the early
seventeenth century.[75]

Using this distinction, Goodwin maintains that election to
eternal life is the end, and everything else is the means; thus, the
objects of election are not human beings as fallen, but as unfallen.[76] God then allows the Fall to happen so that he might reveal

[71] *Works* 10, p. 63.
[72] Ibid., pp. 481–624; *Works* 19, pp. 97–138.
[73] *Works* 19, pp. 21–38.
[74] Goodwin, *Works* 9, p. 154.
[75] See Twisse, *Vindiciae Gratiae* 1, digr. 6.6, pp. 52–3.
[76] *Works*, p. 155.

his own immutable holiness in election in a way that could never have happened had humanity remained sinless.[77] This whole scheme is set within a theological framework which gives absolute priority to the election of Christ over everything else.[78] In his commentary on Ephesians, however, Goodwin is careful to balance this emphasis upon the absolute priority of Christ with the typical Reformed warnings concerning speculation about the possibility of incarnation without sin.[79]

Owen himself is unwilling to go as far as Goodwin. The distinction between end and means is not used by him to develop a supralapsarian doctrine of predestination, and he is decidedly sceptical about debates concerning the ordering of God's decrees. His position is informed more by a desire to hold both divine and human freedom in tension than to develop a scheme which could be interpreted as negating one side or the other. All he will say is that God was not surprised by the Fall and that he had planned to deal with it in eternity. Beyond that he will not speculate.[80] Thus, when in his treatise, *A Declaration of the Glorious Mystery of the Person of Christ* (1679), Owen declares that the person of Christ is the foundation of all the counsels of God, this should not be construed in a supralapsarian manner.[81] Predestination, for Owen, cannot be considered without reference both to Christ

---

[77] 'But it pleased our God permissively to decree those elect to fall together with the rest, as for many other holy ends, so for this one especially that respects the matter in hand, that we might discern the difference of immutable holiness running along with glory, which election brings unto, Eph. I.4, from that of created holiness; which, if we suppose man had not fallen from, but stood by, his free-will grace had not been so manifestly discerned, but the glory of it would have been obscured and attributed unto man's free will, and not the grace of election.' *Works* 9, p. 158.

[78] See Ibid., pp. 93 ff.

[79] *Works* 1, pp. 99–100. Despite the strong Scotistic nature of his discussion of election, sin, and redemption, Goodwin is still happy to use Anselmic arguments when developing his Christology: see *Works* 5, esp. pp. 17 ff. Cf. Muller's comments on Calvin, *Christ and the Decree*, pp. 27–8.

[80] '[A]s we are careful to state the eternal decrees of God, and the actual operations of his providence, so as that the liberty of the will of man, as the next cause of all his moral actions, be not infringed thereby – so ought we to be careful not to ascribe such a sacrilegious liberty unto the wills of any creatures, as that God should be surprised, imposed on, or changed by any of their actings whatever.' *Works* 1, p. 62.

[81] Ibid., p. 54.

and to sin; that is why the decrees cannot be understood as standing at the head of a giant logical construct depending on the sovereignty of God but must be seen as rooted in the intra-trinitarian determination of God to save sinners.[82] It is to this determination that we now turn.

The Eternal Basis of Redemption

The importance of the Trinity

Owen's teaching on redemption has been interpreted as one long exercise in the subordination of Christian faith to Aristotelian causality and teleology.[83] Given the fact that Aristotelian causality is not given the prolegomenal prominence which it has, for example, in the *Methodus Theologiae* of Richard Baxter, it would indeed come as some surprise if such an interpretation of Owen's thought proved to be accurate. In fact, Owen's teaching of redemption parallels in significant ways the other areas of his theology which have already been examined, particularly in the prominence it gives to the role of the Trinity. This should be no

---

[82] The claim that the Reformed Orthodox understanding of the *ordo salutis* is based upon logical inference from God's sovereignty and his decrees is found frequently in the secondary scholarship, especially with reference to Beza's *Tabula Praedestinationis* and its English equivalent in Perkins' *A Golden Chaine*: see J. B. Torrance, 'Strengths and Weaknesses'; A. E. McGrath, *A Life of John Calvin* (Oxford: Blackwell, 1990), p. 214. Such claims represent in general a fundamental misrepresentation of the way in which the Reformed Orthdox developed their arguments, and in particular a basic misunderstanding of how such charts were used in the sixteenth- and seventeenth-century context, a mistake which Karl Barth was careful to avoid: see *CD* 2:2, pp. 77–8. The comment of Paul Helm on such interpretations is devastating: '[They] do not succeed in showing anything other than that in Beza's view each phase of the execution of the decree is intelligible only in the light of what is immediately temporally prior to it; they do not show, nor could they, that any stage in the execution in time of the eternal decree of salvation is logically deducible from the immediately prior stage, nor even from the conjunction of all prior stages. In other words, they confuse a logically necessary condition, consistency, with a logically sufficient condition, deducibility.' 'Calvin (and Zwingli) on Divine Providence', *CTJ* 29 (1994), 388–405, 390. For a careful historical discussion of the issue, see R. A. Muller, 'Perkins' *A Golden Chaine*: Predestinarian System or Schematized Ordo Salutis?', *SCJ* 9 (1978), 69–81.

[83] See Clifford, *Atonement and Justification*.

surprise: the Trinitarian foundations of the whole theological enterprise were quite obvious in Owen's analysis of the principles of theology; furthermore, given his emphasis upon God's acts *ad extra* as acts of the whole Trinity, and upon predestination as a part of providence, it should be obvious that the Trinitarian structure of the former inevitably applies to the latter and thus impacts upon the soteriological scheme as a whole.

Owen's most thorough discussion of the framework of salvation occurs in Book One of *The Death of Death*. At the start of this Book, Owen, using Aristotelian terminology, states that the issue of Christ's death can be discussed in terms of agent, ends and means. This is done very briefly in the first two chapters and represents nothing more radical or sinister than Owen's explicit acceptance of the Aristotelian language and logic of his day.[84] As noted in Ch. 2, the language of Aristotle, and even of causality, functioned within theological systems as heuristic devices not as a priori indications of the presence of certain metaphysical or theological dogmas. Thus, in *The Death of Death*, Owen's initial clarification of terms sets the tone for the organizational structure, though not the content, of Book One.[85] Owen then proceeds to identify the agent as the Trinity, adopting the standard theological notion that all external acts of God can be predicated on God as a unity. He then expands this notion of Trinitarian agency by arguing that all extratrinitarian acts are themselves rooted in intratrinitarian acts. This is, of course, no more than the traditional Trinitarian theology noted earlier, and reflects once again Owen's understanding of God as the eternal causal ground of all that happens in the temporal realm. In Chapters Three to Five, he describes in detail this Trinitarian structure, and it is this which provides the overarching framework of the argument as a whole, and to which his use of Aristotelian logic and terminology is subordinate.[86]

---

[84] For a discussion of Owen's Aristotelianism, see Chs. 1 and 2 above.

[85] *Works* 10, pp. 157–163.

[86] The basic constructive principle behind the argument is, in fact, his understanding of the Trinity, which comes as no surprise when his methodological presuppositions are taken into account: see Ch. 2. It also serves to place him within the broad tradition of Reformed (and, indeed, Western) theological reflection on this issue.

There are then sound reasons internal to Owen's thought for his explication of salvation as lying within the Trinitarian Godhead, but, in addition to these, it is also true that his approach is consistent with the direction of Reformed theology since the late sixteenth century.[87] The predestinarian controversies which divided the Reformed from the Remonstrants are epitomized in the so-called 'five points of Calvinism' as expressed in the Canons of Dordt, but the situation in the seventeenth century was considerably more complex than a surface reading of confessional statements would immediately suggest. Even by the late sixteenth century, Reformed theology had undergone a significant period of systematic elaboration, to the extent that debates over predestination involved far more than the logical relation of God's foreknowledge to his will. Indeed, the Arminian critique of Orthodoxy did not simply involve an altered understanding of the decrees and a modification of Augustinian anthropology, but in fact necessitated a much wider and more radical revision of a variety of key doctrinal loci.[88]

As mentioned above with regard to Owen, the Reformed commitment to acts *ad extra* being acts of the whole Trinity necessitated that Orthodox theologians spent considerable time reflecting upon the implications of salvation for inner life of the Trinity. Combined with their adherence to the order of procession delineated in the catholic Creeds, this inevitably meant that the Orthodox had to work out the decree of predestination in Trinitarian terms, and the focal point of this discussion became the appointment of Christ as Mediator and the relation in which this stood to the predestination of the elect. In Calvin, there are hints only of the later development, as in his commentary on the High Priestly prayer of John 17,[89] but by the time of William Perkins the whole area had received considerable attention, and the appointment of Christ as Mediator was explicitly the foundation of election.[90]

---

[87] See Muller, *Christ and the Decree*.

[88] On this, see R. A. Muller, 'The Christological Problem in the Thought of Jacobus Arminius', *NAKG* 68 (1988), 145–63.

[89] *CO* 47:379.

[90] 'The foundation is Christ Jesus, called of his father from all eternitie, to performe the office of the Mediator, that in him all those which should bee saved, might bee chosen.' *Workes* 1, p. 24.

The importance of this to the Reformed system is indicated by Arminius's development of a scheme which overthrew the anti-Pelagian nature of Reformed doctrine of predestination precisely in the way in which it reconstrued the nature of the divine decree in terms of the relationship between Father and Son. In opposition to the Reformed, Arminius, in his *Declaration* of 1608, argued for four decrees: the first, whereby God the Father appoints Christ as Mediator, etc. to destroy sin; the second, whereby God decrees to receive into favour all who repent and believe in Christ; the third, whereby God decrees to administer in a sufficient and efficacious way the means necessary for faith and repentance; and the fourth, whereby God decrees to save and damn particular persons on the basis of his foreknowledge.[91] It is this element of Arminius' argument which has been identified as having most systematic significance for the development of later Remonstrant theology.[92] The relationship of Father and Son in terms of God's decrees thus lay at the heart of the differences between Orthodox and Remonstrant in the seventeenth century.

Consistent with his orthdox understanding of the Trinity as being one substance in three persons who are distinguished from each other by their relations, Owen sees salvation as rooted in the inner life of the Trinity where the economy of salvation is based upon specific, individual roles for the Father, Son, and Holy Spirit. As mentioned above, it is a basic axiom of his theology that acts *ad extra* mirror the internal intratrinitarian relationships.[93] This is evident in his doctrine of creation where the Father creates by the Son through the Holy Spirit and salvation, as an act *ad extra*, is analogous in this respect to creation. In salvation, the acts uniquely attributed to the Father are the sending of the Son, and the laying upon him of the punishment due to our sin.[94] The sending of the Son consists of the imposition of the office of Mediator upon Christ in setting

---

[91]   Ibid., pp. 653–4.
[92]   Muller, 'The Christological Problem', 148–9.
[93]   'The order of operation in the blessed Trinity, as unto outward works, answereth unto and followeth the order of their subsistence.' *Works* 19, p. 34.
[94]   *Works* 10, p. 163.

him apart for this work and appointing him to it, and also of giving him fullness of gifts and grace. The gifts include those which Christ naturally possessed by virtue of his deity, as well as those which are given to him especially in view of his task as Mediator. The grace refers to that which is communicated to the humanity of Christ by the Holy Spirit through the incarnation.[95] This arrangement is the causal ground of salvation, and as such exerts a decisive influence on all aspects of salvation, including, one might add, the extent of the atonement. Given the fact that Owen builds his case on a specifically Trinitarian doctrine of God which is, by its very nature, above the reach of mere human reason, Aristotle, not surprisingly, is conspicuous by his absence from this doctrinal discussion. Owen bases his case on biblical texts and stands firmly within the framework of Reformed theology.

Christ and the covenant

The whole notion of the sending of the Son and his appointment to the office of Mediator is expressed by Owen in the concept of the 'covenant of redemption'. In his commentary on Hebrews, Owen elaborates at length upon what makes a covenant: it must involve distinct persons; it must be a voluntary arrangement; it must deal with matters within the power of the covenanting parties; and it must dispose matters to their mutual satisfaction.[96] Within this general category of covenant, there is a more specific subset which involves three distinct elements: a proposal of service; a promise of reward; and an acceptance of the proposal.[97] This type of covenant involves a functional subordination of one party to the other, although this is determined by the voluntary terms of the covenant itself and thus involves no necessary natural, ontological subordination. It is to this type of covenant that the covenant of redemption belongs. This is clear from the way in which Owen with his typical precision divides the covenant of redemption into two subsections: the role of God the

---

95 Ibid., pp. 164–8.
96 *Works* 19, pp. 82–3.
97 Ibid., p. 83–4.

Father in appointing Christ as Mediator and promising that he would protect, strengthen, and help him in the accomplishment of his work, and that his mission would be successful and achieve its purpose;[98] and the voluntary acceptance of the role of Mediator by the Son.[99] Thus, the covenant involves the Father and Son as covenanting parties and creates a voluntary hierarchy within the Trinity whereby the Son is officially subordinate to the Father while remaining equal to him in terms of his being or substance.

The distinction between Christ's natural consubstantiality with the Father and his voluntary subordination to him in terms of office is of fundamental importance in understanding the relation of Christ to the decree of salvation. As God, Christ is consubstantial with the Father and thus in no essential way subordinate to him. His acceptance of the office of Mediator is a voluntary act, not something imposed on him by the Father.[100] As a result, Christ's office as Mediator serves to place him, as it were, on both sides of the decree of election: it is his voluntary covenant with the Father which is the foundation of the decree, and so he is the electing God; and his acceptance of the role of Mediator is the causal ground for his entry into history as Jesus Christ of Nazareth, himself now an object of predestination.[101] Owen's resolution of the problem is not innovative but reflects the Reformed tradition on this issue, and finds its counterpart in his adherence to the christological formulation known as the *extra calvinisticum*.[102]

This whole argument has distinct significance for the relationship between the appointment of Christ as Mediator and the particularity of redemption which becomes clear when Owen's discussion of the covenant structure is understood against the background of debates with Arminianism, the explicit context of

---

[98] *Works* 10, pp. 168–71.

[99] Ibid., p. 174; *Works* 19, pp. 86–7.

[100] *Works* 19, pp. 86–7.

[101] For Christ as predestined, see Ch. 4 below.

[102] Cf. Perkins: 'Question: How can Christ be subordinate unto God's election, seeing he together with the Father decreed all things? Answer: Christ as he is a mediatour, is not subordinate to the very decree it selfe of election, but to the execution thereof only.' *Workes* 1, p. 24. On the role of the *extra calvinisticum* in Owen's christological formulations, see Ch. 4 below.

both *A Display of Arminianism* and *The Death of Death*, the two treatises in which the basic outlines and implications of Owen's predestinarian scheme are developed. It was noted earlier that Arminius reconstrued the relationship between the Father and the Son in terms of the decrees of predestination in a manner that separated the appointment of Christ as Mediator from an anti-Pelagian decree regarding predestination. Significantly, this is paralleled in his theology by a subordination of the Son to the Father not simply in terms of office but also in terms of his divinity.[103] Such a subordination allows for the separation of Christ and election in a way in which the Orthodox adherence to equality of essence does not. For the Orthodox, Christ as God stands behind the decree and therefore participates in the election of particular individuals; for the Remonstrants, Christ's role in election only appears in the fourth decree where he is involved in choosing who will enjoy salvation as a consequence of their belief.[104] Such a modification is extremely difficult within an orthodox Trinitarian framework, because Christ as God cannot be separated so radically from the decree of election. Owen's formulation, in line with the Reformed tradition and in a manner more perceptive than some of his later critics, points to the fact that it is the christological problem, the relationship between the Son and the Father in the structure of the decree, which lies at the heart of the predestination debate with the Arminians; as a result, he develops his theology in response to Arminian assaults in this area. At no point is the battle fought over the issue of Aristotelian teleology; rather, the issue at stake is the basic relationship between the decree of predestination and the relationship of the Father and Son demanded by Owen's adherence to orthodox Trinitarianism.

One question which has some relevance to the notion of restricting the Son's subordination strictly to his office as Mediator relates to the implications which Owen's formulation of the covenant of redemption has for the will of God. In proposing

---

[103]   This is clear from, for example, his statements in his *Apology* 21 in Arminius *Works* 2, pp. 29–32; for a discussion of this issue in Arminius, see Muller, 'The Christological Problem'.
[104]   See Muller, 'The Christological Problem', 159.

separate acts of will for Father and Son, is Owen not surreptitiously moving towards an understanding of the two persons having two separate wills? Such a position would clearly endanger the consubstantiality of Father and Son. This is a point of which Owen himself apparently felt the force, as he deals with it in his exercitation on Christ's priesthood in his Hebrews commentary. There, he argues that the distinction in the respective acts of will of the Father and Son does not endanger the overall unity of God's will because internal acts ascribed to particular persons in the Godhead, while involving that person in a special way, are not exclusive to that person and also include the concurrence of the other persons as a result of their mutual in-being. Furthermore, the voluntary relation between Father and Son which arises as a result of this covenant is to be understood as a relational predicate which does not necessarily connote any substantial difference between the two.[105] Owen cites no sources here, but his argument represents a fruitful application of the Boethian tradition of Trinitarian logic to the problems raised by Reformed Orthodox formulations of predestination.[106]

The acceptance of the role of Mediator involves Christ's willingness to take flesh, offer himself as sacrifice, and intercede for the elect.[107] All three elements are part of the one covenant and are thus a unity grounded in the office of Mediator. So central to Owen's case is this unity that he devotes considerable space to establishing this point and to answering objections to it; more space, in fact, than he devotes to any other individual topic in Book One of *The Death of Death*.[108] This emphasis on the importance of the unity of the mediatorial office, with its reference to sacrifice and intercession, obviously includes within itself the unity of the sacerdotal office in these two distinct acts. The thought is not new to Owen in *The Death of Death*: in his earliest published work, *A Display of Arminianism*, the unity of oblation

---

[105] *Works* 19, pp. 87–8.
[106] See Boethius, *De Trinitate*; cf. Aquinas, *ST* 1a.28.
[107] *Works* 10, pp.175–7.
[108] Ibid., pp. 179–200.

and intercession is a key element in his argument that the death of Christ is efficacious for salvation.[109]

In emphasizing this unity, Owen is typical of the Reformed tradition of his time, sensitive as it was to the need to understand Christ's priesthood in terms of the Old Testament types. While this will be discussed in more detail in Chs. 4 and 5, it is worth noting at the outset that the unity of the mediatorial office was considered a thoroughly biblical doctrine, based upon the types of priesthoods of the Levites and of Melchisedec, and not based upon speculative philosophical argument. Indeed, given the antipathy of theologians such as Goodwin to any consideration of Christ's death as complete in itself without reference to its overall context in Christ's mediatorial priesthood, it is those who seek to isolate Christ's death from his intercession who would be regarded as the speculative theologians.[110]

What this emphasis upon the unity of the mediatorial office does, is to make explicit the systematic relationship that exists within Owen's thought between Christ as Mediator and the salvation of the elect and, by implication, the relationship between the appointment of Christ as Mediator and the decree of election. Because the covenant of redemption is the basis for Christ's role as Mediator, and because that mediatorship involves sacrifice and intercession for a particular group, the elect, the covenant of redemption is in fact the causal foundation of the whole economy of salvation. As such, it is ultimately determinative of the structure of that economy, a point which is of vital importance if Owen's position on such issues as the extent of the atonement and the nature of Christ's satisfaction are to be understood correctly.[111] This key role of the covenant of

---

[109] 'His intercession in heaven is nothing but a continued oblation of himself. So that whatsoever Christ impetrated, merited, or obtained by his death and passion, must be infallibly applied unto and bestowed upon them for whom he intended to obtain it; or else his intercession is vain, he is not heard in the prayers of his mediatorship . . . We must not so disjoin the offices of Christ's mediatorship, that one of them may be versated about some towards whom he exerciseth not the other; much less ought we so to separate the several acts of the same office.' *Works* 10, pp. 90–1. For extended discussion of the importance of this unity, see Chapter 5.

[110] See Goodwin, *Works* 4, pp. 57, 60.

[111] See Ch. 5.

redemption is confirmed by the fact that it is in the covenant of redemption that Owen chooses to develop his notion of the particularity of salvation and, more specifically, of the atonement. Commenting on Is. 49:6–12, which he regards as a statement of the Father's commission to the Son in the covenant of redemption, he declares:

> By all which expressions the Lord evidently and clearly engageth himself to his Son, that he should gather to himself a glorious church of believers from among Jews and Gentiles, through all the world, that should be brought unto him, and certainly fed in full pasture, and refreshed by the springs of water, all the spiritual springs of living water which flow from God in Christ for their everlasting salvation. This, then, our Saviour certainly aimed at, as being the promise upon which he undertook the work, – the gathering of the sons of God together, their bringing unto God, and passing to eternal salvation; which being well considered, it will utterly overthrow the general ransom or universal redemption, as afterward will appear.[112]

It is clear from this passage that not only is the atonement's particularity based on this covenant of redemption but that Owen, judging by his final comment, regards the covenant of redemption also as the ultimate basis for the rejection of universal ransom theories. This is entirely consistent with Owen's desire to construct a non-speculative, Christocentric soteriological structure, and merely underlines the connection between the eternal covenant and Christ's work in history which is already clear in his formulation of the mediatorial role of Christ. What Owen does is to provide both election and incarnation with a common causal ground in the covenant between Father and Son, thereby establishing a single framework within which both doctrines must be understood.

Such a connection between Christology and election, whereby the latter must always be understood within the context of the former, is scarcely unique to Owen; it is common in the typically Christocentric constructions of election that are found in Reformed Orthodoxy. For example, in the more vigorously supralapsarian theology of Owen's friend, Thomas Goodwin, speculative considerations about whether it is unfallen or fallen

---

112   *Works* 10, p. 170.

humanity which is the object of predestination, are not allowed to lift the issue of the election of individuals above Christological considerations: Christ as Mediator is the object of God's first decree, and individual persons are then subsequently predestined to union with him. As with Owen's, therefore, Goodwin's theology places Christology in close relation to the decree and points to a common causal ground for both.[113]

In light of arguments concerning the impact of 'one-end teleology' on Owen's soteriology,[114] it is important to grasp that Owen does not here base his argument regarding the relationship between predestination and atonement on Aristotelian logic. Instead, his argument is built upon the notion of the covenant of redemption, which defines Christ's role as Mediator for the elect whom God has given him. This is not a concept which Owen obtains from some textbook on Aristotelian logic but a doctrine he derives from biblical exegesis. It does not mean, of course, that his exegesis is correct – one might indeed wish to fault Owen's interpretation and application of the Isaiah passage – but, if he is in error at this point, he is guilty of bad biblical interpretation, not of a thoroughgoing subordination of theology to Aristotle. As we should expect, given our findings concerning Owen's understanding of the principles of theology, it is the Trinitarian and Christological structures in his thought which provide the foundation for the atonement's particularity, not some Aristotelian methodology. The atonement is limited because the covenant of redemption, the causal ground of all the acts of Christ's mediation, is itself limited in terms of efficacy to the elect thanks to the nature of the transaction between Father and Son.[115]

---

[113] Goodwin, *Works* 9, pp. 93 ff.

[114] For a full discussion of this, see below, Appendix One: The Role of Aristotelian Teleology in Owen's Doctrine of Atonement.

[115] A possible objection at this point could be that Owen does indeed seem to rely upon rational arguments in defence of his doctrine of limited atonement, as, for example, when he declares that God cannot have died for the sins of those who will end up in hell because then he would be punishing the same sin twice, which would be unfair: see *Works* 10, p. 173. We must, however, beware of overemphasizing the importance of this point to Owen's case. Particularity has already been introduced into the argument via the covenant of redemption, which defines the nature of the office of Mediator, and it is within this context that such arguments are to be understood. It is

Baxter on Christ and the covenant: a comparison with Owen

The importance of the particularism of the covenant of redemption to Owen's theology can be confirmed by drawing a comparison with the alternative structure developed by his contemporary, and frequent opponent, Richard Baxter. Baxter, it has to be said, exhibits a far more cautious attitude towards the limits of religious language even than that which is evident in Owen, possibly because of the impact of medieval nominalism upon his thought. This caution is evident in his discussion of the notion of an intratrinitarian covenant between Father and Son, where he emphasizes that he allows the validity of the word 'covenant' strictly as descriptive of intratrinitarian voluntary relations, and not as a concept which should be allowed to take

---

Footnote 115 (*continued*) true that his point here seems to rely on a crudely commercial theory of the atonement, but we must beware of misunderstanding this in crudely quantitative terms (see Ch. 5 below) and be aware that the argument is only a subsidiary point in support of a position which is independently established on other theological grounds. Indeed, it is only in the context of Christ's appointment as Mediator that his sufferings can be said to have any value at all, because it is only thanks to the covenant of redemption that Christ's work can either happen in the first place, or stand in any positive connection to sinful humanity. Discussions of the intrinsic value of Christ's sufferings which fail to set these within the Trinitarian context of mediation are alien to Owen's theology: see Ch. 5. For an example of how failure to set Owen's teaching in its Trinitarian context can lead to misunderstanding, see Clifford, who makes great play of the significance of commercialism in Owen's theory of atonement, but does not set this within the Trinitarian context: *Atonement and Justification*, pp. 126 ff. As we shall see, far more significant in the limitation of the atonement is Owen's emphasis on the unity of Christ's oblation and intercession in the office of Mediator. Compared to this, the Grotian distinction between *solutio tantidem* (which Owen opposes) and *solutio eiusdem* (which Owen accepts) is, *pace* Clifford, of much less significance. In Book Three of the treatise, primacy of place in establishing the limitation of atonement is given to arguments based upon the covenants, and arguments for satisfaction are only dealt with once this basic point has been established: *Works* 10, pp. 236–8. At most, one can argue that notions of satisfaction and the commercial theory of the atonement play an important subsidiary role within the overall argument of the treatise. This is quite clear from Owen's statement in Book Two that Christ's death is the result of the covenant of grace (itself the result of the covenant of redemption, in which, as we have seen, particularity plays a central role), not its foundation, thereby explicitly making the nature of the atonement dependent upon the Trinitarian/covenantal structure of redemption: *Works* 10, pp. 207–8; cf. *Works* 11, p. 303.

on a life of its own.[116] More significant is the fact that Baxter does not link the appointment of Christ as Mediator to a particularist decree of election in the manner of Owen, but instead stresses the universal aspects, arguing that it is corrupt humanity that is the object of Christ's mediation, under certain conditions. The key point to notice is that these conditions, while ultimately providing the ground for distinguishing the elect from the non-elect, do not have the effect of creating an antecedent particularism within the work of Christ as Mediator.[117] There is a certain tension in Baxter's position which leads him at times to speak of Christ's mediation, etc. as being in one sense for all, but in another sense especially for the elect, but there is no need to construe such statements as involving an antecedent particularism rooted in the Father–Son covenant.[118] The covenant between Father and Son

---

[116] 'Et inter Patrem et *logon* aeternum foedus proprie sic dictum intercedere non putandum est: sed cum certum sit, Quaedam per *Filium* esse *facienda*, et quaedam ipsi *Filio* ut incarnato *donanda*, et quaedam *hominibus* donanda *ejus gratia*, Decreta hac seu Volitiones Divinae per *foederis nomen* a Theologis saepe appellantur. Et usui huic ansam dedit etiam Spiritus Sancti in Sacris Scripturis quaedam loquendi formula; dum *Prophetias* scilicet de Christo per *Promissionis* verba saepe exprimit, Quasi Pater haec Filio (non adhuc homini) promittendo dixisset. At notandum est, Locutiones Allegoricas non saepe nimis, et ordinario utendas esse, ne pro propriis ab imperitis habeantur: et quando ex illis Controversiae oriuntur, tunc semper ad locutiones proprias revertendum esse.' *Methodus Theologiae* 3.1. 15–17, pp. 9–10. The point is simple enough, and perhaps insignificant, but it does show that seventeenth-century thinkers were aware of the danger of importing alien concepts into their theology, and had safeguards in place to ensure that they did not fall for the 'root fallacy' which lies at the heart of certain critiques of seventeenth-century thought.

[117] '*Massa corrupta* qua talis, nullius Electionis aut Decreti fuit *objectum effectum*; sed donationis Mediatoris, et Electionis ad eam, fuit *objectum* antecedens *subjectivum*. Massae corruptae, id est, homini peccatori, Lex Gratiae, seu Remissionis et vitae aeternae donatio facta est, sub conditione remissa est, et vita aeterna donata: Ideoque ad haec Massa corrupta tota fuit electa seu destinata.' *Methodus Theologiae* 1.2. 73–74, p. 61.

[118] E.g., 'The Father giveth up to Christ as Redeemer the whole lapsed cursed reparable world (the several parts to several uses) and especially his *chosen* to be *eventually and infallibly saved*, and promiseth to accept his *sacrifice* and *performance*, and to make *him Head over all things to his church*, and by him to establish the *Law of Grace* (in its perfect edition) and to give him the Government respectively of the Church and the world, and to Glorifie him for this work with himself for ever. And the second person undertaketh to assume man's Nature, to do and suffer all that he did, in perfect obedience to his Father's Will, and Law of Redemption, to fulfill all Righteousness, conquer Satan and the world, to suffer in the flesh, and be a *sacrifice for sin*, and to conquer Death, and teach, and rule, and purifie, and raise, and justifie and glorifie all true believers.' *Catholick Theologie* 1.2.3, p. 38.

is distinct from the covenant between God and humanity: the
former provides the basis for the latter, but the latter involves the
conditions which particularize the benefits of the former.[119]

In Owen's theology, the Father–Son and God-humanity covenants are distinguished respectively by the terms 'covenant of
redemption' and 'covenant of grace'. He defines the latter in *The
Death of Death* as having been made with, and embracing, the
elect through the person of the Mediator.[120] Because the election
of individuals is an important part of the covenant of redemption, Owen, unlike Baxter, does not need to use the second
covenant as providing the means for particularizing Christ's
work. Instead, the covenant of grace serves as the bridge between
the specific intratrinitarian arrangement of salvation for the elect
and the application of that salvation to individuals. By distinguishing the covenant of redemption from the covenant of grace
in this way, Owen therefore does not introduce tensions into the
economy of salvation but rather underlines the basic unity of the
soteriological economy and draws attention once again to the
fact that the election of individuals cannot be in any way considered outside of the context of Christology.[121]

Furthermore, this distinction between the covenants of redemption and grace also serves to emphasize the historical movement of the economy of salvation. The covenant of grace is
'established, ratified, and confirmed in and by the death of

---

[119] 'And the *benefits* [of the Father–Son covenant] are *conditionally given*, though the
Spirit of Christ cause us to perform the Condition: For they are called *conditional* from
the *mode* or *form of the Covenant*, which giveth men Right to Christ and Life expressly
on condition of believing . . . [The] *Baptismal Covenant* which is *conditional*, and the
consent to which doth *make us Christians*, must still be distinguished from the *Covenant
between the Father and Christ,* or *his Law of Redemption*: And God promiseth not *to
us*, all that he promiseth *to Christ for us*; nor giveth all to *us* which he giveth *to him*.'
Catholick Theologie 1.2.4, p. 45.
[120] *Works* 10, p. 236.
[121] Cf. Goodwin: 'His Son, the second person, who was predestinated God-man,
simply considered in his person as God-man, and absolutely first decreed; for we are
"chosen in Christ" . . . therefore he is supposed chosen first, as the soil in whom we are
set and chosen.' *Works* 9, p. 94. The difference between Owen and Baxter on the logical
relationship of the appointment of Christ as Mediator and the decree of election finds
a parallel in the different ways the two men construe the logical relationship between
Christ's death and the decree of God which makes it a ransom: see Ch. 5 below.

Christ'.[122] As the one covenant of redemption provides the causal ground for Christ's incarnation, ministry, death and resurrection, so these elements in turn provide the historical point of departure for the covenant of grace. The two covenants both focus upon Christ, and, while made in eternity, both underline the vital centrality of the historical economy of salvation, one prospectively, the other retrospectively.

Salvation and God's immutability

In *The Doctrine of the Saints' Perseverance* (1654), Owen makes a formal distinction within this covenant using the standard Protestant scholastic concepts of the *principium essendi*, the principle of being, and the *principium cognoscendi*, the principle of knowing.[123] The former refers to God; in this case, specifically to his decrees and purposes. The latter refers to God's revelation, meaning specifically his promises. There is obviously a close correlation between the two concepts: God's promises derive their efficacy and their reliability from the fact that they are based upon God himself, and upon the agreements between the persons of the Godhead about the matter of salvation. As God is unchanging, so are his promises and his salvific purposes. This points to the inadequacy of the view of certain theologians that the classic attributes of God, as espoused by the great scholastic thinkers of the seventeenth century, create a picture of God that is metaphysical, abstract, impersonal, and opposed to the biblical picture of a God of salvation history. In fact, as noted earlier, Owen characteristically uses God's attributes, the principles of being for theology, as a means of safeguarding the personal God of history and of salvation, and he is able to do this because of the important relationship in which God's attributes stand to the covenant of grace and thus to God's saving purposes. It is only because God, as the *principium essendi* of revelation, is immutable that humans can have confidence in the constancy of his love and of his saving purposes as revealed in the covenant of grace. In *The Doctrine of the Saints' Perseverance*, Owen says that his

---

122   *Works* 10, p. 236.
123   *Works* 11, p. 205.

argument rests on five foundations: God's nature, purposes, covenant, promises, and oath.[124] In fact, the five are really one, reflecting the two principles of the covenant of grace. The covenant is an unconditional promise of salvation: anchored in the being of God, it reflects both his love and his immutability. Thus, we find the consequences of defining God as pure act being used to underwrite the biblical concept of God's fidelity to his people.

It could be objected at this point that, even if Owen is only using metaphysics to uphold a doctrine of immutability which supports God's saving purposes, he has nonetheless moved beyond the more biblical approach of Calvin and the earlier Reformers who used biblical exegesis, not philosophy, to make their point. Is Owen not thus introducing alien concepts into his doctrine of God? In response to this, it is first of all important to remember that, as noted in Ch. 1, the use of metaphysical language does not necessarily lead to the importation of metaphysical content. It is how the words and ideas are used that is important, not simply the fact of their presence. Second, and more importantly, we must see Owen's use of these categories, etc. within the context of seventeenth-century exegesis. In the context of his own times it was perfectly feasible for Calvin to dismiss literal readings of Gen. 6:6, because his major opponents all agreed with him that God was unchanging, and to deny such a basic doctrine was, by definition, to place oneself on the lunatic fringe of the theological world.[125] For Owen, however, faced with the arguments of the Arminians and the radical biblicism of the Socinians, it was no longer enough to argue that texts referring to God's unchangeableness could be taken at face value, since there were plenty of other texts which seemed to teach that God did indeed change.[126] The Protestant principle of interpreting obscure passages on the basis of clear passages was scarcely of

---

[124] *Works* 11, p. 120.

[125] *CO* 23:118.

[126] See, for example, John Biddle's leading question on this topic: 'Are there not, according to the perpetual tenour of the Scripture, affections or passions in God, as anger, fury, zeal, wrath, love, hatred, mercy, grace, jealousie, repentance, grief, joy, fear?', which is then followed by a judicious selection of proof texts. *Twofold Catechism*, p. 11.

use here; one's decision as to which were clear and which were not probably depended upon prior theological commitments. In such circumstances, Owen's resort to arguments based upon metaphysics can be seen as his attempt to uphold the Orthodox exegesis of passages referring to God's unchangeableness by setting them within the generally accepted, and thus hardly innovative, metaphysical and theological context of the traditional doctrine of God articulated in the language of scholastic theology. This is not in intention an independent, metaphysical doctrine of God which is then allowed to pervert the teaching of Scripture: it is to be understood as an attempt to find ways to defend traditional exegesis of passages referring to God as unchanging, in the face of Socinian attacks.

The role of the Holy Spirit

Having established the respective roles of Father and Son in the economy of salvation, Owen completes the picture by adding the third part of the Trinitarian structure: the role of the Holy Spirit. As the Holy Spirit is the only person of the Godhead who acts immediately in the created realm, he has great significance for Owen's understanding of the historical execution of the eternal covenants. In terms of Christology, it is he who conceives the incarnate Christ in Mary's womb, through whom Christ makes his oblation, and who raises Christ from the dead.[127] From the subjective side, the Spirit is also the one who brings sinners into union with Christ and keeps them there, thus bringing about the individual application of the eternal covenants of salvation.[128] This giving of the Spirit is Christocentric both in its causal ground, Christ's mediation, and in its goal, the spiritual union of the individual person with Christ.[129] As such, it forms an integral part of the overall Trinitarian economy of salvation and repre-

---

[127] *Works* 10, pp. 178–9; for further discussion of Owen's Spirit-Christology, see Ch. 4.
[128] *Works* 11, pp. 336 ff.
[129] This is clear from the fact that Owen treats the mediation of Christ, the indwelling of the Spirit, and the intercession of Christ in consecutive chapters in *The Doctrine of the Saints' Perseverance*. Christology and, by implication, the Trinitarian economy of salvation as expressed in the covenant scheme thus form the context within which the Spirit's work is to be understood.

sents a specifically functional and soteriological application of the *filioque*. The covenants of redemption and grace are between the Father and the Son, and these are the causal ground for the Spirit's saving activity in applying the benefits they entail to the elect. As such, the Spirit's activity does indeed proceed from the Godhead in relation to both Father and Son. The emphasis on the processional order which was so evident in Owen's understanding of the saving appropriation of Scripture's teaching by the believer is evident again in the structure of the economy of salvation, and, indeed, is essential to it. This point is made most clearly not by Owen, but by his friend Thomas Goodwin:

> It is not enough that the Spirit proceeds from the Father . . . that therefore he should have all wholly from the Father, and shew it to you, and pass by the Son of God. No, saith Christ; he must have it from me too; because the order of our subsisting in the Godhead is, that all the Father hath is mine first in order of nature; for my generation by the Father, as his Son, is first, ere the Holy Ghost's procession, for he is the third person; and then, all that the Father hath being communicated to me, thence it is that the Spirit proceeds from both. For even that power to breathe forth the Spirit together with the Father, is one of those things intended when he saith, 'All that my Father hath is mine.' So as it is the account of the order of their subsistence, as the foundation of this their order in working, which he aims at in saying, All that my Father hath is mine, as well as to shew he is God, and that therefore necessarily the Spirit must take of mine, since it is I that send him as well as my Father . . . [W]ere I not God as well as the Father, and that the Spirit proceeded from me, I as merely Mediator, could not have sent him.[130]

Goodwin here makes explicit what is evident throughout Owen's own discussion of revelation and salvation: the order of procession within the Godhead is of crucial importance. It is because the Spirit proceeds from the Father and the Son that there is a basic unity between the decree of election in eternity and the execution of election in time. This procession ensures that the objects of the Spirit's work are defined by the covenant relation that exists between Father and Son and which provides the basis for the Spirit's work. Were it not so, the soteriological structure would have no necessary unity, and the Son would have no way

---

[130]   Goodwin, *Works* 9, pp. 141–2.

of ensuring that the objects of predestination ever came to enjoy the benefits thereof.

In the context of Reformed theology, this model exhibits strong continuities with the tradition as it developed between the mid-sixteenth and seventeenth centuries. The careful delineation of the relative roles of Father, Son, and Holy Spirit is found in Perkins' discussion of predestination, where the Western understanding of the relationship of the persons underlies their role in the soteriological sphere.[131] Indeed, the importance of such arguments became greater as it became necessary to work out in more detail the Trinitarian implications of the interrelationship between predestination and Christ's mediation which is evident in development of the covenant motifs in response to Arminian attempts to reconstruct the relationship of the Father and Son in predestination. In this context Owen's exposition of the covenant scheme can be interpreted as an extended reflection upon the implications which his understanding of God's works *ad extra* being dependent upon Trinitarian relations *ad intra* has for the inner life of the Trinity.

Thus, with the covenants of redemption and of grace, we now have the framework within which to understand Owen's approach to redemption, one which roots both the eternal and historical economies of salvation firmly within the intratrinitarian relations within the Godhead. It is the with the establishment and delineation of these structures that the major part of Book One of *The Death of Death* is concerned, and it is there that they are established as providing the theological context for discussion of the accomplishment of salvation. Any straightforward reading of that text can leave no doubt that it is this Trinitarian structure to which Owen is referring when he says at the start of Book Two:

> The main thing upon which the whole controversy about the death of Christ turneth, and upon which the greatest weight of the business

---

[131] '[I]t is the office of the Sonne, to have the administration of every outward action of the Trinitie, from the Father, by the holy Ghost. 1 Cor. 8:6. And he being by nature the Sonne of the Father, bestoweth this priviledge on those that belleve, that they are the Sonnes of God by adoption.' *Workes* 1, p. 24.

dependeth, comes next to our consideration, *being that which we have prepared the way unto by all that hath already been said.*[132]

The preparation to which he refers is self-evidently not the Aristotelian teleology of which so much has been made by certain scholars;[133] rather, it is the Trinitarian and Christological structures which Owen has taken such pains to expound. This is entirely consistent with Owen's Trinitarian understanding of the analogy of faith as the basis for understanding Scripture, and points us decisively towards the working out of that understanding in the drama of redemption which focuses on the historical person of the Mediator, Jesus Christ.

Conclusion

A number of important points emerge from a close study of how the doctrine of God is worked out in Owen's writings – points which both underline emphases evident in his reflections on the principles of theology and point forward to his subsequent Christological formulations.

The most obvious point is the careful way in which God is distinguished from his creation as cause is from effect. This is reflected both in the logical priority which Owen's appropriation of Thomist metaphysics gives to the Creator as pure act, and in the covenantal structure of redemption. By setting up predestination as a subset of providence Owen is able to carry over the implications of his metaphysics into the realm of soteriology, while then combining this with an Augustinian anthropology and anti-Pelagian understanding of God's grace. In so doing, however, the distinctively Trinitarian orientation of Owen's theology is not lost in a sea of Aristotelian physics. All of God's acts *ad extra* are Trinitarian, and thus predestination is no different. Indeed, Owen's development of the covenantal structure of salvation represents an attempt to do justice to this general theological principle within the specific context of soteriology.

---

[132] *Works* 10, p. 200 [italics mine].
[133] See Appendix One below.

Nevertheless, Owen's teaching on providence and predestination is neither rigidly deterministic nor wildly speculative. His adoption of the notion of secondary causality and contingency, as well as the language of faculty psychology, safeguards him against the first, while he builds a number of safeguards into his system which militate against the second. These safeguards include the logical priority of both sin and, then, the covenant of redemption over the covenant of grace, and a basic concern to stress the centrality of Christ's incarnate ministry to salvation, a stress that matures into an insistence, *pace* Twisse and Rutherford, that God could not, *de potentia absoluta*, forgive sin without satisfaction.

There is clearly a great degree of continuity between this and the principles of theology as Owen understands them. Again it is not just God considered simply as a unity, but God as he exists in Trinity which provides the framework for theological reflection. Also, it is the person of Christ which provides the focal point of salvation as he did of revelation: Father and Spirit both play their respective roles, but their work finds its centre of reference and its unity in the Lord Jesus Christ. Indeed, the covenant structure can be seen as pointing to the *filioque* in the same way as the nature of Holy Scripture does, according to Owen's teaching.

In addition, several interesting factors emerge from all this which will clearly shape the nature of Owen's subsequent Christological and soteriological formulations. First, it is quite clear that his position on the necessity of satisfaction draws him close to the classic statement of the rationale behind the incarnation in Anselm's *Cur Deus Homo*, and arguments which reflect these are, as we shall see, used by Owen at various key points in his discussion of Christology. Second, as the causal ground for the whole economy of salvation, both in terms of Christology and predestination, is found in the covenant of redemption, any subsequent discussion of either the person or work of Christ has to take place against the background of, and in clear continuity with, this covenant. History is not swallowed up by eternity but in fact gains meaning precisely because it stands in positive relation to eternity. This holds true for Owen's general discussion of providence and is particularly relevant to salvation. Quite simply, if there was no eternal covenant there would be no Christ. The terms of his office are defined by the intratrinitarian pact between Father and Son and can only be understood in that context. To see this more clearly, it is now necessary to focus more narrowly on Owen's Christology.

Four

The Person and Work of Christ

Introduction

As examination of both Owen's understanding of the principles of theology and his doctrine of God has shown, an orthodox understanding of the Trinity was fundamental to his whole theological enterprise. While this was a foundation which he arguably shared to an extent with his Arminian opponents, it was, of course, an issue upon which he could have no point of contact with the Socinians, who denied the doctrine outright, and it is in his conflict with them that we find related issues most thoroughly worked out. Given the focus of Owen's doctrine of the Trinity on the soteriological economy, it is not surprising that in his conflict with the Socinians there is little direct discussion of the Trinity as an isolated problem. Instead, the main topic of debate is Christology, for it is the person and work of Christ which, as we can infer from what has already been said, provide the point of intersection for the eternal and the historical Trinitarian structures. Indeed, Owen's commitment to the unity of Trinitarian action in any act of the Godhead demands that his Christology be understood within the larger Trinitarian context. Thus, Socinian attacks on the Trinity have serious implications for orthodox Christology, and Socinian attacks on Christology have serious implications for orthodox Trinitarianism.

In their critique of orthodoxy, Socinians such as John Biddle and the authors of the *Racovian Catechism* therefore attempt to undermine Trinitarianism by rejecting the orthodox notion of the person of Christ. If their rejection of his divinity is valid, then orthodox Trinitarianism is finished. As a result, in his most extensive attack on Socinianism, *Vindiciae Evangelicae* (1655), Owen himself does not develop a comprehensive defence of the ontological Trinity in his response, but, in line with his interest less on speculative and more on soteriological matters, he too focuses on the person of Christ, and mounts a defence of orthodoxy which shows his clear continuity with patristic, medieval and Reformation concerns. It also points unmistakably towards the Trinitarian structure of his soteriology – hardly surprising in the light of all that has been said so far.

The Person of Christ

Socinian criticisms of orthodox Christology

The Christology of Biddle's *Twofold Catechism* is both straightforward and crude, and is expressed through a series of questions to which scriptural references are appended as replies. The basic idea underlying Biddle's thinking at this point is that Christ is not essentially God, but earns his position as Son of God through his work.

The Christology of the *Racovian Catechism* is somewhat more elaborate. The structure of the work approaches Christ in terms of a person–work paradigm, where the orthodox doctrine of his work of salvation is criticized and revised in the light of a prior heretical reconstruction of his person. Whereas the Anselmic approach, which was of great importance in the development of Reformed Christology, facilitated the construction of a doctrine of Christ's person as an inference from the nature of the work he was to do, the *Racovian Catechism* implicitly rejects such an approach. Instead, the whole soteriological structure is built upon a basic rejection of an orthodox view of Christ's person. There is some evidence to suggest that, when expounding his Christology in a non-polemical context, Owen himself preferred to follow the work–person paradigm, but his method in the *Vindiciae Evangelicae* of answering his opponents line by line meant that this was not an option here.[1]

The Racovian rejection of orthodox Christology focuses on a number of key points which serve to counter any notions that divinity can be predicated of the Son in the same way that it can be predicated of the Father. For the Racovians, the reality of Christ's humanity is never in question, and the *Catechism* even points out its agreement with the orthodox tradition on this point.[2] However, while allowing that Christ can be called divine, the *Catechism* insists that the word must in this context be reconstrued in such a way that it does not imply any kind of equality or identity with the Father.[3] Many of the relevant passages in the *Catechism* are taken up with somewhat prolix and tedious expositions of relevant passages, but within these it is easy to identify a number of positive doctrinal concerns.

First, the *Catechism* rejects the notion that an individual can be made up of two separate substances on the grounds that it is logical and metaphysical nonsense.[4] This notion is, of course, Chalcedonian orthodoxy, but, while solving certain problems within the early church, it also generated others which were to preoccupy theologians throughout the Middle Ages and beyond. For example, if Christ possesses both full human substance and full divine substance, how many wills does he have? The orthodox Western resolution of this problem, that Christ has both a human will and a divine will, but that there is no conflict between the two of them, preserves Chalcedonian distinctions, but could be construed as pointing towards a somewhat ambiguous notion of personhood.[5] There are clearly certain aspects of the definition

---

[1] See his comments, *Works* 12, pp. 205, 214. When Owen himself came to write a systematic treatise on Christ, he chose the work–person paradigm: see *A Declaration of the Glorious Mystery of the Person of Christ* (1679) in *Works* 1; cf. Ames, *Marrow*, XVIII; Ussher, *A Body of Divinitie*, pp. 160 ff.; Goodwin, *A Discourse of Christ the Mediator* in *Works* 5.

[2] *RC*, p. 51.

[3] Ibid., pp. 51, 55–6.

[4] Ibid., pp. 56 ff.

[5] On the early church's assertion of two wills in Christ, see B. Studer, *Trinity and Incarnation*, trans. M. Westerhoff, ed. A. Louth (Minnesota: Liturgical Press, 1993), pp. 231–2. The official definition was given by the Third Council of Constantinople of 680–1: 'Et duas naturales voluntates in eo, et duas naturales operationes indivise, inconvertibiliter, inseparabiliter, inconfuse secundum sanctorum Patrum doctrinam adaeque praedicamus; et duas naturales voluntates non contrarias, absit, iuxta quod

which, if not rendering the whole matter incoherent, at least make it somewhat problematic. Thus, when the *Racovian Catechism* attacks the notion of two substances in one person, it is, in many ways, touching a potential Achilles heel of the orthodox position.

This attack on the two-substance notion is two-pronged. If by divine substance is meant the very essence of God, then the notion is repugnant both to right reason and to Holy Scripture, the two basic principles of Socinian thought.[6] According to reason, it is impossible for two substances with diverse properties to be ascribed to one individual.[7] Alternatively, from the Scriptures a variety of reasons can be gathered for rejecting Christ's consubstantiality with the Father: the Scriptures themselves distinguish between God and Christ; they assert that Christ was only human; they describe his divine nature as a gift; Christ himself prayed to the Father; he himself said he was not the ultimate object of human worship; he was sent by the Father; he was ignorant of the timing of the Day of Judgment; and he declared the Father to be greater than himself.[8] Later in the *Catechism* it is also argued that Christ's subordination to the Father, implicit in the notion of the Father giving him all things, points to a difference in essence.[9]

Owen's response

Owen's response to the Socinian criticisms of the orthodox position on the two substances in one person amounts to a careful restatement of orthodoxy which draws upon the rich heritage of historic christological concepts to make a number of rarefied doctrinal points. First, he stresses that the hypostatic union does not involve a mingling or cancelling-out of the diverse properties of the two substances involved. Instead, the diverse properties to

---

Footnote 5 (*continued*) impii asseruerunt haeretici, sed sequentem eius humanam voluntatem et non resistentem vel reluctantem. sed potius et subiectam divinae eius atque omnipotenti voluntati. Oportebat enim carnis voluntatem moveri, subici vero voluntati divinae iuxta sapientissimum Athanasium.' *Denz.* 291. see also Aquinas *Summa* 3a.18 arts. 1 and 5; Turretin, *Institutes* 13.7.14.

[6] *RC*, p. 55.
[7] Ibid., p. 56.
[8] Ibid., pp. 57–60.
[9] Ibid., pp. 57 ff.

which the *Catechism* refers must be seen as referring to the two natures, with each retaining their integrity while subsisting within the one person.[10] In this context, Owen introduces the notion of Christ's anhypostatic human nature:

> We deny that the human nature of Christ had any such subsistence of its own as to give it a *proper personality*, being from the time of its conception assumed into subsistence with the Son of God . . . If by *natures constituting persons* they mean those who, antecedently to their union, have actually done so, we grant they cannot meet in one person, so that upon this union they should cease to be two persons. The personality of either of them being destroyed, their different beings could not be preserved. But if by 'constituting' they understand only that which is so in *potentia*, or a next possibility of constituting a person, then, as before, they only beg of us that we would not believe that the person of the Word did assume the human nature of Christ, that 'holy thing that was born of the Virgin,' into subsistence with itself; which . . . we cannot grant.[11]

In other words, before the Logos assumed the human nature, that human nature had no personal subsistence of itself. This idea is impeccably orthodox and has its origins in questions raised concerning the Chalcedonian definition by Leontius of Byzantium.[12] The problem was that of maintaining the full humanity of Jesus Christ without falling into the error of breaking the unity of his person. If both his humanity and his divinity possessed individual personhood, then the union of the two would lead to an incarnation involving two separate persons. As a result, it was argued that Christ's humanity was identical to that of everyone else (sin excepted) but that it had no personal subsistence outside its union with the Word. A useful idea, it was subsequently a christological commonplace, although it was not without its detractors in the Middle Ages who considered that it undermined the real humanity of Christ.[13] The idea then later found favour amongst Reformed theologians who, like Owen,

---

[10] *Works* 12, pp. 209–10.
[11] Ibid., p. 210; cf. p. 211. Owen does not use the term anhypostatic at this point, but he does do so in a later treatise, *A Declaration of the Glorious Mystery of the Person of Christ* (1679): *Works* 1, p. 233.
[12] A. Grillmeier, *Jesus der Christus im Glauben der Kirche* 2.2 (Freiburg: Herder, 1989), p. 210.
[13] The concept is found in Peter Lombard, *IV Libri Sententiarum* 3.5.3, and in Aquinas, *ST* 3a.2.5; it is criticized by Duns Scotus in *Opera Omnia*, 26 vols (Paris: Vives, 1891–5), 14, pp. 210–98.

found it necessary to elaborate and defend orthodox Christology against the background of Socinian reductionism.[14] In this context it serves to counter allegations that two natures implies two persons. Later in the *Vindiciae Evangelicae*, Owen uses the philosophical distinction between existence and essence to make the same point, again pointing to the way in which the metaphysical distinctions of medieval Scholasticism could be deployed in the defence of Reformed Orthodoxy.[15]

In his later christological treatise, *A Declaration of the Glorious Mystery of the Person of Christ* (1679), Owen again presupposes this notion in his discussion of incarnation. He distinguishes between the *assumption* of the human flesh by the Word, and the subsequent *union* of the two natures in the one person: the former imparts personality, where the humanity is made one person with the Word, while the latter is that whereby the two natures then subsist in mutual relation. In line with the notion of anhypostatic human nature, and with his understanding of God as immutable, Owen here stresses that the union is an act solely of the divine nature: the humanity is purely passive.[16] Again, Owen's Christology is building upon medieval distinctions which were developed to clarify and defend orthodoxy, and which can now be used to good effect in the face of new Christological heresies.[17]

This notion also goes some way to underlining the anti-Pelagian structure of a salvation that in its very foundation in the incarnation is all of God, all of grace, and not based upon any prior merit in mankind. This last point is reflected in Owen's emphasis on the notion of Christ as predestined, whereby the incarnate Christ is regarded as the primary focus of predestination.[18] This points clearly to the underlying structure as deter-

---

[14]   For example, Turretin, *Institutes* 13.6.5; Goodwin, *Works* 3, pp. 53 ff.
[15]   'Because Christ is the Son of man, it follows that he is a true man, but not that he hath the personality of a man or a *human personality*. Personality belongs not to the *essence* but to the *existence* of a man.' *Works* 12, p. 230. In this statement the problems generated by catholic Christological formulations are obvious.
[16]   *Works* 1, pp. 225–6; cf. *Works* 3, p.165.
[17]   For the distinction between assumption and union, see Aquinas, *ST* 3a.2.9; on the activity of God and the passivity of the human nature in this assumption, see *ST* 3a.2.10.
[18]   *Works* 12, pp. 246, 247.

mined by the covenant of redemption and is again an indication that it is only within the context of this covenant that Christ's work can be understood: the assumption of the human nature was part of God's eternal purpose, and this incarnation is the foundation of the election and salvation of all others.[19] Such a view is perfectly consistent with, and is an implication of, the eternal covenant structure whereby the covenant of redemption, which defines Christ's role as Mediator, is the foundation of the covenant of grace. This serves once again to focus attention on the incarnation as the focal point of both eternal and historical economies, underlines the anti-Pelagian structure of Owen's soteriology, and indicates the decisive importance of the single causal ground for both Christology and predestination in the intratrinitarian covenant relations.[20]

The problem of the union of two substances in one person is only one of the various Christological problems raised by the Socinians. The issue of the consubstantiality of the Father and the Son points towards two other important theological issues: the eternal preexistence of Christ; and the role of Christ in creation. On these issues, the *Racovian Catechism*'s position is based to a large extent upon the validity of its arguments concerning the absurdity of the notion of the hypostatic union, although it does deal extensively with the passages alleged by the orthodox in defence of the catholic positions.[21] Nevertheless, the

---

[19]   Cf. Goodwin, *Works* 9, pp. 93 ff.

[20]   'The cause of this [hypostatical] union is expressed in it, i.e., the phrase, "grace of union". This is the free grace and favour of God towards the man Christ Jesus – predestinating, designing, and taking him into actual union with the person of the Son, without respect unto, or foresight of, any precedent dignity or merit in him, 1 Pet. 1:20' *Works* 1, p. 227. Owen then quotes from *On the Predestination of the Saints* 15 (*NPNF* [First Series] 512–13).

[21]   *RC* pp. 62 ff. For Owen, the key passage on preexistence is the opening section of John's Gospel. He regards this passage as having been specifically written to refute Gnostic attempts to ascribe creation to the activities of a demiurge. Secondly, he regards *logos* here as necessarily referring to Christ because of the reference (v. 11) to the *logos* being made flesh and (v. 14) being the only-begotten of the Father. Then, Owen sees the clear relationship drawn in this passage between the Word and creation as pointing to his preexistence. While Owen accepts that the phrase, 'In the beginning . . .' does not automatically imply *eternal* preexistence, he sees this as an inference from the use of the verb 'to be': in the beginning, the Word was not created, he simply *was*. See *Works* 12, pp. 216–19.

arguments it musters exhibit a kind of methodological apriorism which rejects orthodox doctrinal formulations on the basis that presupposed standards of human rationality are to be used as the ultimate criteria of theological coherence. For example, the *Catechism* argues that the notion of generation is incoherent on the basis that, if part of the Father's essence is communicated to the Son, then it is divided, which is an impossibility; alternatively, if all of the essence is communicated, then the Father himself must cease to be God; and, in any case, the whole notion of the perfect unity of the divine substance makes such communication impossible.[22]

In this context, Owen, consistent with what was noted earlier concerning his understanding of the relationship of faith and reason, makes the interesting methodological point that that which God has revealed to be the case must therefore be a possibility.[23] By implication, human rationality can be no competent judge of what is metaphysically impossible in an absolute sense, and revelation must have final authority over human reason. This is precisely the methodological priority of revelation over reason, and of Scripture over human notions of rationality, that ran throughout Owen's discussions of the principles of theology and which is evidence of a fundamental continuity with the Reformation emphasis on the Scripture principle. It is the

---

[22] *RC* p. 70.

[23] 'That which God hath revealed to be so is not impossible to be so. Let God be true and all men liars.' *Works* 12, p. 237. In light of attempts by some to emphasize the 'rationalistic' bent of seventeenth-century Reformed Orthodoxy, it is worth noting that Owen's comment here points quite clearly to the need to distinguish between a notion of human reason as a separate, autonomous basis for judging the truth of doctrinal statements, and as a means of exploring the structure of doctrine grasped by faith: see the comments of Muller, *PRRD1*, pp. 88–97. There is throughout Owen's theology a strongly antispeculative thrust, as is clear, for example from a later work, *A Discourse Concerning the Holy Spirit* (1674), where he states quite explicitly that, while the unity of God is a truth self-evident to all, knowledge of the Trinity is only available via revelation: *Works* 3, p. 152. Such a view clearly delimits the competence of unaided human reason and points to the basic inadequacy of natural theology even in an objective sense. There is no evidence to suggest that Owen's views in the 1650s were any different. By way of a contrasting example, Baxter's views on metaphysics point directly towards the destruction of the kind of limits which Owen imposes on human reason in relation to doctrines such as the Trinity: see Ch. 2 above; also, Trueman, 'A Small Step Towards Rationalism.'

Socinians, not Owen, who are operating on the basis of rational a prioris at this point: Owen seeks not to criticize the orthodox understanding of the Trinity on the authority of human reason, but to show its inner rationality in the light of divine revelation, with his approach being perhaps akin to the modern notion of a philosophical defence rather than a proof, whereby an idea is shown to be coherent and plausible rather than proved to be true and necessary.

Owen also objects to the straightforward extrapolation from the finite to the infinite which he sees in the *Racovian Catechism*'s arguments and which fails to take account of the radically different orders of being involved in the two realms. It is true, he allows, that finite essences cannot be subject to division without multiplication or diminution, but these rules do not apply in relation to the infinite:

> We say, then, that in the eternal generation of the Son, the *whole* essence of the Father is communicated to the Son as to a *personal existence* in the same essence, without multiplication or division of it, the same essence continuing one in number; and this without the least show of impossibility in an infinite essence, all the arguments that lie against it being taken from the properties and attendancies of that which is finite.[24]

This passage is very important for an accurate understanding of the way in which Owen construes the relationship between human reason and Christian doctrine, and the closely related issue of how human language relates to divine realities. On the first point, what he says clearly corresponds to his stated belief that possibility in the realm of divine truths must be judged by actuality, and that revelation is therefore to have priority over human reason; on the second point it is obvious that Owen is acutely aware of the radically limited capability of human language and logic to reflect the inner realities of God. From the patristic age onwards, theologians had acknowledged the basic poverty of human language when dealing with the doctrine of the Trinity.[25] Here we see Owen arguing that the infinite nature of the divine essence means that God exists on a fundamentally

---

[24] *Works* 12, p. 237.
[25] For example, Augustine, *On the Trinity* 5:9 (*NPNF* [First Series] 3:92).

different level of being to finite creation and that the logical rules to which finite essences are subject do not apply to the infinite essence of God. Of course, the same language is used to describe both Creator and creation, but this is only in an analogous or, arguably, equivocal way. There is little here to suggest that Owen's theology is at all 'rationalistic' in some quasi-Cartesian sense; indeed, his sensitivity to the limits of language on this issue indicate that he is only too aware of the limitations of his systematic formulations. This clear sensitivity to the fragility of language is evident, for example, when Owen challenges the Racovian exegesis of Ps. 2:7. The *Catechism* places great emphasis upon the word 'today', stressing that the word means a fixed period of time and therefore stands in contradiction to notions of eternal generation.[26] Owen's reply presupposes the Boethian notion of eternity as an eternal present, without past or future. As such, the words do not refer to an act within time, but point to the eternally present act of generating the Son – scarcely an interpretation suggested by a literal rationalist reading of the text.[27]

Christ and creation

Another aspect of Owen's Christology which arises from his commitment to the full deity of the Son, and the Trinitarian implications thereof, is that of the Son's role in creation, and in its close relation, providence. Traditional Christian theology, taking its cue from various New Testament passages, in particular the opening verses of John's Gospel, had always maintained a close connection between God's acts of creation and providence and the role of the Son as agent in these.[28] Such a position, of course, requires a prior belief in the consubstantiality of the Father and the Son, and, as such, is not an option open for those

---

[26] *RC* pp. 72–3.

[27] *Works* 12, p. 241. Owen's arguments here do, arguably, stand in tension with his discussion of divine justice where a much closer analogy is assumed between the divine attribute of justice and the human concept of justice.

[28] See, for example, Irenaeus, *Against Heresies* 5.18 (*ANF* 1:546–7); Athanasius, *On the Incarnation* 4 (*NPNF* [Second Series] 4:38). For Calvin on creation as a Trinitarian work, see Schreiner, *The Theater of His Glory*, pp. 15–16.

of Socinian persuasion. As a result, the *Racovian Catechism* explicitly rejects the agency of the Son in creation, and seeks to reinterpret those biblical verses which do at first glance appear to assign him such a role.

In the Racovian Catechism 4.1 there is an extended discussion of biblical passages referring to Christ as an agent in creation, such as Jn. 1:3,10; Col. 1:16; and Heb. 1:2, 10–12. In line with their basic Christology, the authors of the *Catechism* make a series of important distinctions: the passages refer to 'making', not 'creating'; Christ is only a secondary cause, an instrument in this process; and, more significantly, the passages should be understood as applying to the new moral creation effected by Jesus Christ, and not to the creation of the world out of nothing.[29]

If valid, this Socinian attack on Trinitarian agency has devastating consequences for the Reformed Orthodoxy which Owen is committed to defending. It was noted in discussion of the covenant scheme that the order of procession within the Trinity was vitally important because the works *ad extra* reflect the order *ad intra*, in line with typical Western teaching. Therefore, denial of the Son's agency in creation means at the very least that the Trinitarian order in regard to external works (the Father working by the Son through the Holy Spirit) is disrupted. In fact, and more seriously, the Racovian rejection of the Son's agency in creation is simply one more aspect of the larger agenda aimed at rejecting Trinitarianism outright, and dispensing with the preexistence of Christ, a point which is obviously foundational not only to Owen's understanding of creation but, perhaps more significantly, to his whole soteriological scheme, depending as it does upon the intratrinitarian covenant between Father and Son.

Faced with this denial of Trinitarian agency in creation, Owen claims that the plural forms in the opening verses of Genesis and in Ecc. 12:1, Ps. 149:2, and Job 35:10 all point towards a plurality of agents. In addition, he cites Jn. 1:3, 1 Cor. 8:6, and Rev. 4:11 as speaking of the Son as Creator, and Gn. 1:1, Job 26:13, and Ps. 33:6 as referring to the Spirit in the same way.[30] In seeing signs

---

29 *RC*, pp. 86 ff.
30 *Works* 12, pp. 142–3.

of the Trinity in the opening verses of Genesis, Owen is of course adopting an exposition which differs from that of Calvin at this point, but it is entirely consistent with the Trinitarian orientation of an understanding of the analogy of faith and is also scarcely radical within the tradition as there were historical precedents for using this verse as part of the biblical evidence for Trinitarianism.[31] No doubt the pressure of controversy was an added incentive to Owen to find help on this issue wherever he could.

Within this Trinitarian understanding of creation Owen is careful to provide a specific Christological focus in order to preserve the axiomatic relationship of God's external acts to his internal acts. Identifying the Wisdom in Pr. 8:23 as Christ, Owen uses the language of Aristotle in order to explicate and clarify the orthodox position, arguing that Christ was the efficient cause in creation, a view he supports with citations of Jn. 1:3 and Heb. 1:10.[32] He then proceeds to see Heb. 1:10–12 as describing Christ the Creator in terms of attributes applicable only to the one who is God: the name 'Jehovah', eternity, omnipotence, immutability, and sovereignty.[33] Following on, and as the obvious implication of Christ's role in creation, Owen argues that Christ must be regarded as the disposer of providence as well.[34]

There are two major points of significance in Owen's treatment of creation in this way. The first is that he is very careful to stress that creation and providence are to be assigned to Christ as he is God and not as he is Mediator.[35] At an earlier point in the *Vindiciae Evangelicae*, he has made the traditional distinction between Christ as God being equal to the Father in terms of essence but being subordinate to him in terms of office, a distinction which is quite clear in the structure of the covenant of redemption.[36] The distinction becomes important at this point

---

[31] For Calvin, see his *Commentarius in Genesin*, *OC* 23.15. By way of contrast, cf. Ussher, *A Body of Divinitie*, p. 76; also Zacharias Ursinus, *Commentary on the Heidelberg Catechism*, trans. G. W. Williard (Phillipsburg: Presbyterian and Reformed, n.d.), p. 133; for similar arguments in Lutheran Orthodoxy, see Preus, *Post-Reformation Lutheranism* 2, pp. 133–4.

[32] *Works* 12, p. 271; cf. p. 243.

[33] Ibid., p. 273.

[34] Ibid., pp. 278–83.

[35] Ibid., p. 279.

[36] Ibid., p. 171.

because Owen now wishes to refute Socinian attempts to refer biblical passages which speak of Christ's dominion purely to his role as Saviour.[37] If the Socinian arguments are allowed to stand, this would amount to a serious concession on the issue of the eternal preexistence and deity of Christ, a doctrine which obviously stands central in Owen's entire theological enterprise. Instead, Owen's position clearly points once again to the pivotal causal role of Christ as God in all acts *ad extra*. Underlying Owen's argument at this point, but something which is not made explicit, is the Reformed, and indeed, basic Western idea, that the Word is united to the flesh in the incarnation, but is not comprehended by it. If this were not the case, then it would be impossible for Christ to continue to play a role in providence simply as God and not as Mediator, as anything predicated of Christ as Mediator must be predicated of both natures. As it is, Owen's adherence to the basic pattern of catholic Christology which runs from the patristic era, through the Middle Ages and the Reformation (excepting the Lutherans) and into Reformed Orthodoxy, provides him with the theological framework for attacking Socinian attempts to restrict Christ's rule to his role as Mediator.[38]

This leads directly to the second point of significance: if Christ is involved in all acts *ad extra* by virtue of his deity, his consubstantiality with the Father, then he can and must also play a causal role in election; there can be no reduction of Christ to a mere instrument in the soteriological structure. While the incarnation may well be the object of predestination, Christ as God is also involved in the decree which stands prior to the incarnation and which defines the office of Mediator. Such an inference from Christ's consubstantiality with the Father confirms once again the basic soteriological structure defined by the covenant of redemption. This is confirmed yet further when we remember that Owen, following the typical definition provided by medieval

---

[37]   See *RC*, pp. 109–10, 153, 360–8.
[38]   For a discussion of this aspect of catholic Christology, see H. A. Oberman, 'The "Extra" Dimension in the Theology of Calvin' in his *The Dawn of the Reformation*, pp. 234–58; also E. D. Willis, *Calvin's Catholic Christology* (Leiden: Brill, 1966).

Scholasticism, considers predestination to be a subset of providence.[39] As such, it shares in the same Trinitarian foundation,
with Christ as eternal Efficient Cause, as does providence in
general. In other words, while Christ as Mediator stands below
the decree, Christ as God stands above it, and, as he is not
comprehended by the flesh, continues to do so even after the
incarnation. Thus, Owen's debate with the Socinians over the
deity of Christ is obviously consistent with the Trinitarian structures which we saw him developing in his various discussions of
the doctrine of God.

With this we are now at the point where discussion of the
person and of the work of Christ become one and the same.
Predestination points unequivocally towards the work of Christ
and the soteriological framework, where these implications of
Owen's understanding of the person of Christ and his work in
creation and providence are made explicit.[40] Interestingly
enough, it is therefore Owen's commitment to the scholastic
definition of predestination as a subset of providence which is
one of the factors that makes the christological basis of predestination so clear.[41]

---

[39] *Works* 10, pp. 53–4; see Ch. 3 above.

[40] This point is further underlined by Owen's emphasis upon the fact that Christ is
Mediator in his incarnation, and that his humanity is itself predestined: *Works* 12, pp.
247, 347.

[41] It is worth noting at this point that, to a large extent, Owen's refutation of Socinian
theology is simply a restatement of the orthodox Christological framework and presupposes the validity of his defence of eternal generation, etc. The problem is fundamentally that of the relationship of doctrine to exegesis. Owen and the Socinians are
interpreting the relevant biblical texts within two totally different theological frameworks and therefore arriving at totally different conclusions, a point which indicates
that it would be inaccurate to interpret the Protestant notion of *sola scriptura* in such
a way as to regard it as a sufficient safeguard in and of itself to safeguard the church
against heresy in the seventeenth-century context. In fact, Owen's defence of orthodox
Christology in the face of the radically biblicist attacks of the Socinians clearly depends
upon setting the notion of *sola scriptura* and scriptural exegesis within the ongoing
catholic theological tradition. This is not to deny that the Scriptures do not possess
normative authority for Owen when he comes to formulate doctrine, but simply to
point out that this must be seen as standing in positive relation to the doctrinal and
exegetical tradition. It is the Socinians' radical break with the tradition that makes the
theological results of their exegesis so heterodox.

The Work of Christ

Introduction

While Owen's choice of the *Racovian Catechism* as the primary target of his wrath in his controversy with the Socinians led him to adopt an approach to Christology in the *Vindiciae Evangelicae* which moved from the person of Christ to the work of Christ, it is obvious from what has been said so far that his attacks on the Socinian reconstruction of the person of Christ is based upon the fact that the Christ of the Racovian Catechism is simply not capable of performing the work of salvation as understood by the Reformed Orthodox. It is therefore true to say that, even in his discussion of the person of Christ, Christ's work possesses a position of theological even logical, priority. That this is the case should be no surprise when it is remembered that the causal ground for incarnation is the covenant of redemption, a covenant with a specific salvific purpose, and that, as Owen shifts his position on the nature of God's justice, the soteriological basis of Christology is strengthened yet further.[42] Nevertheless, this soteriological focus is inevitably brought out most clearly in discussions devoted explicitly to the work of Christ.

Patterns of explication

Within the tradition of Reformed Orthodoxy, two basic patterns of explicating Christ's work were available to Owen: that of the two states of humiliation and exaltation, and that of the threefold office. The two patterns are in no way mutually exclusive, but happily coexisted within the same system, both serving to emphasize the historical movement within Christ's saving work.[43]

---

[42] One sign of the soteriological–functional nature of Owen's Christology, which points clearly to the importance of the covenant of redemption in Christology, is his contention that Christ is Mediator according to both natures: see *Works* 12, pp. 375, 386. This is typical of the Reformed tradition: cf. Calvin, *Inst.* 2.14.3; Perkins, *Workes* 1, p. 27; Ames, *Marrow*, XVIII; see also Muller, *Christ and the Decree*, pp. 31 ff., 98 ff., 140 ff.

[43] E.g. Perkins, *Workes* 1, pp. 26–31.

In the seventeenth-century context the humiliation/exaltation theme was understood in significantly different ways in Lutheran and Reformed Orthodox systems, and marked a fundamental point of difference between the two traditions. For the Lutherans, the distinction was a way of bringing their understanding of the communication of properties into line with the historical movement depicted in the gospels. Consistent with their understanding of the communication of properties in the *genus maiestaticum*,[44] they considered the active subject of the state of humiliation to be the incarnate person of Christ who willingly renounced the glory that belonged to him as God. As such, this state was inaugurated at conception and continued until Christ's burial.[45] The state of exaltation then started with the descent into hell.[46] The Reformed on the other hand, had no such problem with the communication: the so-called *extra calvinisticum* precluded the problem faced by the Lutherans, and so their use of the state of humiliation was somewhat different. For a start, the incarnation *per se* did not involve humiliation; it was not the assumption of human flesh that constituted the state of humiliation, but Christ's submissive obedience to the will of the Father throughout his ministry, particularly as this focused upon his suffering and death, as is epitomized in the *Leiden Synopsis* 25:3.[47] The state of exaltation, then, started not with the descent into hell, which was understood by the Reformed to refer to

---

[44] The term *genus maiestaticum* was used by the Lutheran Orthodox to refer to the participation of Christ's human nature in the divine attributes, a participation which involves a real communication of the divine attributes to the human nature: see Mueller, *Christian Dogmatics*, pp. 275 ff; Muller, 'communicatio idiomatum/communication proprietatum' in *DLGTT*, pp. 72–4.

[45] See Mueller, pp. 287 ff.; Schmid, pp. 376–9; W. Elert, *The Structure of Lutheranism*, trans. W. A. Hansen (St Louis: Concordia, 1962), pp. 236 ff.

[46] Mueller, pp. 295 ff.; Schmid, pp. 379–81.

[47] 'De hoc statu humiliationis ut nunc dicamus, ordinis ratio postulat. Quo nomine in genere, intelligitur tota illa oeconomia. Qua Christus accepta forma servi, Patri fuit obediens usque ad mortem, mortem autem crucis, Phil. 2:7, et lata significatione totam Filii incarnati humilitatem, omnesque ejus gradus comprehendit; proprie vero extremam illam submissionem, seu ultimum vitae actum usque ad mortem, quae vulgo etiam recepta in Scripturis significatione, *kat' exochen* passio appellatur.' *Synopsis Purioris Theologiae*, ed. H. Bavinck (Leiden: Donner, 1881), p. 262.

Christ's death and thus to be part of the state of humiliation, but with the resurrection.[48]

The two-states structure underwent significant modification at the hands of Jacob Arminius who defined the state of humiliation in terms of the Creed, and thus as commencing with Christ's suffering under Pontius Pilate.[49] The effect of this modification was the exclusion of Christ's active obedience during his earthly ministry from his work of salvation, a point which facilitated his synergistic doctrine of justification.[50] As such, it could possibly have provided a dogmatic context for Owen's Christological debates with the Remonstrants. In fact, however, the humiliation–exaltation pattern plays a relatively minor structural role in many of Owen's discussions of Christ's work, although the exaltation motif does shape his extended Christological reflections in *Meditations on the Glory of Christ* (1684/91).[51]

The reasons for this relatively minor role are indicative more of the specific kind of debates in which Owen is engaged than of any theological idiosyncracy. First, in his attack on Arminianism the question raised in regard to Christology is that of the efficacy of Christ's work, a point which is discussed far more conveniently in relation to the threefold office, where specific attention can be given to the nature of mediation and priesthood, than in relation to the two states, where the immediate questions raised concern the content of Christ's work without necessarily touching on its effectiveness.[52] Second, much of Owen's debate with the Arminians is combined with sharp criticisms of the Socinian position. As the *Racovian Catechism* used the threefold office to organize its own Christological discussion, as well as having no doctrinal need for the humiliation motif, Owen's responses somewhat inevitably meet his opponents on this common terminological ground.[53]

---

[48] E.g. Perkins, who lists Christ's descent into hell as part of his humiliation, stressing that 'wee must not understand that hee went locally into the place of the damned, but that for the time of his abode in the grave, he was under the ignominious dominion of death.' Perkins, *Workes* 1, p. 29; see also the sources cited in Heppe, pp. 488–509.

[49] See *Private Disputation* XXXVII, I–III in Arminius, *Works* 2, p. 384.

[50] Muller, 'The Christological Problem', 154–5.

[51] *Works* 1, pp. 274–415.

[52] See, for example, the argument of *The Death of Death*.

[53] See *RC*, pp. 168–368.

The threefold office

The level of disagreement between Owen and his Socinian opponents on the issue of the threefold office is evident from the
relative space which they each in turn devote to each office: in
the *Racovian Catechism*, it is the prophetic office which receives
by far the longest exposition;[54] in Owen's works, it is the priestly
office, in many ways the climax of his soteriology, which receives
the most extended attention.[55] The difference in emphasis is a
direct reflection of a difference in underlying Christology. For
Biddle and the *Racovian Catechism*, their denial of Christ's divinity serves as the critical premise for all they have to say about
his work. Thus, the nature of Christ's threefold office is reinter-
preted on this basis and Christ's primary, if not his only, importance lies in his task of revealing the Father's will to humanity
through example and teaching, i.e. those tasks covered by the
prophetic office. For Owen, it is Christ's work in expiating sin
through his position as Mediator between God and humanity
that serves as the basic premise for his understanding of the
person of Christ, and it is this soteriological concern that finds
its most detailed exposition in the threefold office.

The importance of the threefold office for Owen's theology is
evident from the way in which he uses it as the basis for structur-
ing his Christological discussion in his major work on the person
of Christ, *A Declaration of the Glorious Mystery of the Person of
Christ* (1679).[56] Owen regards the threefold office as providing a
framework for an exhaustive statement of all Christ's mediatorial
dealings with the church, and, as such, as implying certain things
about Christ: he must stand in relation to those on whose behalf
he executes his office, and he must therefore share their nature.
He must also be human if he is to be subject to the law and to
fulfil it. But he must be more than a mere human because he is
to mediate between humanity and God, and he must therefore
also be God.[57] As we shall see, these basic premises are worked

---

54 *RC*, pp. 168–347; cf. Biddle, *Twofold Catechism*, pp. 42–52.
55 E.g. *Works* 11, pp. 397–551.
56 *Works* 1, pp. 3–272.
57 Ibid., pp. 86–7.

out in detail when Owen comes to a separate treatment of each part of the office.

Christ's prophetic office: communication of properties and Spirit-Christology

This basic difference between the Christ of Owen and the Christ of the Socinians is evident from the different ways in which they each understand his prophetic office. For the Socinians, Christ's prophetic office consists of his making God the Father's will known to humanity, '[i]n perfectly manifesting to us, confirming, and establishing the hidden will of God'.[58] This position is, superficially at least, similar to that of Calvin and of the Reformed tradition, although there is obviously an objectivity to Calvin's view of Christ's anointing to the office which presupposes the hypostatic union and which is emphatically not present in that of the Socinians.[59] Indeed, it is the basic reality of the hypostatic union set within the context of an orthodox doctrine of the Trinity which provides the ground for this revelation of the Father's will. This point is basic to Reformed understandings of the office, and is reflected in Owen's own statements on the issue, for example that in his *Greater Catechism* (1645), where the concept is expounded in Chapter Thirteen in the form of three questions and answers:

Q.1: Wherein doth the prophetical office of Christ consist?
A: In his embassage from God to man, revealing from the bosom of his Father the whole mystery of godliness, the way and truth whereby we must come to God.
Q.2: How doth he exercise this office towards us?
A: By making known the whole doctrine of truth unto us in a saving and spiritual manner.
Q.3: By what means doth he perform all this?
A: Divers; as, first, internally and effectually, by his Spirit writing his law in our hearts; secondly, outwardly and instrumentally, by the Word preached.[60]

---

[58] *RC*, p. 169.
[59] See Calvin, *Inst.* 2.15.2; J. F. Jansen, *Calvin's Doctrine of the Work of Christ* (Edinburgh: James Clarke, 1956), p. 43.
[60] *Works* 1, p. 483.

These three brief questions contain a wealth of theology and point to the profound way in which Christ stands at the centre of Owen's theology. First, we see yet again the intimate connection between the eternal and historical dimensions of Christ's work which is presupposed in Owen's answer to the first question; second, both explicitly and as an implication of the first point, we see the Trinitarian framework of the prophetic office, in that the Son is sent by the Father and performs his task through the Holy Spirit; and third, we see that the prophetic office continues to function as providing the content of the Christian gospel through the preaching of the Word and its individual application through the Spirit.

The connection between Christ's consubstantiality with the Father, his earthly ministry and his eternal appointment as Mediator is crucial to the Reformed understanding of the prophetic office.[61] The purpose of the prophetic office is to reveal the will of the Father, and it is self-evident that he must know the will of his Father and stand in such a relationship to other humans that he is then able to communicate it to them. In the *Vindiciae Evangelicae*, the humanity of Christ is not at stake and so Owen only stresses the argument for Christ's divinity: he counters Biddle's bizarre contention, that Christ as human must have been taken up to heaven to have the will of God revealed to him, by pointing to Christ's eternal subsistence in the bosom of the Father and his consubstantiality with the Father, as the basis for Christ's knowledge of the Father's will.[62] Being consub-

---

[61] E.g. the comment of Perkins: 'His propheticall office, is that whereby he immediately from his Father, revealeth his word and all the meanes of salvation comprised in the same. Ioh. 1.18. *The Sonne, which is in the bosome of his Father, he hath declared unto you.* Ioh. 8.26. *Those things which I heare of my father, I speake to the world.* Deut. 18.18. *I will raise them up a prophet, etc.*' *Workes* 1, p. 30. Cf. Ames, *Marrow* 1.19.15, pp. 132–3.

[62] *Works* 12, pp. 351, 355. Biddle's question is as follows: 'Can you further cite any passages that prove that Christ as a man ascended into heaven, and was there, and came from God out of heaven, before he shewed himself to the world, and discharged his Prophetick office; so that the talking of Moses with God in the person of an angel bearing the name of God was but a shadow of Christ's talking with God?', in reply to which he cites such texts as Jn. 3:13, 6:38, etc. *Twofold Catechism*, p. 44. The idea of Christ's supernatural knowledge as dependent upon a rapture experience is not found in the *Racovian Catechism*, but is certainly hinted at in the works of Crellius: see *De Uno Deo Patre*, pp. 130–4.

stantial with the Father, Christ as God was a party to the making of the covenants of redemption and grace and thus had no need to be informed of their content as if he were a third party. This, of course, reiterates the point that Christ was also electing God and that the Arminian separation of election from the appointment of the Mediator is not possible.

While the divinity of Christ secures his knowledge of the Father's will, it is his humanity which is necessary for the communication of that knowledge to other human beings. Underlying this is Owen's concern for the epistemological problem behind the incarnation. Because God is immaterial, therefore incomprehensible in himself, and the finite cannot comprehend the infinite, humans can have no intuitive knowledge of him and must make do with the shadowy representations of himself which God condescends to make through material phenomena. In Christ, however, this distance between God and humanity is overcome, and, as he is true God manifest in the flesh, there can be seen in him a true representation of the Father as the Father wishes to be towards us as an object of faith. In Christ there is a revelation of all the attributes of God necessary to faith and obedience in a form in which human beings can comprehend them.[63] Christ not only overcomes the gap between Creator and creature which exists on account of sin but also overcomes the ontological gap between the infinite and the finite. The incarnation thus possesses epistemological as well as soteriological significance. On this point, Owen's thinking stands in continuity with the traditional belief that God must accommodate himself to human capacity in order for humans to comprehend him, and that the incarnation is a central part of this accommodation. As with Calvin, however, it is the need to deal with sin that is the decisive motive behind the incarnation; unlike some medieval scholastics, he does not indulge in speculation about whether

---

[63] *Works* 1, pp. 65–9. Owen does allow that Christ discharged his prophetic office before the incarnation through personal appearances in the likeness of human nature, through the ministry of angels, through the Holy Spirit, and through the ministry of holy men. Then, as now, he was prophet by the ministry of Spirit and Word: *Works* 1, pp. 88–90; cf. *Works* 20, pp. 21–3.

Christ would have become incarnate had humanity not sinned.[64]

This emphasis upon Christ as the revealer of the Father's will reflects the Christocentric presuppositions of Owen's theology which we noted earlier, and provides the basis upon which Owen is able to build his Christ-centred doctrine of Scripture:

> A mere external doctrinal revelation of the divine nature and properties, without any exemplification or real representation of them, was not sufficient unto the end of God in the manifestation of himself. This is done in Scripture. But the whole of Scripture is built on this foundation, or proceeds on this supposition – that there is a real representation of the divine nature unto us, which it declares and describes . . . [T]his is done in the person of Christ. He is the complete image and perfect representation of the Divine Being and excellencies. I do not speak of it absolutely, but as God proposeth himself as the object of our faith, trust, and obedience.[65]

This passage is of the utmost importance in understanding Owen. In line with his belief that the problem of the relationship of humanity to God is one of both sin and finiteness, he stresses that Christ is himself the presupposition and focal point of scriptural revelation. Owen emphasizes that in Christ we do not have a revelation of God's essence but of God as he is towards us. Again, Owen's concern is not for some abstract, metaphysical notion of God, but for God as he acts towards us as Saviour. This the same emphasis we noted earlier in Owen's discussion of God's attributes, that of God *for us*.[66]

The prophetic office of Christ is therefore the basis for objective revelation of God as Redeemer in the world after the Fall. The reasons which were noted in Owen's discussions of the nature of theology as making such revelation necessary, and shaping its form, are precisely those which guide Owen as he formulates his understanding of the office, pointing clearly to the importance of the nature of Christ's work as determinative of the nature of his person. Furthermore, it is apparent from this that the cluster of problems surrounding salvation and revelation have a common focal point in the person of the incarnate

---

[64] *Works* 12, p. 214; cf. Calvin, *Inst.* 2.12.4.
[65] *Works* 1, p. 69.
[66] See Ch. 3 above.

Mediator. Nevertheless, as the related issues of revelation and mediation must be understood within a Trinitarian context, both presupposing specific divine acts *ad intra* and *ad extra* to be assigned to the three persons, the prophetic office itself must also be understood within such a framework.

While Christ's divinity secures the reliability of his revelation of the Father, and his humanity is the medium of that revelation, the Trinitarian dimensions of the prophetic office emerge most clearly in Owen's understanding of the communication of properties within the person of the Mediator. This communication is the presupposition of the communication of full revelation to humanity, and serves to give revelation both its objective and subjective reliability: objectively, it is utterly reliable because it is a full revelation of God as he is towards us; subjectively, it is reliable because Christ, as God, has the authority to send the Holy Spirit into human minds to make his Word effectual.[67] Again, the Western order of procession within the Trinity is of crucial importance: the Father is revealed by the Son through the Holy Spirit. It is precisely the same point noted earlier in the context of Owen's clash with the Quakers: Christ stands at the centre of any saving revelation of the Father; and it is the dual procession of Spirit from both Father and Son which binds the whole structure to its centre in Christ. Biddle's merely human prophet, however exalted, is inevitably inadequate for the task as Owen understands it: he cannot bridge the infinite gap between Creator and creature, nor put away sin, and so can provide no reliable revelation of the Father's will.[68]

The nature of this communication in relation to Christ's prophetic office receives its fullest exposition in Owen's works in his comments on Heb. 1:1–2 in his massive *Commentary on Hebrews*. Here, in line with the basic distinction between archetypal and ectypal theology, Owen is careful to stress that, while the Son as God knew God's will in its entirety, this infinite knowledge is not communicated in its entirety to the human nature:

---

[67] *Works* 1, pp. 94–5.
[68] *Works* 12, p. 351.

The Lord Jesus Christ, by virtue of the union of his person, was from the womb filled with a perfection of gracious light and knowledge of God and his will. An actual exercise of that principle of holy wisdom wherewith he was endued, in his infancy, as afterwards, he had not, Lk. 2:52; nor had he in his human nature an absolutely infinite comprehension of all individual things, past, present, and to come, which he expressly denies as to the day of judgment, Mt. 24:36, Mk. 13:32; but he was furnished with all that wisdom and knowledge which the human nature was capable of, both as to *principle* and *exercise*, in the condition wherein it was, without destroying its finite being and variety of conditions, from the womb.[69]

From this it is clear that Owen sees the assumption of flesh by the Son as being entirely in accordance with human finiteness, and as such his views reflect the general character of Reformed Christology. There is also a historical–dynamic element which is built into his Christology and indicated by his statement that, while Christ's humanity possessed this gracious wisdom from the moment the flesh was assumed, he did not exercise it until later.

This historical focus in Owen's Christology stands in contrast both to Socinian Christologies and the formulations of medieval Scholasticism. For Socinians, such as the authors of the *Racovian Catechism* and John Biddle, rejection of the notion that Christ was eternally generated by, and consubstantial with, the Father, led to Christologies which rooted his 'divinity' in his perfect union with the Holy Spirit, a union more perfect than that enjoyed by anyone else, and one which was paradigmatic for everyone else. The participation referred to in 2 Pet. 1:4 is cited to support this view.[70] It is thus true that Jesus Christ, while not being essentially God, is nonetheless somewhat elevated above the rest of humanity: he is the only-begotten Son, and his virgin birth, his sanctification by the Father, his resurrection, and his subsequent dominion and authority all point to his possessing a certain resemblance to God which the rest of the human race lacks.[71]

The purpose underlying the Christological arguments of the *Racovian Catechism* is the establishment of the fact that Christ

---

[69] *Works* 20, p. 28; cf. *Works* 1, pp. 93–4.
[70] *RC*, pp. 55–6.
[71] Ibid., pp. 52–5; Biddle, *Twofold Catechism*, pp. 26–33; Crellius, *De Uno Deo Patre*, pp. 213–9.

was not the Son of God by eternal generation from the Father, but because of the miraculous dimensions of his birth, ministry, and death: Christ becomes Son of God by adoption; and the union between God and Christ is different in degree, though not in kind, from that which exists between God and other believers. Socinian Christology thus has a radical historical focus which roots its understanding of Christ's divinity in his personal development over time through his life and ministry.

Faced with the radical historical focus of the Socinians in their argument for Christ's work leading to his adoption as Son of God, Owen presents a Christology which distinguishes between the Son as he is eternally God and the Son as Mediator, a distinction which is made possible, as we have seen, by the Trinitarian basis and implications of the eternal covenant of redemption. In this context, he introduces the notion of the exaltation of the Mediator in his kingly office, a theme to be picked up again later in the treatise.[72] Thus, while Owen argues that Christ is Son by his very essence and not as the result of any work he has done, he does not hold to some static Christology which eclipses the historical economy of salvation through an overarching emphasis upon eternity; his Christology gives due allowance to the dynamic movement of the work of the Mediator in history. For example, Owen makes clear that he does not regard the hypostatic union, in itself, as sufficient for the communication of the divine knowledge to the human nature.[73] Any consequences of the assumption of flesh by the Son, other than the personal union, are entirely voluntary and not ontological necessities which can be inferred from the nature of incarnation.[74] As he argues in the *Vindiciae Evangelicae*, it is his anointing with the fullness of the Spirit at his baptism that gave Christ all that he needed for the fulfilment of his task, rendering a subsequent rapture, of the kind suggested by Biddle more than superfluous.[75] This anointing preserves the importance of the historical economy: the hypostatic union by itself is not enough; the office of

---

[72] *Works* 12, p.191.
[73] *Works* 20, p. 29.
[74] *Works* 3, pp. 161, 180.
[75] *Works* 12, pp. 355–6, 359–60.

Christ as Mediator is established and confirmed by the anointing with the Spirit at his baptism. Thus, salvation cannot simply be swallowed up into an eternal divine decree: the terms of the divine decrees themselves, as they determine the nature of the incarnation, exclude such a possibility.

As well as countering the radical historical emphasis of Socinian Christologies, Owen's approach also stands in contrast to medieval discussions of the knowledge of Christ. In an attempt to deal with the problems raised for the incarnate Christ's knowledge of God, the medievals argued for the existence of a number of different kinds of knowledge in Christ. For example, according to Aquinas, Christ had a fourfold knowledge by virtue of the hypostatic union: created, beatific, infused, and acquired.[76] Thus, while Christ could be said to gain acquired knowledge *via* his senses, he never came to know anything which he did not know before in some other mode of knowledge because that would imply some lack of perfection within his human nature.[77]

Such a view was clearly unacceptable within the framework of Reformed Christology. In line with the basic understanding of the communication of properties, with its axiom that the finite cannot comprehend the infinite, the notion that Christ's humanity could be omniscient in any way, had to be rejected. Thus, the incarnation involved a certain self-emptying on the part of God whereby the incarnated Word was not omniscient as the Word in and of itself outside the flesh was. This view of Christ's self-emptying is that of Calvin,[78] and is also that of Owen. In direct contrast to the medieval position which involved a static, metaphysical view of the incarnation and which could not as a consequence take seriously the scriptural verses which speak of the Father revealing himself to the Son after the human flesh has been assumed into union with the Son, Owen argues that, while the Son as God knew all things by virtue of his eternal generation, and while the human nature was the means by which the Son carried out his work as Mediator, there was nevertheless a real

---

[76] *ST* 3a.9.3.

[77] *Ibid.*

[78] *Inst.* 2.14.2; see also the discussion by Willis, *Calvin's Catholic Christology*, pp. 80–2. Cf. Turretin, Institutes 13.13.

growth in knowledge in terms of his human nature, both because of his nature as a human being and because of the activity of the Holy Spirit. As a human being he was essentially rational, and therefore was guided by his reason and gained knowledge experimentally. So, it would have been quite possible to place something before Jesus of which he had no previous knowledge and then to say that, as a result, he had come to know that object and that his knowledge had therefore increased.[79]

This discussion of the communication of properties helps draw attention to the fundamentally pneumatological emphasis of Owen's Christology, an emphasis which is inevitable, given his adherence to the notion that the Spirit is the agent of God in the realm of creation. Christ's humanity, of course, being a creature, was subject to the same basic framework of divine activity as any other part of the created realm. In terms of the activity of the Holy Spirit in relation to the incarnation, while it was true that Jesus Christ received the Spirit at conception, this Spirit became progressively more active in terms of the gifts and knowledge he endowed him with throughout his life. It was not until his baptism, and the inauguration of his public ministry, that he received the fullness of the Spirit.[80] This allows for the growth in wisdom which numerous biblical texts predicate of Jesus of Nazareth, and also meets the exegetical difficulties presented by texts which speak of Christ's not knowing the timing of the end of the world, something which the human nature cannot know except by a special act of revelation.[81] Thus, while the hypostatic union does not itself automatically lead to any communication of properties, this role is fulfilled by the Spirit. This is made crystal clear in Owen's vigorous emphasis upon the fact that the assumption of the flesh is the only immediate act of the Son upon the human nature, and the only necessary consequence of this is the personal union.[82] Then, in line with his view that the immediate agent in all acts within the created realm is the Spirit, Owen

---

[79] *Works* 3, p. 170.
[80] Ibid., pp. 171–4; 20, pp. 30–1.
[81] *Works* 1, p. 93, where Owen correlates Mk. 13:32 with Rev. 1:1.
[82] *Works* 3, p. 160; for a similar position, see Goodwin, *Works* 6, pp. 10–13.

argues that all other actions of the Son on the human nature are performed *via* the Spirit as intermediary – although, in line with the traditional view that God's acts *ad extra* can be ascribed to all three persons, he does stress the concurrence of the Father and the Son. In this argument, the *filioque* is used as his explicit premise, this time with a specifically incarnational twist.[83] Herein lies the consistency and strength of Owen's Spirit-centred Christology: it emphasizes the fundamentally Trinitarian nature of the incarnation, paralleling the Trinitarian causal ground of incarnation in the eternal covenant scheme, by emphasizing that the Son never acts within the created realm except as he works through the Spirit. Christ's conception is the work of the Spirit, as is the sanctification of the human flesh.[84] Indeed, it is not the virgin birth which guarantees Christ's sinlessness for Owen, but the supernatural infusion of grace by the Holy Spirit.[85] By the same token, Christ's resurrection and glorification were also the acts of the Spirit.[86] Now that Christ has ascended to heaven, he continues his prophetic office in this world exclusively via the Word and the Spirit, and it is the Holy Spirit which holds both the objective completeness of salvation in Christ and the moral responsibilities of the Christian life together.[87] Thus we see once again the clear structural parallel and continuity between the Trinitarian acts of God *ad intra* and the Trinitarian acts of God *ad extra*.

The dynamic nature of the communication of properties has one other significant implication for Owen, and this brings us

---

[83] 'The Holy Spirit is the *Spirit of the Son*, no less than the Spirit of the Father. He proceedeth from the Son as from the Father . . . And hence he is the immediate operator of all divine acts of the Son himself, even on his own human nature. Whatever the Son of God wrought in, by, or upon the human nature, he did it by the Holy Ghost, who is his Spirit, as he is the Spirit of the Father.' *Works* 3, p. 162.

[84] Ibid., p. 162.

[85] Ibid., pp. 168–9. Owen refers here to 'supernatural endowments of grace, superadded unto the natural faculties of our souls' to enable Christ as man to live to God. Owen here borrows the language of the *donum superadditum* from medieval Scholasticism to underscore the radical disjunction between the Creator and the creature and thus to remind his readers of the ontological dimension of his anti-Pelagian theology.

[86] Ibid., pp. 181–3.

[87] Ibid., p. 640.

back again to the nature of the kind of God that is revealed, and the Christological focus of that revelation: in the incarnation, there is a complete revelation of all the properties of the divine nature necessary for present obedience and future blessedness; thus, the God who is revealed therein is the God *for us*.[88] This is precisely the relational understanding of the nature of theology which Owen articulated in his basic definition of theology as covenantal. Thus the doctrine of the incarnation focuses attention on the close connection that exists in Owen's theology between doctrine and piety: Christian piety depends upon the objective reality of the incarnation, as this provides the basis for our knowledge about God, about how he relates to us and how we are to relate to him. Doctrine and piety cannot be divorced. The actual content of the revelation of God, which constitutes Christ's prophetic office, is twofold: the revelation of God's grace and love; and the revelation of God's will and commands.[89] God's grace and love are seen in the objective gift of salvation that Christ himself embodies. God's will and commands are seen in Christ's radicalizing of the law to include inner obedience and not just outward conformity. Thus, Christ in his prophetic office serves as both Saviour and teacher, and the two cannot be separated. Of course, the objective epistemological problem of relating the infinite to the finite was not the only reason that humans could not grasp God: sin also darkened hearts and minds so that humanity was unreceptive to the teaching of Christ. This is why Christ's prophetic office includes the authority to send the Holy Spirit to take the Word and apply it to the hearts of individuals.[90] As such, the prophetic office of Christ, as an act of the Trinitarian God, therefore stands in fundamental continuity with all that Owen had to say concerning the nature of theology itself, both in terms of its objective reality and subjective application.

---

[88] *Works* 1, p. 69.
[89] *Works* 3, p. 361.
[90] *Works* 1, p. 95.

The office of king

The regal office of Christ is not something upon which Owen dwells at great length. In *Christologia* he declares that his major treatment of the topic occurs in his commentary on Heb. 1:3, but even the discussion in this work is brief and elliptical.[91] Nevertheless, the issue does form one of the points of significant disagreement with the Socinians, as expressed in his work, *Vindiciae Evangelicae*.

The point of departure for discussion is the view of the regal office found in the *Racovian Catechism*. The authors of the *Catechism* considered Christ's office as king to start with his session at the right hand of the Father after God has raised him from the dead and drawn him up to heaven.[92] The office is therefore something which Christ does not possess by nature, does not possess during his earthly pilgrimage, and which does not play a large role in the *Catechism*'s theology.

There are indeed superficial similarities between the position of the Reformed Orthodox and the Socinians, as both regard the regal office as being inaugurated by Christ's ascension.[93] There are also, however, significant differences. For the Reformed, the inauguration is set within the context of the two states and therefore represents part of the exaltation after the humiliation. The doctrine thus assumes the framework of an orthodox Christology and serves as part of the way in which the historical movement of Christ's mediation is emphasized while the continuity of his person in terms of who and what he is is also maintained. This is made clear by Owen:

> As for his exaltation at his ascension, it was not by any investiture in any new office, but by an admission to the execution of that part of his work of mediatorship which did remain, in a full and glorious manner, the whole concernment of his humiliation being past. In the meantime, doubtless, he was a king when the Lord of glory was crucified, 1 Cor. 2:8.[94]

---

[91] Ibid., p. 96; 20, pp. 117–21.
[92] *RC*, p. 360; cf. Biddle, *Twofold Catechism*, pp. 55–63.
[93] Cf. *RC*, pp. 360–8 (Section VII) with Perkins, *Workes* 1, p. 31; Ussher, *A Body of Divinitie*, p. 185.
[94] *Works* 12, p. 373; cf. *Works* 20, p. 117.

This statement contains a number of important points. First, the admission to the regal office does not involve some kind of ontological change on the part of the Son. It represents rather a particular phase in the historical economy of salvation, an economy which derives its unity from the fact that each of the offices of prophet, priest, and king are not really a separate office but that the three offices are three parts of one task of mediation. The investiture as king is not therefore something entirely new, but reflects the move from humiliation to exaltation which is implicit in the structure of mediation as determined by the covenant of redemption. Indeed, in Owen's engagement with the Socinians on this issue there is no extensive discussion of the usual aspects of Christ's regal office, such as his protection of, and authority over, the church. This is not theologically significant; rather, it reflects the nature of the point at issue: Owen is concerned with a correct understanding of the regal office as it relates to an orthodox Christology and the doctrine of the two states rather than in an exposition of the office in itself.

It is clear from this that Owen's understanding of the regal office reflects the concerns of the *extra calvinisticum* in its emphasis upon Christ's subordination to the Father solely in terms of his voluntary acceptance of the office of Mediator. Owen, as is clear from the last quotation, maintains that Christ, as God, is always king even during the humiliation of the incarnate Logos. This is the necessary implication of his Trinitarianism, whereby the Father always acts *ad extra* by the Son through the Holy Spirit. Thus, the role of Christ as king in terms of guarding and guiding the church belongs to him as much by the fact that he is God as by the fact that he is Mediator.[95] It was noted earlier that Owen rejected Socinian attempts to restrict biblical texts which speak of Christ's dominion to times after the resurrection; he insisted that these spoke of Christ's eternal deity. The same basic point is made in the quotation above, where Christ is asserted to be king before his ascension. There is in fact a dual focus in Owen's Christology, reflecting his understanding of the relationship of Word to incarnation, which stresses, on the one hand,

---

[95] See *Works* 20, p. 98; cf. The discussion of Christ and providence in Ch. 3.

Christ as king and sovereign by nature, as he is God, and, on the other hand, Christ as king and sovereign by delegation, within the structure of mediation.[96] One result of this dual focus is that, as the office of Mediator will cease in the eschaton, so will the administration of the regal office based upon that mediation: drawing on the imagery in 1 Cor. 15, Owen speaks of the Son giving up the kingdom to the Father.[97] This does not, of course, mean that Christ himself ceases to have authority – his divinity precludes that possibility – or that the incarnation ceases to have relevance – Owen's belief in the fact that the finite can never comprehend the infinite ensures that God's incarnational accommodation retains its importance even after the Day of Judgment. All it means is that Christ's regal office as defined by his specific role as Mediator, and thus by the covenant of redemption, will cease.[98]

While Owen's positive exposition of the regal office in *Vindiciae Evangelicae* is brief, it is important because it is in this context that Owen raises the issue of the interconnection between Christology and piety in its most acute form. The background to this issue lies in Socinian attempts to maintain the worship of Christ despite their rejection of orthodox Christology.[99] For Owen, this is nonsensical, as divine worship requires divinity as its object if it is to avoid being anything but idolatry. The

---

[96] 'The power that Christ hath upon the account of his divine nature is not *delegated*, but *essential* to him . . . We grant that *the judiciary power* that was delegated to Christ as mediator, he being appointed of God to judge the world, was given him "because he is the Son of Man," or was made man to be our mediator, and to accomplish the great work of salvation of mankind.' Works 12, pp. 374–5; cf. p. 391.

[97] Works 12, p. 391; cf. Works 1, p. 271.

[98] On the relationship of the regal office to the eschaton, see Muller, 'Christ in the Eschaton', 31–59. Muller draws attention to the fact that the Socinian understanding of the regal office raised in an acute form the problem of the duration of the office in eternity and raised the matter to the status of a doctrinal locus in Reformed systems, *op. cit.* 55 ff. The key text is 1 Cor. 15:28 which was used by the Socinians to indicate the eternal, and thus essential, subordination of the Son to the Father. In his reply to the *Racovian Catechism*, Owen does not deal with the *Catechism*'s exposition of this text, although he does relate 1 Cor. 15:27 to the two states, which provides an obviously orthodox framework for understanding the following verse: see *Works* 12, p. 214; cf. *RC*, p. 60.

[99] E.g. *RC*, pp. 189 ff.; cf. *Works* 12, pp. 377–9.

Socinians' attempts to maintain the worship of Christ without an orthodox understanding of his person and work are, he argues, the Achilles' heel of their Christology.[100] This observation is interesting if for no other reason than the fact that it draws attention to the intimate connection between doctrine and piety that exists within Owen's thought.

This issue pushes Owen to a greater precision in terms of the relationship he describes between the incarnate Christ and the nature of Christian worship. He is adamant that Christ cannot be considered the formal cause of worship in terms of his office of Mediator. In the polemical context, this position stands in stark contrast to the Socinian Christology, where it is only as a result of his mediation that Christ can be an object of worship – if it were not for his mediation, he would, after all, be no more than any other mere mortal.[101] For Owen, however, Christ is incarnate God. It is Christ's divine nature that provides the basis for his being the object of divine worship. Owen distinguishes in this context between the formal, or fundamental, reason for worshipping Christ, and the motive thereunto. The former is Christ's divinity; the latter is his mediation.[102] Mediation cannot be the formal cause for a variety of reasons: only the infinite can be the object of worship, but Christ is infinite prior to his appointment as Mediator and incarnation; as Mediator, he is partaker of God's nature, not God pure and simple; as Mediator, Christ depends on God and receives his power from him by delegation; as Mediator, Christ is subordinate to the Father; and as Mediator, Christ is not eternal and thus cannot be the cause of worship – if he were, then worship of God will cease when the office of Mediator ceases in the eschaton.[103]

In fact, only divine excellence can be the formal cause of worship.[104] In light of this, Christ can be said to have a twofold relation to divine worship: formally, as he is God; and causally,

---

[100] *Works* 12, pp. 391–2.
[101] *RC*, pp. 154 ff., 189 ff.
[102] *Works* 12, p. 388.
[103] Ibid., pp. 390–1.
[104] Ibid., p. 385.

as the means of all the good which believers receive from God.[105]
We see here the functional nature of Owen's Christology,
whereby the incarnation is seen as the means to a specific end,
the bridge between finite humanity and infinite God. Furthermore, we find once again the fundamental distinction within
Owen's theology between the ontological and the economic aspects of the Trinity, the same distinction which was of such
importance in distinguishing between Christ as God and Christ
as appointed Mediator in the covenant of redemption, and which
defines the relationship between Christology and predestination.
Here the distinction is used to articulate the specifically Trinitarian nature of worship. In the context of worship, we find once
again a confluence of epistemological and soteriological concerns
in the person of the Mediator. In the order of knowing, Christ as
Mediator reveals the Father as the object of worship for the
believer through the work of the Holy Spirit; in the order of
being, the procession of the Son from the Father, and of the Spirit
from both, means that when the believer's mind is fixed upon the
Father, via the work of the Spirit and of Christ, there is then a
subsequent worshipping of the Son and Spirit which derives from
their consubstantiality with the Father. What happens in worship
is that Christ as Mediator provides access to God the Father as
the formal object of adoration but, having done so, further gives
the believer an understanding of the ontological Trinity whereby
all the three persons, as they are God, become the objects of such
adoration. The Western Trinitarian structure once again undergirds the unity of the salvific economy.[106] God is revealed as a
Trinitarian object of worship precisely through the economy of
salvation that depends upon the covenant of redemption, and
upon the order of procession within the Trinity. The mature fruit
of this Trinitarian perspective is, of course, found in Owen's great
treatise, *Of Communion with God the Father, Son, and Holy Ghost*
(1657), a work whose entire structure is shaped by the Western
order of procession within the Trinity.[107]

---

[105]   Ibid., p. 387.
[106]   Ibid., pp. 392–3.
[107]   *Works* 2, pp. 3–274.

Owen's discussion of the regal office is therefore significant not only for understanding the work of Christ as Mediator in a purely doctrinal sense, but also in understanding the link there is between doctrine and piety in his thought. Nevertheless, both the prophetic and regal offices point beyond the ontological problem of human finiteness in the light of God's infinity and towards a deeper need for humanity: the need to deal with the objective problem of sin and its subjective impact upon the believer. These issues are only resolved when the third part of the mediatorial office is taken into consideration: the high priesthood of Christ.

The high priestly office

There is no doctrine with which Owen's name is associated which has proved more controversial than that of limited atonement, the teaching that Christ only died to save the elect. Indeed, in Owen's 1647 treatise, *The Death of Death in the Death of Christ*, the doctrine can be said to have been given its most exhaustive and elaborate exposition, with the result that one modern author goes as far as to say that the doctrine stands or falls upon the cogency of Owen's arguments.[108] As such, it is hardly surprising that Owen has been singled out for attack by those who wish to deny the doctrine.[109] This study, as historical rather than dogmatic, will not deal with the question of the ultimate truth or falsity of the doctrine, but aims simply to clarify the nature of the argument proposed by Owen and thereby to refute certain misinterpretations of his position which have been put forward by other scholars.

Before discussing the doctrine, however, a number of preliminary remarks must be made. The first is that Owen's major statement on this issue, *The Death of Death*, is not a treatise about the limitation of the atonement as such. Rather, as James Packer

---

[108] See J. I. Packer, ' "Saved by his Precious Blood": an Introduction to John Owen's "The Death of Death in the Death of Christ" ' in *Among God's Giants*, p. 178.
[109] E.g. Clifford, *Atonement and Justification*; J. B. Torrance, 'The Incarnation and "Limited Atonement".'

observes, it is a piece of positive theological construction primarily aimed at establishing the efficacy of Christ's death for the salvation of the elect.[110] The extent of the atonement, while providing the initial reason for writing, is actually part of a much bigger question, that of whether Christ died simply to make salvation possible or to make it actual. In this context, limitation of the atonement can, on one level, be seen as an inference from other doctrines: if the death of Christ is efficacious for salvation, then those who do not come to enjoy that salvation cannot be numbered among those for whom Christ died.

In light of both this last point and everything which was said earlier regarding Owen's understanding of theology and of the doctrine of God, it should be obvious that the death of Christ cannot be examined in isolation from other theological concerns. Indeed, Owen himself sets Christ's death within the context of his role as the great high priest; this priestly role is itself set within the context of his role as Mediator; and this mediatorial role is set within the context of the two economies of salvation, the eternal and the historical, which find expression in the intratrinitarian covenant relations and the incarnation. Thus, students of Owen's thought cannot divorce Christ's death from the broader structures of his Christology.[111] One does not have to agree with Owen's arguments to see that he treats atonement as part of the high priestly office of Christ and thus as one more aspect of his understanding of the Trinitarian structure of salvation; therefore, if his arguments are to be

---

[110] ' "Saved by his Precious Blood" ', pp. 175 ff.

[111] In this respect, the analysis of Alan Clifford is seriously deficient in that the high priesthood of Christ, so crucial as a determining factor in Owen's Christology and thus in his understanding of atonement, is virtually bypassed, while the lion's share of the blame for the doctrine of limited atonement is ascribed to Owen's Aristotelian 'one-end teleology'. That this one-end teleology (understood inclusively by Owen, not exclusively, *pace* Clifford) was used by all kinds of theologians in the seventeenth century, Orthodox, Arminian, and all points in between, should alert students of the period to the danger of ascribing too much causal power to it in terms of the resulting theological content. It is, in fact, peripheral to an understanding of Owen and cannot be conveniently dealt with at this point. It will be dealt with in more detail in Appendix One below.

understood and expounded fairly, that is how the student of Owen's thought must deal with them.[112]

As Christ's priesthood is just one aspect of his role as Mediator, so his appointment to the office is, in the same way as his appointment to the offices of prophet and king, simply one aspect of his appointment as Mediator. Thus, the eternal and the historical economies are again of crucial importance: Christ's high priesthood finds its ultimate causal ground in the intratrinitarian covenants, and its historical inauguration in the earthly ministry of Christ.

The priesthood of Christ, while not dominating Owen's theology, appears to have been something of a preoccupation with him. In devoting more space to discussing this aspect of Christ's mediatorial work, Owen stands in basic continuity with the

---

[112] Dr Clifford (see *Atonement and Justification*, p. 94 n. 97) does make one reference to the priesthood of Christ when he discusses the arguments about the relationship between oblation and intercession in Calvin raised by R. T. Kendall (*Calvin and English Calvinism*, pp. 13–14) and P. Helm (*Calvin and the Calvinists* [Edinburgh: Banner of Truth, 1982], pp. 32–50). The theologian under discussion is Calvin, and so need not delay us long here, although a brief comment on the reference given as proof for Dr Clifford's position is in order. This reference, to Calvin's commentary on Jn. 17:9, is somewhat misleading as this passage does not say that Christ prayed for all indiscriminately at Lk. 23:34. Rather, in the context of the argument, it presents that interpretation of the Lucan verse as an objection to Calvin's interpretation of the verse in John. As such, it may or may not represent Calvin's views; there is no way of telling from the narrow context of this passage in isolation, and a glance at the commentary on Lk. 23:34 in the *Harmony of the Gospels* reveals a far more cautious view of the passage. If, for the sake of argument, we allow that Dr Clifford is correct in his view of Calvin (and it is beyond the scope of this study to examine this in the necessary detail), he still cannot rely on this text as proof: see *OC* 47:380–1 and *OC* 45:767–8. Interestingly, neither Dr Clifford nor R. T. Kendall attempts to explore the implications of what they have to say about the relationship between intercession and oblation in terms of the consubstantiality of the Father and the Son, a doctrine with clear implications for the understanding of the role of Christ's will in human salvation. These implications were arguably not fully worked out by the early Reformers and the consequent loose ends provided much of the background to the way in which the later Orthodox developed their formulations of Christology in relation to soteriology. They understood that individual doctrines stand in positive relation to other doctrines and have consequences which reach far beyond their immediate sphere; thus, they have to be integrated within the catholic theological framework as a whole. Consequently, piecemeal treatment of isolated doctrines which takes no account of the wider context inevitably leads to serious distortion. For a careful exposition of Calvin's understanding of Christ's work set (refreshingly!) within the larger theological context, see Muller, *Christ and the Decree*, pp. 17–38.

Reformed Orthodox tradition of his time. There were sound internal reasons for this: Orthodox Augustinian understanding of sin and anthropology, as well as the Anselmic roots of Orthodox Christological patterns, meant that the objective problem of sin and its cure was central to the soteriological scheme.[113] There were also good polemical reasons for this emphasis. The priesthood of Christ, involving as it does an understanding of the nature of Christ's death and its relationship to salvation and to the church, was a point of key difference between the Reformed and their Arminian, Socinian, and Catholic opponents. The Arminian ordering of decrees, which placed individual election after faith, clearly precluded any direct causal relationship between the priestly work of Christ and the salvation of any particular individual.[114] The Socinians, by denying that Christ was divine in the traditional sense, radically reduced the objective importance of atonement.[115] The Catholics were problematic on various fronts, particularly in the relationship they drew between Christ's death and the Mass, and also in the development of Pelagianizing tendencies within their ranks, tendencies susceptible to the same strictures from the Orthodox viewpoint as those of the Arminians.[116]

The importance which Owen attached to a correct understanding of Christ's priesthood is apparent right from the start of his theological career. Indeed, in an early work, *The Duty of Pastors and People Distinguished* (1644), he alludes to a book in which he discusses priesthood, for which a marginal note

---

[113]   See Calvin, *Inst.* 2.12–17; Ames, *Marrow*, XI–XXIII; Ussher, *A Body of Divinitie*, pp. 127–186; Goodwin, Of Christ the Mediator, Works 5.

[114]   E.g. Arminius, *Works* 1, pp. 653–4.

[115]   E.g. *RC*, pp. 303 ff.

[116]   The close relationship between Arminianism and parallel tendencies such as Molinism in the Catholic Church was a commonplace of English Reformed polemic in the seventeenth century, as is evident from the full title of Twisse's 1632 treatise, *Vindiciae gratiae potestatis ac providentiae Dei, hoc est, Ad Examen Libelli Perkinsiani de praedestinationis modo et ordine, institutum a Iacobo Arminio Responsio scholastica tribus libris absoluta. Una cum digressionibus ad singulas partes accommodatis in quibus illustriores in hoc negotio quaestiones fusius pertractantur et accurate discutiuntur, veritasque adversus Bellarminum, Didacum Alvarez, Gabrielem Vasques aliosque tum Papistas tum Pelagianos asseritur. Nec non opiniones nonnullae quorundam modernorum Theologorum modeste examinantur.*

provides the title, *Tractatu de Sacerdotio Christi, contra Armin. Socin. et Papistas, nondum edito.*[117] As stated in the title, the work had not been published at that point; in fact it appears never to have been.[118] Nevertheless, the title itself is enough to suggest that Owen realized that the priesthood of Christ was a focal point of disagreement between the Orthodox and their Arminian, Socinian and papist opponents. The reasons for this are not hard to find: in the priesthood of Christ we find the central act of the drama of redemption, and a key doctrine which acts as controlling factor in biblical interpretation.

Both of these points can be seen clearly in Owen's most extensive and systematic treatment of the priesthood of Christ: his commentary on Hebrews.[119] This work contains not only extensive exegesis of passages which speak of Christ's priesthood but also an extended preliminary essay on this topic which serves to draw together the various doctrinal issues involved and thus provides a framework which both arises out of, and serves to shape, his biblical exegesis.

For Owen, the nature of all priesthood is encapsulated in Heb. 5:1. This verse defines two basic criteria for anyone who is to be a priest: they have to be from among the people; and they have to be appointed to act on behalf of others in the matters of God.[120] These two aspects of priesthood can be found in Christ's incarnation, whereby Christ as man can be said to be taken from among the people, and in the covenant of redemption, whereby the Father appoints the Son as Mediator, and the Son willingly accepts the office. In this context, Owen does not hesitate to see

---

[117] *Works* 13, p. 18.

[118] No manuscript appears to have survived, and none is listed in *Bibliotheca Oweniana*. The nineteenth-century editor of Owen's complete works speculates that it may have been incorporated into 'Exercitation on the Christ's priesthood' in the Hebrews commentary (*Works* 19, pp. 3–259): see his comment in the prefatory note, *Works* 13, p. 2. This is quite possible, but the change in Owen's understanding of God's justice in the late 1640s/early 1650s means that the content would have to have been significantly modified as the Hebrews commentary reflects the later understanding: cf. *Works* 10, p. 205 with Works 19, p. 105.

[119] Owen regards Christ's priesthood as the most important element of Hebrews: see *Works* 19, p. 3.

[120] Ibid., pp. 16–17; cf. *Works* 12, pp. 398–9.

the covenant as constituting the call of Christ to the office, citing Heb. 5:4–6 as evidence.[121] This, of course, merely confirms what was stated earlier, that it is the eternal covenant which is both the causal ground of Christ's priesthood and, therefore, the basic theological structure which defines the nature of that priesthood. Nevertheless, this eternal foundation is only half of the story: at the same time, Owen is careful to maintain the historical and pneumatological dimensions of Christ's ministry by distinguishing this call to the office from its actual inauguration. This distinction is very important because it reflects Owen's refusal to allow the logical and metaphysical problems raised by God's eternity to negate the significance of the historical movement of salvation. This is of great importance when he comes to discuss satisfaction, as the cogency of his rejection of eternal justification and the Grotian alternative depends upon just such a distinction. It is important to note, therefore, that this is a basic pattern running through Owen's theology, and not some kind of *deus ex machina* introduced in controversy to circumvent specific problems.

With regard to Christ's priesthood, Owen sees three moments of 'inauguration': at his conception, where he received fullness of gifts from the Holy Spirit; at his baptism, where he was filled with the Spirit (these two moments apply also to Christ's role as prophet and king); and his special, personal self-dedication to the specific office of priesthood in the so-called 'High Priestly prayer' of Jn. 17.[122] The dynamic nature of Owen's Christology is once again explicit in the notion of historical movement within Christ's role as Mediator: while the causal ground of Christ's mediation lies in the eternal covenant, this does not serve to eclipse the importance of Christ's entry into history – eternity does not swallow up time but instead is necessary in order to give meaning and purpose to Christ's historical person and ministry; thus, the incarnate acts of Christ are important. As noted above, Owen does not devote much time to discussing the common dogmatic distinction of humiliation/exaltation to convey the idea

---

[121] *Works* 19, pp. 152–3.
[122] Ibid., pp. 153–5.

of the historical movement of Christ's mediation, but his emphasis on the threefold office obviously serves the same purpose.

Owen sees the nature of Christ's priesthood as being analogous to that of the Old Testament Levites, consisting of two basic, inseparable elements: sacrifice and the offering of that sacrifice to God, or oblation and intercession as he prefers to call them.[123] That Christ is denominated a priest in the order of Melchisedec is no objection to this basic definition of priesthood, as Owen regards the mysterious king of Salem as a sacrificer (an inference he draws from Gn. 14:20).[124] Indeed, Owen regards sacrifice as of the essence of the priestly office to the extent that, he claims, if there were no need of sacrifice, there would be no need of a priesthood, shown by the absence of priesthood in pre-Fall Eden.[125] This view is reflected in Owen's analysis of Christ's oblation: in terms of its nature it is a bloody sacrifice for sin, and in terms of efficacy it achieves pardon from sin and freedom from the curse.[126] It is sin, therefore, that makes Christ's priesthood necessary. In his commentary on Hebrews, Owen elaborates this picture by analysing the necessity for atonement in terms of a fourfold causality: its meritorious cause is sin; its supreme efficient cause is God himself; its instrumental cause is the curse of the law, as this defines the nature of the separation between God and sinners; and the external cause Satan, as he now holds power over humanity. These four factors therefore define the nature of God's response: sin must be expiated, God's justice must be satisfied, the curse must be removed, and Satan's power must be destroyed.[127] Given the central role played by sin in this scheme, Owen is able to use the sacerdotal office of Christ as further evidence of his view that there would have been no incarnation had there been no sin, and therefore to reinforce the anti-speculative foundations of his Christology.[128]

---

[123] Ibid., p. 195.

[124] Ibid., p. 12.

[125] Ibid., pp. 12, 16–17.

[126] Ibid., p. 195.

[127] *Works* 23, p. 283.

[128] *Works* 19, pp. 21 ff. Owen's position here also allows him to develop a Christological theodicy argument: sin was permitted because the greatest glory of which the original order of things was capable was far inferior to that of which restoration by the incarnation was capable: see *Works* 19, p. 28.

This last point is closely related to Owen's arguments that, given the reality of sin and of God's desire to save, the incarnation of Christ is absolutely necessary and that salvation cannot even theoretically be accomplished by a mere act of God's will. As has already been noted several times, this position is first developed by Owen in *A Dissertation on Divine Justice* (1653), in opposition to the views of the Socinians and certain of the Orthodox.[129] What is important to notice in this context is the way this point once again reinforces the tendency against abstract speculation in Owen's Christology which is evidenced by the way in which he develops his thought so as to retain the integrity of both the eternal and historical dimensions of salvation while clearly pointing out their mutual dependence. While it is true that the eternal covenant provides the causal ground for Christ's mediation, it cannot be interpreted as weakening the importance of the incarnation, or of Christ's historical ministry, because the very being of God which stands behind the covenant requires that the Son assume human flesh if salvation is to be accomplished. Covenant and incarnation are equally vital in the overall soteriological structure.

The basis for the necessity of incarnation in the need to deal objectively with human sin points towards the fundamental difference between Christ's priesthood and that of any other human priest: unlike his human antecedents, Christ is both the sacrificer and the sacrifice. Owen makes this point by turning to the elements which constitute a sacrifice: adduction, or the bringing of the offering to the place of sacrifice; mactation, or the slaughtering of the offering, which was itself subdivided into the laying on of sins and the sprinkling of blood; and the burning of the sacrifice.[130] To the first element correspond Christ's going up to Jerusalem, his going to Gethsemane, and his prayers and sufferings in the Garden. To the second and third elements corresponds his death on the cross, which constituted in a single act the many separate acts of the Levitical sacrifices. Finally, as the Levitical

---

[129]   See Ch. 3; also Trueman, 'Owen's *Dissertation on Divine Justice*'.
[130]   *Works* 19, pp. 155–6.

high priest entered the Holy of Holies, so Christ now goes before God on behalf of sinners, uniting in one person the offering and the one who offers.[131] This structure of oblation is paralleled, as one would expect given the unity of the office, by Owen's analysis of Christ's intercession: begun on earth, with oral prayers, it now continues now in heaven in a virtual, or real sense, whereby Christ directly intercedes with the Father in a transcendent way without the use of language.[132] Once again, the notion of historical movement is not swallowed up by, or radically subordinated to, the eternal dimensions of salvation but rather helps to focus and define Christ's role as Mediator.

Given all that has been said so far concerning both the eternal causal ground of Christ's mediation in the covenant of redemption, and the historical movement within his incarnate life as Mediator, it should be no surprise that it is the interrelationship between the eternal and the historical which provides the real key to understanding the sacerdotal office. Again, this is no new theme in Owen's theology: in his reflections on the nature of theology, in his doctrine of God, and in his development of basic Christological structures, we have seen a consistent effort both to distinguish and to correlate eternity and time. This is most clearly evident in Owen's consistent Christocentrism, his constant emphasis upon God manifest in the flesh as the centre of Christian theology.

The priesthood of Christ is, of course, no exception to this, and it is vital that the end of Christ's priesthood should not be divorced or considered in isolation from either its cause in the eternal covenant of redemption, or its means in the incarnation and work of Christ. The importance of the cause and means of

---

[131] Ibid., pp. 157–9.

[132] Ibid., p. 196–7. The earthly and heavenly intercession of Christ are fundamentally continuous, the difference lying in the mode not the content: 'The whole matter of words, prayers, and supplications, yea, of internal conceptions of the mind formed into prayers, is but accidental unto intercession, attending the state and condition of him that intercedes. The real entire nature of it consists in the presentation of such things as may prevail in the way of motive or procuring cause with respect unto the things interceded for. And such do we affirm the intercession of Christ as our high priest in heaven to be.' *Works* 19, p. 197.

Christ's priesthood has already been demonstrated, and so all that remains is to see how they relate to the end: salvation.

On one level, the answer to this question is very simple: the covenant of redemption contains conditions which, when fulfilled, lead to the salvation of the elect; the obedient oblation and intercession of Christ are those conditions; therefore, when these have been fulfilled, the elect are saved.[133] The covenant serves to provide a unity to the mediatorial acts, and thus to the priesthood of Christ: all aspects of his priesthood are to be understood as part of the fulfilment of the conditions stipulated in the covenant and thus as united both in their cause and in their end.[134] This understanding of Christ's priesthood is reflected in Owen's emphasis upon the unity of Christ's oblation and intercession: Christ both dies and intercedes for the same group of people, the elect.[135] This is extremely important for an understanding of how Owen relates Christ's death to the overall soteriological structure: Christ's death can only be understood correctly if it is set within the whole context of the covenant of redemption and within the whole context of Christ's priesthood; indeed, to attempt to isolate the salvific nature of Christ's death from this

---

[133] E.g. *Works* 10, pp. 168 ff.

[134] 'The call of Christ unto his offices of king, priest, and prophet, as it respects the authority and love of the Father, was but one and the same. He had not a distinct call unto each office, but was at once called unto them all, as he was the Son of God sent and anointed to be the Mediator between God and men. The offices themselves, the gifts and graces to be exercised in them, their powers, acts, and duties, were distinct, but his call unto them all was the same.' *Works* 19, p. 182. To point to the fundamental unity of purpose behind Owen's conception of Christ as Mediator is not to argue, following Clifford, that Owen's theology is driven by a 'one-end teleology' but to point to the conceptual unity which the covenant (and not Aristotle) provides. Indeed, Aristotle, not being a covenant theologian, is conspicuous by his absence from much of what Owen has to say about the unity provided by the covenant. For a critique of Clifford, see Appendix One below.

[135] 'His intercession in heaven is nothing but a continued oblation of himself. So that whatsoever Christ impetrated, merited, or obtained by his death and passion, must be infallibly applied unto and bestowed upon them for whom he intended to obtain it; or else his intercession is vain, he is not heard in the prayers of his mediatorship . . . We must not so disjoin the offices of Christ's mediatorship, that one of them may be versated about some towards whom he exerciseth not the other; much less ought we so to separate the several acts of the same office.' *Works* 10, pp. 90–1.

overall framework, is to make a speculative theological move in which Owen himself never indulges.[136]

Owen finds justification for this view of the unity of oblation and intercession in the Old Testament Levitical priesthood, which he regards as a type of Christ.[137] While the Levitical priests had to perform a variety of procedures during sacrifices, Owen regards this as God's accommodation to earthly limitations which prevents the whole richness of Christ's priestly acts from being represented by a single type.[138] This unity is also expressed in relation to the particularity of Old Testament sacrifices:

> The blood was offered [by the Levites] . . . for the people of God, the church, the whole congregation. And as the high priest herein bore the person of Christ, so did this people of all the elect of God, who were represented in them and by them. It was that people, and not the whole world, that the high priest offered for; and it is the elect people alone for whom our great high priest did offer and doth intercede.[139]

Thus, Owen's profound sense of the continuity between the Old and New Testaments, and the typical–antitypical relation of Levitical sacrifice to that of Christ, provides a further confirmation of the particularity of the atonement. As the Levites only offered sacrifices for the people of Israel, so Christ only offers for the church. Of course, it is self-evident that this aspect of Owen's argument does not operate as an autonomous line of theological reasoning in support of the atonement's particularity but does itself stand in relation to the covenant of redemption as its ultimate principle of being. Levitical sacrifices are particular in scope because the sacrifice of Christ, which they foreshadow and upon which they depend, is particular. What is important is that, in the order of knowing, they can be given a certain logical priority over, and an interpretive role in, the understanding of Christ's own sacrifice. Seeing such a close relationship between Levitical sacrifice and Christ's priesthood is scarcely innovative – it would seem

---

[136] Thus, modern questions about 'limited atonement' which take no account of the Trinitarian framework of redemption would be, in a seventeenth-century context, highly speculative.

[137] *Works* 19, pp. 159–60.

[138] *Works* 23, p. 231.

[139] Ibid., p. 232.

to be essential to any credible interpretation of the book of Hebrews – and it cannot be claimed as an example of the intrusion of Aristotelian metaphysics into theology; yet it plays a significant role in Owen's formulation of limited atonement. Here, it is not metaphysical concerns but the biblical–historical focus so typical of Owen's thought which is again of the utmost importance, this time as it touches on the hermeneutical importance of understanding Christ's sacerdotal office against the background of the Levitical priesthood.

Despite this clear, antispeculative, historically oriented and biblically grounded approach to Christ's priesthood, it is here, in the oblation and intercession of Christ, that it is argued by some that Owen's theology is at its most speculative in its emphasis upon the nature of the efficiency and, therefore, the particularity of Christ's work as Saviour.[140] These claims focus on particular aspects of Owen's formulation of Christ's priesthood, to which we shall turn in the next chapter. Nevertheless, it is worthwhile noting that the basic structures which we have so far delineated as providing the theological context and basic shape of that priesthood are remarkable for their non-speculative nature: the covenant of redemption, which cannot be understood as logically prior to the existence of sin, represents the causal ground of Christ's mediation, and thus of his priesthood, and is itself the result of reflection upon the Trinitarian implications of an Augustinian understanding of predestination; the necessity of incarnation, given both the reality of sin and God's desire to save, prevents the kind of radical voluntarism that serves to eclipse, or at least weaken, the importance of the incarnate person of Christ for salvation; the crucial importance of the historical movement within Owen's Christology serves to underline the vital importance of Christ's incarnate life and ministry to the overall economy of salvation; and Owen's use of the biblical teaching on priesthood as typical of the priesthood of Christ. In terms of its basic foundations at least, the priesthood of Christ hardly represents wild, unbiblical speculation.

These then are the basic structures that inform Owen's under-

---

[140]   E.g. Clifford, *Atonement and Justification, passim.*

standing of Christ's priesthood: doctrinally, the Trinitarian determination of the office of Mediator; biblically and historically, the contextualization of Christ's ministry against the backcloth of Old Testament teaching on priests and priesthood. The obvious inference from this, and one which pervades Owen's work, is that the death of Christ cannot be understood in isolation but must be understood within the framework of mediation which is defined by the covenant of redemption and the threefold office, particularly that part which refers to Christ's priesthood. This point is vital as a preliminary to a correct understanding of the explicit point of conflict between Owen and his great opponent, Richard Baxter, over Christ's death which we shall examine in the next chapter.

Conclusion

In opposition to heretical positions which sought to deny the orthodox doctrine of Christ's person and work, Owen's christological reflections represent a restatement of orthodox Christology which stands in fundamental continuity with the Reformed tradition, particularly in its use of the so-called *extra calvinisticum* and of the threefold office of Christ. Nevertheless, Owen's Christology does not simply use the Reformed tradition, but also utilizes numerous concepts, of which the *extra calvinisticum* is in fact one, from the broader Western tradition, such as the anhypostatic nature of Christ's humanity and the importance of the order of Trinitarian procession for establishing various Christological points, from the relationship of Christ to revelation, to Owen's so-called Spirit-Christology. As in his reflections upon the principles of theology and upon the doctrine of God, it is quite clear from his statements on Christology that Owen's theology cannot be understood simply in terms of its narrow seventeenth-century context but that we must also take into account medieval and patristic sources.

What is perhaps more significant from a theological viewpoint, however, is not the sources of Owen's Christology, but the rigorous way in which this is related to its causal foundation in the covenant of redemption. Of course, Owen's emphasis upon the *extra calvinisticum*, the resulting Spirit-Christology, and his discussions of Christ's threefold office, with their emphasis upon historical movement, serve to prevent a complete and radical subordination of the historical Christ to the eternal decree. What emerges is a Christology which is decisively shaped by the intra-trinitarian relations defined by the covenant of redemption and which preserves, both in its historical and eternal dimensions, the thoroughgoing Trinitarian emphasis found in Owen's doctrine of God. It is in the context of this covenant that his understanding of Christ as Mediator is defined and thus within this same context that all aspects of that mediatorship, humiliation and exaltation, and Christ's respective roles as prophet, priest, and king are to be understood. Indeed, to divorce any of these from their causal ground in the covenant of redemption is to do violence to the structure of Owen's thought and to cut a key doctrine free from its theological moorings. It is with this in mind that the most controversial aspect of Owen's Christology, his understanding of atonement, must be approached.

Five

The Nature of Satisfaction

Introduction

At the heart of Owen's discussion of Christ's priestly office, and at the heart of negative critiques of Owen's thought, lies the problem of Christ's satisfaction. The problem in its seventeenth-century context focused on two separate, but related points: the way in which Christ could be said to have died for all (if indeed he could be said to have done so); and the relationship between what Christ suffered on the cross and the penalty due to sinners under the law. The two points are ultimately very closely connected, and analysis of Owen's treatment of these issues will reveal the common doctrinal foundation which lies behind his thinking on both.

The Sufficiency of the Atonement

The Christological context

While most of Owen's work on the atonement focuses on the efficiency and intent of the work of Christ, it is worthwhile spending a little time reflecting on his understanding of its sufficiency, if only to clarify the foundations of his thinking on this point. There is, of course, a great temptation to move straight to citations of various proof texts to establish Owen's view on this issue, but such a move is scarcely adequate in that it removes these isolated statements from their context within Owen's thought, within contemporary debate, and within the Western tradition of discussion of the sufficiency of Christ's work.

The commonplace Western distinction regarding the relationship of the sufficiency of Christ's work to its efficiency was provided by Peter Lombard in his *Four Books of Sentences*, where he described Christ's satisfaction as sufficient for all but efficient only for the elect.[1] In context, this distinction can be seen as an attempt to relate an Anselmic understanding of satisfaction, which makes Christ's work of infinite value by virtue of the hypostatic union of the divine and human natures, to the problem of why all are not saved. This is important, because it points clearly to the fact that the distinction itself stands in close relation to broader Christological concerns which determine its function and meaning. It is not considerations internal to the person of Christ that make his satisfaction effective for the salvation of any given individual person, but the salvific will of God.

In seventeenth century Reformed theology, basically the same connection between Christ's person and the sufficiency of satisfaction is found in the Canons of Dordt, where its infinite sufficiency is regarded as a corollary of the hypostatic union.[2] In the English Reformed context the same is true, for example, of the theology of James Ussher.[3] Such a view is closely

---

[1] 'Christus ergo est sacerdos, idemque et hostia pretium nostrae reconciliationis; qui se in ara crucis non diabolo, sed Trinitati obtulit pro omnibus, quantum ad pretii sufficientiam; sed pro electis tantum quantum ad efficaciam, quia praedestinatis tantum salutem effecit.' *IV Libri Sententiarum* 3.20.3. The distinction is oft cited, but seldom, if ever, with any reference to the primary source: see, for example, R. T. Kendall, *Calvin and English Calvinism*, p. 16.

[2] 'III. Haec mors Filii Dei est unica et perfectissima pro peccatis victima et satisfactio, infiniti valoris et pretii, abunde sufficiens ad totius mundi peccata expianda. IV. Ideo autem haec mors tanti est valoris et pretii, quia persona, quae eam subiit, non tantum est verus et perfecte sanctus homo, sed etiam unigenitus Dei Filius, ejusdem aeternae et infinitae cum Patre et Spiritu S. Essentiae, qualem nostrum Servatorem esse oportebat. Deinde, quia mors ipsius fuit conjuncta cum sensu irae Dei et maledictionis, quam nos peccatis nostris eramus commeriti.' Schaff, *The Creeds of Christendom* 3, p. 561.

[3] 'Although they were not everlasting, yet in regard of the worthiness of the person who suffered them, they were equivalent to everlasting torments; forasmuch as not a bare man, nor an Angell did suffer them, but the eternall Son of God, (though not in his Godhead, but in our nature which he assumed) his Person, Majesty, Deity, Goodnesse, Justice, Righteousnesse, being every way infinite and eternall, made that

connected to the Reformed understanding of the communication of properties, whereby predicates that find their principle
in one specific nature can yet be predicated of the acts of the
whole person. This point is made quite clear in Thomas Goodwin's discussion of the worth of Christ's satisfaction:

> And though the human nature (which is itself finite) be the *principium
> quo*, and the instrument by which and in which the second person doth
> all that he doth; and therefore answerably the physical being of those
> actions is but finite *in genere entis*, yet all those articles being attributed
> to the person who is *principium quod*, the principle which doth, and unto
> which all is to be ascribed (for *actiones sunt suppositorum*, actions are
> attributed to the persons, because that is said only to subsist), therefore
> the moral estimation of them is from the worth of the person that
> performs them. And thus though the immediate principle, the human
> nature, be finite, yet the radical principle, the person, is infinite.[4]

The important point to note here is that the value of Christ's
death in this context is based upon the person of Christ, and not
upon any will of God that might lie behind his work. It is simply
by virtue of the fact that Christ is the incarnation of the infinite
God that the finite physical sufferings of his finite human nature
gain infinite value. Such infinite sufficiency therefore says nothing about the nature or limits of God's salvific will. This latter
issue is raised in an acute form by various English writers in the
seventeenth century who wish to go beyond the so-called 'internal sufficiency' of the atonement and to give the universal sufficiency a positive connection with the world of the non-elect. One
example of this is provided by John Davenant, an English
representative at Dordt, who argues that to restrict the atonement's universality to a mere sufficiency, with no positive con-

---

Footnote 3 (*continued*) which he suffered of no lesse force and value then eternall
torments upon others, yea, even upon all the world besides. For even as the death of a
Prince (being but a man, and a sinfull man) is of more reckoning then the death of an
Army of other men, because he is the Prince; much more shall the death and sufferings
of the Son of God the Prince of all Princes, not finite but every way infinite, and without
sin; much more I say shall that be of more reckoning with his Father, then the sufferings
of all the world, and the time of his sufferings of more value (for the worthinesse of his
person) then if all the men in the world had suffered for ever and ever.' *A Body of
Divinitie*, pp. 173–4.

[4] Goodwin, *Works* 5, p. 105.

nection to a an equally universal aspect in God's will to save, is simply to make meaningless distinctions.[5]

Owen on sufficiency and atonement

Since Owen's theology incorporates an orthodox Christology into an economy of salvation which finds its causal ground in the covenant of redemption, it is hardly surprising to find that he argues for an infinite sufficiency in the atonement while rejecting any unconditional connection between this and God's salvific will. The universalist note is struck on a number of occasions throughout Owen's writings, but he is careful to make clear that this depends specifically, and only, upon the person suffering in line with a Reformed understanding of the communication of properties.[6] Such a view is clearly compatible with the ongoing development of the Reformed tradition throughout the sixteenth and seventeenth centuries.[7] Indeed, for Owen as for Calvin, it is

---

[5]   *A Dissertation on the Death of Christ* (London: Hamilton,1832), pp. 408 ff.

[6]   E.g. 'It was, then, the purpose and intention of God that his Son should offer a sacrifice of infinite worth, value, and dignity, sufficient in itself for the redeeming of all and every man, if it had pleased the Lord to employ it to that purpose . . . This sufficiency of his sacrifice hath a twofold rise: First, The dignity of the person that did offer and was offered. Secondly, The greatness of the pain he endured . . . It was in itself of infinite value and sufficiency to *have been made a price* to have bought and purchased all and every man in the world. That it did formally become a price for any is solely to be ascribed to the purpose of God, intending their purchase and redemption by it.' *Works* 10, pp. 295–6.

[7]   On this issue, see Muller, *Christ and the Decree, passim.* Particularly helpful is his discussion of the mischief done and confusion caused by the way in which some modern scholars persist in imposing on Calvin's thought categories such as 'atonement' which have no precise counterpart in his thinking and which serve merely to cloud the issues: see pp. 34–5. Other works which adopt developmental, as opposed to the unhistorical and anachronistic Barthian, neo-Calvinist, and Amyraldian models of interpretation on this issue include: W. R. Godfrey, 'Tensions Within International Calvinism: The Debate on the Atonement at the Synod of Dordt', unpubl. PhD diss. (Stanford University, 1974); J. H. Rainbow, *The Will of God and the Cross: An Historical and Theological Study of John Calvin's Doctrine of Limited Redemption* (Allison Park: Pickwick, 1990); and, on the related topic of reprobation, D. Sinnema,'The Issue of Reprobation at the Synod of Dordt (1618–19) in Light of the History of this Doctrine', unpubl. PhD diss. (Toronto School of Theology, 1985). The complete failure to engage with any of the increasing flow of material which adopts an historical, developmental approach to the whole subject of Reformed Orthodoxy has seriously undermined the cogency of recent restatements of the old scholarly orthodoxy.

the intercession of Christ set in the whole context of his office of Mediator, as we have seen, that makes this infinite sufficiency efficient for the elect and which provides the unity and continuity between the eternal covenant and the historical economy.[8]

It is worth asking at this point why Owen does not adopt the position of such as Davenant whereby the universal sufficiency of atonement does stand in some positive relation to God's will to save, a view given an even more radically constructive role in the soteriology of Richard Baxter.[9] Clifford argues that this is because of Owen's adherence to Aristotelian teleology, but, as Aristotelian teleology was used in both Arminian and Orthodox systems to produce mutually exclusive positions, and was even elevated by Baxter, Owen's opponent on the nature of atonement, to the level of a theological prolegomenon, this is unlikely.[10] That Baxter does not attack Owen on the issue of teleology is yet further proof that the answer must be found elsewhere. An additional point of interest is that Owen does not apparently adopt the medieval distinction between God's antecedent and consequent salvific wills which one finds in, say, Thomas Aquinas. In this scheme, God antecedently wills that all be saved on condition that they first meet certain criteria necessary for salvation, but he wills that only some (the elect) will actually fulfil this condition. Consequently, he wills the salvation only of some. This distinction is useful to Aquinas. It provides a

---

[8]   Clifford comments that 'For Owen, the atonement is only sufficient for those to whom it is efficient.' *Atonement and Justification*, p. 74. This is true, of course, only if one sets Christ's death within the overall context of the soteriological economy, as Richard Muller does with Calvin's view of atonement, an approach which allows him to comment that, regarding Calvin's theology, '[i]t is superfluous to speak of a hypothetical extent of the efficacy of Christ's work beyond its application.' *Christ and the Decree*, p. 35. Much the same could indeed be said of Baxter's own view of atonement, as universal satisfaction nowhere leads to universal salvation, which, in the overall context of salvation, gives claims about the former a somewhat strained appearance. Indeed, if Owen can be accused of playing with words concerning sufficiency, then surely Baxter is vulnerable to a similar stricture: his claim that 'Christ . . . *died for all*, but not *for all equally*, or with the *same intent, design or purpose*' seems somewhat analogous to the Orwellian dictum that 'All animals are equal, but some are more equal than others.'

[9]   See *Catholick Theologie*, pt. 2, pp. 51 ff; cf. *Universal Redemption, passim.*

[10]   *Atonement and Justification*, Chapter Six *passim*. For a full discussion of this claim, see Appendix One below.

coherent theological framework for interpreting those biblical passages which speak of God willing not the death of a sinner, loving the world, etc. and, set within a system which stresses both the uncoerced causal priority of God over creation and a vigorous Augustinian anthropology, it cannot slip into semi-Pelagianism.[11] The distinction was adopted by sixteenth- and seventeenth-century theologians, including Orthodox, such as Zanchi, and Arminians, including Arminius himself who deployed it within a system that significantly modified the original Thomist understanding of God and of anthropology.[12]

In Owen's mind there was a definite connection between this distinction between God's antecedent and salvific wills, and a consequent Arminianism, although he regarded the Arminian use to which the term was put as a perversion of its original purpose. For this reason, it would seem, and not out of conscious disagreement with other Reformed theologians, Owen avoided such terminology in order to give no quarter to such abuse.[13] In fact, in his emphasis upon the universal sufficiency of the atonement as the basis for the universal offer of the gospel he comes very close to the original Thomist distinction while yet being very careful to avoid making any explicit connection with God's will.[14]

---

[11] *ST* 1a.19.6; 1a.23.4.

[12] Muller, *Arminius*, pp. 185 ff.

[13] 'Many more effectual reasons are produced by our divines for the denial of this natural affection in God, in the resolution of the Arminian distinction (I call it so, as now by them abused) of God's antecedent and consequent will, to whom the learned may repair for satisfaction.' *Works* 10, p. 323.

[14] The following passage is worth quoting in full in this connection: '[The oblation of Christ] was every way able and perfectly sufficient to redeem, justify, and reconcile, and save all the sinners in the world, and to satisfy the justice of God for all the sins of mankind, and to bring them every one to everlasting glory. Now this fulness and sufficiency of the merit of Christ is a foundation unto two things: First, The general publishing of the gospel unto "all nations" . . . because the way of salvation is wide enough for all to walk in. If there were a thousand worlds, the gospel of Christ might, upon this ground, be preached to them all, there being enough in Christ for the salvation of them all, if so be they will derive virtue from him by touching him in faith.' *Works* 10, p. 297. The conditional structure of Owen's argument here parallels the Thomist distinction of antecedent/consequent will but without the language of willing being used. In the context of mid-seventeenth-century England, it would appear that Owen regarded such language as too open to abuse.

The vital clue to understanding what lies behind Owen's thinking on this issue is provided by his statement in *The Death of Death*: '[I]t is denied that the blood of Christ was a sufficient price and ransom for all and every one, not because it was not sufficient, but because it was not a ransom.'[15] It is the character of Christ's death as *ransom* that gives it its particularity, and thus it is the thing that makes it a ransom which really lies behind its limited efficiency. What is this? Is it Aristotelian teleology? No – in the light of all that has been said throughout this book, it should come as no surprise that it is the intratrinitarian covenant of redemption, not Aristotelian teleology, that brings Christ's death into positive relation to God's will to save: Christ's death is part of his priesthood; his priesthood is part of his mediatorial office; and the mediatorial office is created and defined by the covenant of redemption. This is obvious from all that was said concerning the intratrinitarian covenant relations and the constitution of the Mediator,[16] and the connection is made explicit by Owen in his *Of the Death of Christ*, while discussing a closely related doctrinal point.[17] While Christ's suffering is of infinite worth simply by virtue of the fact that he is God incarnate, it has relevance to salvation only as Christ is Mediator, and so his death, in terms of its salvific efficacy, must be set within the theological context of his mediation, i.e. within the economy of salvation based upon, and determined by, the covenant of redemption.

This brings us to the real root of the difference between Owen and others such as Baxter. Baxter, while naturally suspicious of making distinctions between decrees of God, given God's utter simplicity, argues using the Thomist terminology that Christ dies to gain salvation antecedently for all and consequently for those who will believe.[18] Thus, the death of Christ, in terms of its antecedent universal purpose, has logical priority over, and is thus separable from, the decree of election, while Baxter's careful

---

[15] *Works* 10, p. 296.
[16] See Chs. 3 and 4 above.
[17] *Works* 10, p. 441. For a discussion of this, see below, 'The Nature of Christ's Satisfaction'.
[18] *Methodus Theologiae*, 3a.1, dist. 16 (pp. 55–7).

formulation of the latter, in conjunction with his Augustinian anthropology, prevents him from slipping into Arminianism.[19] In Owen, this is not the case: as we have seen, the covenant of redemption includes both the appointment of Christ as Mediator and an essential particularity in its reference to the elect, a particularity which is strengthened by its close connection to the covenant of grace. This is what makes Christ's death a payment or satisfaction for sin and what prevents the universal sufficiency of Christ's oblation from having any straightforward positive connection, even in an antecedent sense, with God's will to save. It is thus a difference in the construction of the relationship between the covenant of redemption and election which is the underlying cause of the difference here between Owen and Baxter.

The Nature of Christ's Suffering

The polemical background

In his teaching on Christ's satisfaction there is one concern which lies behind almost everything Owen has to say and which exerts a profound influence on his thinking in this area: his need to refute the Socinian objection that the whole notion of satisfaction for sin is antithetical to the notion of God's free forgiveness. If salvation is earned, according to the Socinians, then it is not an act of grace.

The argument had received its most sophisticated and significant expression in Faustus Socinus' masterpiece, *De Jesu Christo Servatore*.[20] In a stimulating analysis of this work, Alan Gomes has outlined Socinus's grounds for rejecting satisfaction in terms of four categories: theological, exegetical, logical, and moral.[21] Of these, the objections of most immediate significance to understanding Owen are those which are classified as logical.

---

[19] *Catholick Theologie* Pt. 1, p. 123; cf. the separation of the appointment of Christ as Mediator and the decree of election noted in Baxter's theology in Ch. 3 above.
[20] Cracow, 1594.
[21] Alan W. Gomes, '*De Jesu Christo Servatore*: Faustus Socinus on the Satisfaction of Christ', *WTJ* 55 (1993), 209–31.

According to Socinus, the notion of satisfaction is incoherent because, first, as soon as a debt is paid, it ceases to exist, and so there is no place left for remission,[22] and, second, Christ's death can in no way be an equivalent for the debt owed because every sinner is obligated to endure eternal death; Christ, as one individual, could only undergo one death.[23]

These objections strike at the very heart of the Orthodox understanding of the relationship of Christ's death to salvation, and provide part of the background to the development of English views on atonement in the seventeenth century, particularly in terms of Richard Baxter's critique of the Orthodox position on Christ's death as that position was espoused by, amongst others, John Owen. First, however, there is a further aspect of the seventeenth-century background which must be understood: the impact of Antinomian ideas on the Reformed view of atonement.

Two leading examples of the way in which basically Orthodox theological structures could be developed in an Antinomian direction are provided by the theological writings of Tobias Crisp (1600–42) and John Saltmarsh (*c.* 1612–47).[24] In Crisp's writings, we have an underlying Orthodox foundation upon which certain distinctive emphases are built. These concern the timing of justification and the role of faith, both of which in turn tie in with his understanding of Christ's death, which Crisp understood to be the punishment for human sin. The key element in his argument here is that human sin is really transacted upon Christ, and that when God punishes Christ, he is actually punishing human sins in a real sense.[25] As a corollary of this doctrine, Crisp then

---

[22] 'Neque enim illi remittitur, alius vero pro eo satisfacit; nihil dixeris. Nam quid opus est remissione, aut quomodo ea consistere potest, ubi nullum est amplius, ubi iam plene pro ipso satisfactum est.' De Jesu Christo Servatore 3.2, p. 240.

[23] *De Jesu Christo Servatore* 3.3, pp. 250–1.

[24] On Crisp and Saltmarsh, see P. Toon, *Hypercalvinism* (London: Olive Tree, 1967); C. Daniel 'Hypercalvinism and John Gill' (unpubl. PhD diss., University of Edinburgh, 1983); Boersma, *A Hot Peppercorn*.

[25] 'God not only inflicted the desert of sin on Christ, in wounding him for it, but also he laid even iniquity itself on him; I mean the iniquity of his elect.' Tobias Crisp, *Christ Alone Exalted* 1, p. 267; 'It is iniquity itself, even the sins themselves of those for whom God intends shall reap benefit by Christ, that are laid on him.' Ibid., p. 269.

developed a doctrine of justification which placed justification emphatically before faith in the order of salvation.[26] In the resulting scheme, faith serves not as a means of grasping Christ's righteousness nor as any kind of cause of justification, but as a means of manifesting prior justification in Christ.[27] The same kind of emphases are evident in Saltmarsh, whose radically Christocentric approach to the covenant leads to a similar stress on the objective fulfilment of salvation in Christ and a consequent diminution of emphasis upon the human response.[28] Saltmarsh too regards faith as manifesting what is already true of the elect through the person and work of Christ.[29] The shift is perhaps not as rationalistic, nor as radical, as it has sometimes been portrayed, but it does represent one way in which the Orthodox theory of atonement could be used to exert a distinctive influence on other areas of theology. While Socinian attacks on the satisfaction theory of atonement pointed to the problem of placing it in coherent relation to God's attributes of justice and

---

[26] '[T]here is not now a new thing to be done by the Lord in the transferring the sins of believers to Christ; as if, when they begin to be called out of darkness into marvellous light, just then God begins to transfer sin from them, and lay it upon Christ; so that the act of God's laying sin upon him, is not a continued act, but what he hath done long before.' *Christ Alone Exalted* 1, p. 268.

[27] '[Faith] serves for the manifestation of that justification which Christ puts upon a person by himself alone: that you by believing on him, may have the declaration, and manifestation of your justification.' *Christ Alone Exalted* 1, p. 91.

[28] 'All the ground of a beleevers righteousnesse and salvation, and exemption from the Law, sin and the curse, is from the nature, office, and transaction or work of Christ, and Gods accounting, or imputing; Christ stood clothed in our nature, betwixt God and man, and in that with all the sins of beleevers upon him, God having laid on him the iniquities of us all: In his Office he obeyed, suffered, satisfied, and offered up himself, and now sits as a Mediator to perpetuate or make his sacrifice, obedience, suffering, and righteousnesse everlasting; and thus bringing in everlasting righteousnesse: And God he accounts, reckons or imputes all that is done in our nature, as done by us, calling things that are not, as if they were; and in his person, as in our person: And thus he is made sin for us who knew no sin, that we might be made the righteousnesse of God in him.' *Free Grace* (London, 1646), p. 143; 'The Covenant that is called the new covenant that God makes with his now under the Gospel, is all on his own part, without anything on mans; he makes himself ours, and makes us his; all is of his own doing.' *Free Grace*, p. 152.

[29] 'Christ hath taken away all sin by his offering up one sacrifice once for all . . . and that faith in the believer doth nothing, no not instrumentally as to justification, but as by way of revelation and manifestation of that justification.' J. Saltmarsh, *Sparkles of Glory* (London: Huntington, 1811), pp. 161–2.

mercy, the developments evidenced in Crisp's writings point to the problems of relating the theory to the nature of individual salvation and the way it could be used to weaken the stress on (though not, at least in Crisp's case, the necessity of) personal response.[30] Moreover, this development in the understanding of the order of salvation and of faith in relation to the satisfaction theory of the atonement was not confined to the radical fringes of Reformed theology. Curt Daniel cites Bunyan, Witsius, Hoornbeck, Twisse, Pemble, Chauncey, and Ames as advocating the doctrine of eternal justification, and Hans Boersma has also shown that the placement of justification prior to faith was far from uncommon in English Reformed Orthodoxy.[31] In the case of Twisse the doctrine is explicitly taught in his magisterial work, *Vindiciae Gratiae*, but is closely related to the causal structure of the order of salvation, thus precluding any notion that it might undermine the importance of human faith.[32]

---

[30] Eternal justification, while moving yet another part of the order of salvation into eternity, still does not, at least in the theology of Crisp, undermine the importance of personal faith and thus of the historical dimension of salvation, e.g. 'There is no person under heaven shall be saved till he have believed.' *Christ Alone Exalted* 1, p. 90. Furthermore, while it is true that critiques of the later hypercalvinism which the theology of Crisp adumbrated at numerous points have generally stressed the role of logic and inference within the hypercalvinistic systems (see Toon, *Hypercalvinism*, pp. 146–8; Daniel, *Hypercalvinism and John Gill*, pp. 306–7, 768 ff.), it must nevertheless not be forgotten that while many so-called hypercalvinists, such as Crisp and, from a later era, John Gill, were primarily scriptural exegetes, there is, as yet, no major study of hypercalvinist exegesis by which such claims about their incipient rationalism can be evaluated. Gill in particular deserves study in this regard, as one of the foremost Hebraists of his day, and the author of one of the most ambitious commentaries on the whole Bible ever written. Indeed, his proficiency in Hebrew earned him a DD from the University of Aberdeen, an honour which he could not receive in his own country because of his non-conformity.

[31] Daniel, 'Hypercalvinism and John Gill', p. 305; Boersma, *A Hot Peppercorn*, Pt. 3 *passim*.

[32] 'Quare ante fidem, haec Christis justitia nostra fuit, quatenus ex intentione Dei Patris et Christi Mediatoris pro nobis praestita; et quia pro nobis praestita, ideo suo tempore Deus, daturus est nobis et gratiam cujuscunque generis, ipsamque etiam fidem inter alias, et tandem aliquando caelestis gloriae coronam. Sed adveniente fide, quam in cordibus nostris Spiritus Sanctus accendit, tum demum agnoscitur et percipitur hic amor Dei erga nos in Christo Jesu. Unde dicitur justitia Christi imputari nobis per fidem, quia non nisi per fidem dignoscitur, a Deo nobis imputari: et tum demum justificari dicimur, ejus generis justificatione, atque absolutione a peccatis nostris, quae pacem ingenerat conscientiis nostris.' *Vindiciae Gratiae* 1.2.25, p. 197.

These two strands, then, of the Socinian criticism of the notion of atonement and of the Orthodox restructuring of the order of salvation, provide the necessary backcloth to Owen's own development of the doctrine of satisfaction which inevitably had to take account of both if it was to be at all adequate or coherent in its seventeenth-century context. There is still, however, a third dimension to the whole debate, and that is the response of Hugo Grotius to the Socinian critique, a response which was picked up by Richard Baxter and used to attack both the Socinian criticism and the Orthodox understanding of Christ's satisfaction.

Grotius's critique and Owen's response

Well before Owen came to write on the death of Christ, the Socinian critique of the satisfaction theory of atonement had already met with vigorous responses from Protestants. One of the most important of these was that of the Dutch theologian Hugo Grotius (1583–1645), both because of the clever way in which it outmanoeuvred Socinus and because of its introduction of a key distinction into the notion of satisfaction, which in the hands of Baxter was to be given a wider reference. In *A Defence of the Catholic Faith concerning the Satisfaction of Christ against Faustus Socinus* (1617), Grotius argued for the so-called governmental theory of atonement.[33] Central to his theory was a distinction he made between the different ways of paying a debt. Debts could be paid by giving the creditor either exactly what was owed, or something of a different kind which was deemed to be an equivalent.[34] The distinction was hardly a radical innova-

---

[33] The text I have used for the *Defensio* is that contained in volume 3 of his *Opera omnia theologica* (Amsterdam, 1679), hereafter *Opera* 3. The work exists in a good English translation as, *A Defence of the Catholic Faith*, trans. F. H. Foster (Andover: Draper, 1889).

[34] 'Ubi ergo idem solvitur aut a debitore, aut ab alio nomine debitoris, nulla contingit remissio: nihil enim circa debitum agit creditor, aut rector. Quare si quis poenam pertulerit quam debet, liberatio hic erit, remissio non erit . . . Alia vero quaevis solutio ipso facto non liberat, puta si aliud quam quod in obligatione est, solvatur . . . Sed necesse est actum aliquem accedere creditoris aut rectoris, qui actus recte et usitate remissio appellatur. Talis autem solutio quae aut admitti aut recusari potest, admissa in jure, speciale habet nomen satisfactionis, quae interdum solutioni strictius sumptae opponitur.' *Opera* 3, p. 319.

tion, as such a procedure regarding debt was recognized in Roman law.[35] What Grotius did was to apply this concept to the satisfaction wrought by Christ, arguing that Christ paid the debt for human sin by offering a satisfactory equivalent, a *solutio tantidem*.[36] For Grotius, understanding Christ's satisfaction in this way allows him to reject the Socinian criticisms of the satisfaction theory of atonement: in denying the automatic equivalence of humanity's debt and Christ's satisfaction, he manages to circumvent the problems which Socinus argued lay at the heart of the orthodox satisfaction theory. First, satisfaction and remission are not radically opposed: the acceptation of Christ's satisfaction as equivalent payment for human sin is based not on anything inherent in the satisfaction itself but upon a separate act of God's loving will which graciously declares that it may stand as equivalent payment for human sin.[37] Secondly in response to Socinian objections that, if the debt is paid, then release from the debt must occur immediately afterward, Grotius is able to point out that *solutio tantidem* places the release from debt entirely in the hands of the one who pays and of the creditor, and they are free to set up whatever conditions or timetable for the release of the actual debtor they choose, a point which Grotius then uses as support for his Arminian soteriology.[38] It is

---

[35] E.g. *Code of Justinian* VIII. xliii.

[36] 'At Christus *lytron* [*redemptionem*] dedit vitam suam pro nobi . . . Et pretio empti, hoc est, solutione aliqua liberati sumus . . . Non est ergo hic acceptilatio: non est etiam solutio rei ipsius debitae, quae ipso facto liberet; nostra enim mors et quidem aeterna erat in obligatione; non est etiam novatio aut delegatio; neque enim post nos liberatos alid simile debitum aut debitor alius succedit: sed est remissio antecedente satisfactione . . .' *Opera* 3, p. 320.

[37] This is quite clear from Grotius's explication of the analogous situation of debts between humans: 'Est enim in obligatione afflictio ipsius qui deliquit: unde dici solet, noxam caput sequi: quod in aliis quoque obligationibus ad factum mere personalibus videre est, ut in sponsalium contractu, et in obligatione operarum officialium . . . In his enim omnibus, si alius solvat, ipso facto liberatio non sequetur, quia simul aliud solvitur. Quare ut ex poena unius alteri liberatio contingat, actus quidam rectoris debet intercedere: Lex enim ipsum qui deliquit puniri imperat. Hic actus respectu legis est relaxatio sive dispensatio, respectu debitoris remissio.' *Opera* 3, p. 319.

[38] 'At ubi alius solvit pro debitore, et ubi aliud solvitur quam quod debebatur, hic ad liberationem duplex actus voluntatis requiritur. Nam et qui solvit hoc velle debet ut debitor liberetur, alioqui non contingit liberatio . . . et alterius rei pro altera solutionem debet creditor aut rector velle admittere. Quare cum unusquisque actui ex sua voluntate

also worth noting here that this whole idea is obviously suggestive as a basis for criticizing doctrines of eternal justification, a
fact, as we shall see, that is not lost on Richard Baxter.

When Owen came to write *The Death of Death* (1647) he
addressed this issue of the precise relationship between the nature
of Christ's satisfaction and the nature of humanity's debt in some
detail. While not mentioning Grotius by name, there can be no
doubt that it is his argument which Owen is addressing and that
he is the person alluded to at various points in the relevant
passages.[39] Underlying Owen's arguments at this point is his clear
belief that Grotius has conceded too much to the Socinian cause
by allowing that their objections have some strength. For Owen,
the Socinian arguments can be adequately refuted without having to resort to a significant reconstruction of the orthodox
theory of satisfaction.

Owen has no doubt that Christ's satisfaction is *solutio eiusdem*
and he sees no problem in holding this view in the face of the
various Socinian objections. He does not, for example, regard
this as raising a question concerning the chronological relationship between satisfaction and remission. While the two are logically inseparable, they do occur at separate points in time: it is
not until individuals receive Christ's righteousness through faith
that their sins are actually remitted. To prove his point, he uses
the analogy of a prisoner for whom a ransom has been paid: until
the warrant arrives at the prison and the prisoner learns of his
pardon, the freedom purchased is not a reality.[40] The analogy
docs, however, leave the door open to a doctrine of eternal
justification, as it appears to imply that the decisive moment of
faith is simply the point at which believers realize that they have

---

Footnote 38 (*continued*) pendenti legem possit imponere, sicut id quod pure debetur,
novari potest sub conditione . . . ita etiam possunt, is qui solvit pro alio, et is qui rei
alterius pro altera solutionem admittit, pacisci, ut aut statim sequatur remissio, aut in
diem, item aut pure aut sub conditione. Fuit autem et Christi satsifacientis, et Dei
satisfactionem admittentis hic animus ac voluntas, hoc denique pactum et foedus, non
ut Deus statim ipso perpessionis Christi tempore poenas remitteret, sed ut tum demum
id fieret, cum homo vera in Christum Fide ad Deum conversus, supplex veniam
precaretur, accedente etiam Christi apud Patrem advocatione sive intercessione.' *Opera*
3, p. 320.
39 *Works* 10, pp. 268 ff.
40 Ibid., p. 268.

already been pardoned. That Owen rejects this position, however, is quite clear from his late treatise, *The Doctrine of Justification by Faith* (1677), where he points to the vital need of union with Christ, a union effected through faith, in order for Christ's righteousness to be imputed to sinners, and thus for those sinners to be truly forgiven. The basic problem is solved, according to Owen, if one does not attempt to isolate one element of the economy of salvation from another: the death and satisfaction of Christ, and the application of this to the believer, both depend upon God's will, and God's will has arranged that they will happen at two separate moments of time.[41] The distinction parallels similar distinctions such as those between God's eternal decree and its execution in time, and between Christ's death and his intercession. It was noted above that Christ's sacrifice is made efficacious only upon Christ's entry into the Holy of Holies and his intercession before the Father, and that this limited the fruitfulness of discussing that death in isolation from the whole context of priesthood somewhat. The same applies here: Owen does not use Christ's objective satisfaction as some kind of logical axiom which forces him into placing the actual justification of individuals in eternity or at the moment of Christ's death.

As for the argument that satisfaction makes merciful remission a nonsense, Owen points out once again that Christ's satisfaction and the subsequent remission of sins must be understood within the whole framework of salvation: God's grace and mercy lie in his free appointment of Christ as Mediator, his free acceptance of Christ's satisfaction in mankind's stead, and in his free application of Christ's death to us.[42] While Owen does not make it explicit at this point, it should be obvious that these three points rest directly upon the Trinitarian covenant structure which shapes his entire soteriology. Grotius locates the act of God's will which makes Christ's satisfaction a payment for human sin in a position which is logically subsequent to the death of Christ, a position which comports nicely with his Arminian soteriological concerns. Owen, however, locates the act of God's will logically prior to Christ's death, in the covenant of redemption: the act of

---

41 *Works* 5, pp. 216–18.
42 *Works* 10, pp. 268–9.

appointing the Mediator by the Father, and the susception of that office by the Son, are both acts which are entirely free and uncoerced, rooted in grace, love, and mercy. It is only because of this that Christ becomes incarnate and makes satisfaction. That this satisfaction has an intrinsic relation to the debt owed by sinful humanity is still, in terms of its origin, the result of God's grace, and therefore the fact that it saves any given sinner is because that sinner is covered by the covenant.

Baxter's critique and Owen's response

In the context of the mid-seventeenth century, Owen clearly saw no need to adopt the Grotian model of satisfaction in order to counter Socinian objections to atonement and to avoid Antinomian doctrines of justification. Not everyone agreed, however, and his adherence to a doctrine of *solutio eiusdem* provoked the wrath of Richard Baxter who attacked Owen first in his 1649 work, *Aphorismes of Justification*, and again in his *Universal Redemption of Mankind*, a work published posthumously in 1694, but the manuscript of which dated back to 1657.[43] In these works Baxter argued, *contra* Owen, for the Grotian *solutio tantidem* notion.[44]

For Baxter, the major problems with Owen's understanding of satisfaction as *solutio eiusdem* are, first, that the doctrine is indeed vulnerable, *pace* Owen's claims to the contrary, to the Socinian arguments about the mutual exclusivity of satisfaction and remission, and, second, that it also undergirds Antinomianism.[45] Baxter's criticisms of Owen focus on the question of

---

[43] In his preface to the work, Joseph Read states that the transcription of Baxter's notes which went to make up the text for this work was one of the first acts assigned to him when he went to Kidderminster as Baxter's assistant in 1657: see the unpaginated 'To the Reader' at the start of *Universal Redemption* (London, 1694). The work thus dates from the time when the issue was being hotly debated by Owen and Baxter.

[44] It would appear, however, that Baxter's reading of Grotius confirmed and clarified his understanding of satisfaction rather than led him to his convictions: see Boersma, *A Hot Peppercorn*, p. 246 n. 351.

[45] 'Where the proper debt is discharged, or penalty undergone, in Law-Sence by the person himself who was obnoxious, there is no room for pardon to such a Person: But according to the Doctrine which I oppose, the proper debt is discharged, or the penalty undergone, in Law-Sence by the Person himself who was obnoxious: Therefore according

whether Owen's rejection of *solutio tantidem* is based upon a misunderstanding of the term. In *The Death of Death*, Owen interprets the term as referring to a satisfaction which 'is not the same or equivalent unto it [the debt], but only in the gracious acceptation of the creditor'. Baxter has the following to say about this:

> If he mean 'not of equal value', then he fighteth with a shadow; he wrongeth Grotius (for ought I can finde in him) who teacheth no such doctrine. . . . But if he mean that it is not equivalent in procuring its end, *ipso facto*, delivering the debtour without the intervention of a new concession or contract of the creditour, (as *solutio eiusdem* doth) then I confesse *Grotius* is against him; and so am I.[46]

Owen responded to Baxter's criticisms in *Of the Death of Christ* (1650) where he clarified exactly what he meant by *solutio eiusdem*. Owen's argument is based overwhelmingly on references to Scripture rather than on debates concerning the precise meaning of the legal terminology: citing Gal. 3:13, he points out the explicit reference to Christ being made a curse, the same sanction of the law under which sinners are placed; he refers to Rom. 8:3 as the condemning of sin in the flesh, Christ's flesh; he refers to the penalty of sin as being death, Gn. 2:17, and as Christ tasting death, Heb. 2:9; he reads Is. 53 as being a Christological reference to sins being placed upon Christ, and 2 Cor. 5:21 as laying the very punishment due to sinners upon Christ, etc.[47] What is different is that the duration of the penalty is altered with respect to Christ's person: as he is perfect man and infinite God, death cannot hold him and thus he does not perish eternally but is resurrected.[48] This difference in temporal duration Owen refers to as one of the accidents of the punishment which do not effect its essence: 'When I say *the same* [penalty],

---

Footnote 45 (*continued*) to that Doctrine, there is no place for Pardon to such.' *Universal Redemption*, p. 69; '[T]hese two together (that Christ paid the *Idem*, the debt it self and not the value, by personating us in his sufferings, so that in Law Sence, we satisfied in him) are the very foundation of the whole frame of that Religion commonly called *Antinomian*, but much more fitly Antievangelical.' Ibid., p. 80.
[46] *Aphorismes of Justification*, Appendix p. 138.
[47] *Works* 10, pp. 448–9. To point out the basis of Owen's arguments in biblical texts is not, of course, to argue that his position is correct but merely to establish what means he uses to build his case.
[48] Ibid., pp. 269–70, 442.

I mean essentially the same in weight and pressure, though not in all accidents of duration and the like.'[49]

This statement has been ridiculed as using unreal and meaningless Aristotelian distinctions, with David Hume (!) and Bertrand Russell (!!) cited in support.[50] While it is hardly surprising that Owen fails to use the logical procedures of eighteenth-century empiricism or twentieth-century analytic philosophy to rid his theology of its alleged Aristotelian leaven, it is worth pointing out that the presupposition behind the idea which Owen is here trying to convey is simply that, for sinners, the infinite duration of death is the result of humanity's finiteness; this problem is overcome by orthodox notions of Christ as Mediator where the infinite aspects of the debt are resolved, not by an infinite duration of time, but by an infinite divine nature, as we noted above. This is perfectly consistent with the Reformed understanding of the communication of properties and, furthermore, lies at the heart of Anselm's classic rationale for the incarnation. This Anselmic model plays a crucial role in Reformed Christological constructions, to which Owen is no

---

[49] Ibid., pp. 269–70.

[50] *Atonement and Justification*, pp. 129, 138 n. 40. Several comments are in order here. First, Clifford assumes that Owen's use of distinction can be equated with Aristotle's own use (see, e.g. Clifford's uncritical use of Aristotle as a source for his definition, ibid. p. 138, n. 40). This may be the case, but can hardly be assumed when one considers how medievals, for example, Thomas Aquinas, modified the distinction when applying it to doctrines such as transubstantiation, and in how many diverse ways Renaissance and post-Renaissance scholars reworked Aristotelian language and themes. Secondly, and somewhat ironically, Clifford himself appears to use a distinction which mirrors that of accidents and essence in this very same context when he introduces the terms *qualitatively* and *quantitatively* on pages 128–9, arguing that Owen sees Christ's death as payment of the same quantitative debt owed to God while Baxter sees it as the same qualitative debt. The introduction of these terms in fact serves merely to obscure the clarity which, to the seventeenth-century mind, the language of Aristotle provided, and to make a complicated issue even more obscure. In his discussion, Clifford fails to see that Owen is working on the assumption that *death* and not *eternal punishment* is the penalty demanded by the law (cf. *Works* 10, p. 448 with Clifford, p. 129), and that Christ's death was, in this respect, *qualitatively* identical with what the law required, albeit, if we must use such language (not, in this case at all helpful), in terms of duration, not quantitatively so. This, *pace* Clifford, Owen justifies, of course, with recourse to biblical exegesis and not Aristotelian metaphysics. The language of Aristotle merely helps to organize and present that which Owen regards as the biblical teaching.

exception.[51] The Reformed understanding of the communication of properties also plays an important role, as we have seen, specifically in Owen's understanding of the infinite sufficiency where, because Christ is God, his suffering is of infinite value. This is surely what lies at the back of Owen's mind when he talks about the law being relaxed because of the person. At the very worst, Owen's language might be unclear – but only to those not acquainted with seventeenth-century terminology and Western teaching on atonement and Christology. Indeed, as far as the essence/accidents distinction is concerned, few in the seventeenth century would have had much difficulty in understanding what Owen intended by these terms, even if they did not agree with what he was saying.[52]

A further line of criticism that Baxter makes of Owen is the reiteration of the Socinian charge that satisfaction in the same kind and pardon are incompatible.[53] To this, Owen responds by reaffirming his commitment to an understanding of Christ's satisfaction based upon the covenant of redemption: the free, merciful, and gracious character of Christ's work is rooted in the covenant; Christ's acceptance of the role of representative of humanity is voluntary; and the only way in which Christ's work has significance for the believer is because God has freely agreed to accept the death of Christ as satisfaction and then to apply it.[54]

---

[51] In using the Anselmic argument for generating his Christology *via* a work–person paradigm, Owen is, of course, consistent with the Reformed tradition stemming from Calvin which eschewed metaphysical speculation in favour of a more soteriologically oriented understanding of the person. For the importance of the Anselmic argument, refracted through a Scotist lens, to Calvin's own Christology, see *Inst.* 2.12 ff.; cf. Muller, *Christ and the Decree*, pp. 27–9.

[52] For example, it plays a somewhat significant role in Baxter's own theology in the context of his teaching concerning the new law of grace and, if criticism of Owen were to be allowed as sound (which I do not allow), then, on the eminently equitable basis that what is good for the goose is good for the gander, Baxter's soteriology would be guilty of the same charge of incoherence: see *Universal Redemption*, pp. 14–15. Such usage is, of course, not unique to either Owen or Baxter but is commonplace in a world of thought dominated by Aristotelian vocabulary.

[53] *Aphorismes of Justification*, pp. 140 ff.

[54] *Works* 10, pp. 444–6. When Owen later comes to stress the absolute necessity of Christ's satisfaction if God is to forgive sin, it is clear that his position here must undergo some modifications, but not any of great significance. The whole of Christ's work is still dependent upon the covenant of redemption for its nature and efficacy: no covenant, no Christ.

On this issue, then, the difference between Owen and Baxter is rooted in a difference of logical order they ascribe to the decrees: Owen sees the death of Christ as determined by the covenant of redemption, which is also the causal ground of election, while Baxter places the death of Christ, and the decree of God which makes it salvific, logically prior to any consideration of the election of individuals.

Baxter's second major criticism of the satisfaction theory is addressed specifically against Maccovius, although he also criticizes Owen who responds in *On the Death of Christ*. This objection is that Christ's death, on the Orthodox interpretation, delivers the elect *ipso facto* from the penalty due to sin and therefore has a doctrine of eternal justification as its consequent.[55] Baxter's criticism of Owen focuses upon the time-lapse in the latter's theology between Christ's death and individual justification. Picking up on the weakness in Owen's analogy of the prisoner, Baxter makes the following points:

1. Whether a man may fitly be said actually, and *ipso facto*, to be delivered and discharged, who is not at all delivered, but onely hath a right to deliverance. I doubt.

2. Knowledge and possession of a deliverance, are farre different things. A man may have possession and no knowledge in some cases; or if he have both, yet the procuring of knowledge is a small matter, in comparison of possession.

3. Our knowledge therefore doth not give us possession; so that the similitude failes; for it is the Creditors knowledge and satisfaction that is requisite to deliverance. And our Creditour was not in a farre and strange countrey, but knew immediately and could either have made us quickly know, or turned us free before we had knowne the cause.

4. Nor can it easily be understood, how God can so long deny us the possession of Heaven, if wee had such absolute actuall Right (as he speaketh) so long ago; which seemeth to expresse a *jus ad rem et in re*.[56]

The criticisms here expressed exploit in an obvious way the inadequacy of Owen's imagery, but fail to engage with the details of his argument. In response, Owen breaks down his position into

---

[55] *Aphorismes of Justification*, Appendix pp. 146 ff. On Maccovius, see M. D. Bell, '*Propter Potestatem, Scientiam, ac Beneplacitum Dei*: The Doctrine of the Object of Predestination in the Theology of Johannes Maccovius', unpubl. ThD diss. (Westminster Theological Seminary, 1986).

[56] *Aphorismes of Justification*, Appendix pp. 156–7.

various components which can be treated generally under three headings: the will of God towards the elect prior to the death of Christ; the will of God towards them immediately upon the death of Christ; and the way in which salvation is actualized for individual elect. Under the first heading Owen makes it quite clear that if Christ's death has any salvific value it is only because of its relationship to the covenant, and therefore Christ's satisfaction, with all of its consequents, cannot be given a place logically prior to the covenant of redemption in eternity. True, God loves the elect from eternity, but God's love is not by itself sufficient to give them the right to those things which Christ's satisfaction is ordained to obtain for them.[57] Under the second heading Owen argues that Christ's death does not lead to immediate remission for the elect, not because the payment is refusable, as with a *solutio tantidem*, but because of the terms of the covenant which stands behind the whole economy of salvation, whereby God decrees to discharge the debtor when and how he pleases.[58] As Owen himself makes patently clear at this point, abstracting the payment from the covenant is a speculative move which makes the whole thing a nonsense.[59] Under the third heading Owen simply points to the fact that the covenant, the same one which gives Christ's death meaning, includes not only the objective satisfaction of Christ, but also the time of the application and imputation of Christ's righteousness through faith.[60] While the connection is not made explicitly by Owen in *Of the Death of Christ*, this clearly parallels his view of the believer's union with Christ which is wrought by faith. The notion of eternal union of the elect with Christ is a fundamental

---

[57] *Works* 10, pp. 454–7.
[58] Ibid., pp. 457–8.
[59] 'Absolutely, as in itself, abstracting from the consideration of any covenant or compact thereabout; and so it cannot be said to be a refusable payment; not because not refusable, but because no payment. That any thing should have any such reference unto God as a payment or satisfaction, whether refusable or otherwise, is not from itself and its own nature, but from the constitution of God alone.' Ibid., p. 458. Again, it is worth noting that the later shift in Owen's understanding of righteousness does not substantially affect this position, as it is still the covenant of redemption which establishes Christ's appointment as Mediator and defines his work.
[60] Ibid., pp. 468–71.

building block of the kind of Antinomian and hypercalvinist
views which Baxter wishes to impute to Owen,[61] and yet Baxter
makes no reference to the latter's views on union with Christ in
his strictures at this point, even though, as we saw, this doctrine
was central to Owen's separation of the objective accomplishment of redemption from its subjective application. Instead,
Baxter prefers to exploit the weakness of Owen's metaphorical
imagery, thus missing the real crux of the argument.

The significance of the debate

Two of the recent works on Owen, those of Clifford and Boersma, focus on the issue of *solutio tantidem/solutio eiusdem* as
being of great importance for an understanding of the structure
of Owen's doctrine of satisfaction, and so it is worth assessing
their arguments to see whether their conclusions have any validity. Clifford's argument is that Owen's adherence to *solutio
eiusdem* is a major element of his doctrine of limited atonement.[62]
A number of comments are in order here. First, it must be
understood that the debate between Owen and Baxter on this
issue is not about the extent of the atonement but about the
problem of how Christ's death relates to such issues as eternal
justification; in addition, the various Socinian criticisms of the
satisfaction theory also lurk just below the surface. Baxter's
concern is to avoid the errors of Antinomianism which he sees as
flowing as the logical consequences from *solutio eiusdem*, not, at
this point anyway, to strike at the atonement's particularity or
limitation. Clifford's failure to make any reference to the wider
polemical background at all in his analysis of this point allows
him to misconstrue the exact agenda behind the discussion, and
even to declare that 'Owen saw clearly that his doctrine of limited
atonement hung upon the "sameness" between Christ's sufferings and those deserved by the elect.'[63] This is not a connection
Owen ever appears to make explicit in his discussion of the
distinction, and, as we have repeatedly seen, the particularism of
redemption, and the consequent particularity of atonement, are

---

[61] On this issue, see Daniel, 'Hypercalvinism and John Gill', pp. 264–7.
[62] *Atonement and Justification*, pp. 128–30.
[63] Ibid., p. 129.

based upon the Trinitarian covenant structure of Owen's soteriology, and of the logical priority of this over considerations about the efficacy of Christ's satisfaction, and not upon any consideration of the atonement in isolation from this context. In the entire discussion of the *eiusdem/tantidem* distinction in *The Death of Death* and *Of the Death of Christ*, Owen's particularism is conspicuous only by its absence as a logical premiss for his argument.[64]

Nor, one might add, is commercialism a significant factor in Owen's arguments.[65] The debtor–creditor analogy is, of course, prominent, but the whole point of the two kinds of *solutio* is that both provide suitable ways of resolving a situation which can be construed in commercial terms. Pure commercialism then points neither one way nor the other on this issue and that is why, when replying to Baxter's *Aphorisms*, Owen bases his case for adhering to *solutio eiusdem* not on any speculative premiss but on exegesis of specific biblical texts which use the same language to speak of the penalty for sin and the penalty paid by Christ. It is these texts, interpreted in line with an analogy of faith determined by his Trinitarian concerns, and not the language and concepts of commerce, which make up the substance of his case, and to attempt to argue otherwise is to do gross violence to what Owen actually says.

Of course, by the time he comes to write *Vindiciae Evangelicae* in the 1650s, Owen has made the significant modification in his understanding of God's righteousness which was noted earlier. As he now regards Christ's atonement as absolutely necessary if God is to forgive sin, this has been interpreted by Boersma as strengthening the need for *solutio eiusdem* in his understanding of satisfaction and as fitting in much more neatly with his commercial view of atonement.[66] Nevertheless, a number of observations are in order also in this context. First, it must be remembered that the shift in Owen's understanding of divine

---

[64] Limitation of atonement is mentioned by Owen in connection with *solutio eiusdem*, but this is at the end of this particular argument and does not operate as a major constructive principle of his position: see *Works* 10, pp. 272–3.

[65] See Clifford, *Atonement and Justification*, pp. 126–7; cf. Boersma, *A Hot Peppercorn*, pp. 245 ff.

[66] Boersma, *A Hot Peppercorn*, p. 247.

righteousness is not motivated in any way by commercialist considerations, but simply by his desire to leave no opening whatsoever for Socinian ideas of atonement within Orthodox theology. His reason for changing his mind on this issue is to establish the necessity of atonement in the face of Socinian attempts to reject, and Reformed attempts to water down, the necessity of atonement.

Second, the arguments of Clifford and Boersma which stress the commercialist ideas within Owen's theory of atonement emphasize this one strand of his thought in isolation from the broader theological context, ignoring others which are equally, if not more, pertinent to the issue in hand, such as the Trinitarian context of salvation and the high priestly office of Christ. Claims that Owen's commercialist metaphors are allowed to control his thinking on atonement simply do not reflect the emphases in his relevant writings, and it is no doubt significant that such claims have so far been supported only with highly selective 'proof texts' and not theologically contextualized analyses of Owen's arguments. A clear example of the way in which the commercial metaphor is not allowed to lead Owen to logical conclusions is his continued insistence in the *Vindiciae Evangelicae* that, in one respect, Christ's sacrifice is of infinite value:

> [I]t may be said, 'If only the human nature of Christ was offered, how could it be a sacrifice of such infinite value as to [satisfy] the justice of God for all the sins of all the elect, whereunto it was appointed?'
> *Ans.* Though the thing sacrificed was but finite, yet the person sacrificing was infinite, and the *apotelesma* of the action follows the agent, that is, our mediator, *Theanthropos*, – whence the sacrifice was of infinite value.[67]

This statement, coming as it does after his change of mind on the issue of divine justice, clearly undercuts much of the nonsense spoken about the impact of Owen's commercialism. What underlies Owen's argument here is a view of atonement, based upon Anselmic principles, where the objective value of the atonement is derived from the person of the Mediator, and is thus still infinite.

---

[67] *Works* 12, p. 431.

This leads to a further point. Boersma argues that Owen's new understanding of God's justice means that there can be no difference between *satisfactio* and *solutio*, a distinction which Owen was just about able to maintain in *The Death of Death* because of his belief that Christ's death gained its penal character only as a result of a separate decree of God.[68] The distinction between the two is important because the former allows for the gracious interposition of God's agreement to accept Christ's death as satisfying his wrath against sin and thus of the free, gracious nature of salvation. In fact, the distinction is still possible, indeed, necessary, within Owen's later view on satisfaction both because of his adherence to the atonement's infinite sufficiency and because of the overall structure of salvation. Because the atonement is of infinite sufficiency, its particular efficiency (the point at which it becomes a *solutio* for specific sins of specific sinners) is still based upon decrees of God: the covenants of redemption and grace. Christ's atonement is part of his high priestly office, an office to which he was appointed by God the Father and which he willingly accepted. The value of his death is, in one sense, infinite, and so its application to the elect must still depend upon God's decision in eternity to save some and not others. It is only if a person fails to see either the continuing Trinitarian foundations of atonement or the impact of the Anselmic view on Owen's thinking at this point, and consequently misunderstands his commercial view of atonement as leading to crudely quantitative sufficiency in payment for the sins of the elect, that the change in Owen's understanding of God's justice can be construed as leading to the effects outlined by Boersma.[69] The really significant point of difference between Owen and Baxter is, again, the logical ordering of the decrees. Christ's satisfaction is not refusable as a payment because of what it is

---

[68] Boersma, *A Hot Peppercorn*, p. 247.

[69] Owen makes precisely this point about the Trinitarian context of atonement when discussing the *solutio eiusdem/tantidem* distinction in his reply to Baxter appended to the end of *Vindiciae Evangelicae*: see *Works* 12, pp. 613–614. Here he refers the reader back to his earlier statements on these issues, which presumably include those in *The Death of Death* and *Of the Death of Christ*, written before his new understanding of God's justice. Obviously Owen himself felt that his change of mind had little substantial impact upon this issue.

solely in reference to itself, but because it takes place within the context of the covenant of redemption, a covenant which always has logical and causal priority over the historical economy of salvation in Owen's thought, throughout his career and which is unaffected by his change of mind on the issue of God's righteousness.

For Owen, then, the significance of *solutio eiusdem* does not lie in the positive constructive impact which it has on his theology – it is rather a consequence than a premiss in his scheme – but in the fact that this is what he regards, rightly or wrongly, as Scripture's plain sense. Furthermore, he does not see that it is vulnerable to the Socinian criticisms or that it necessarily leads to the kind of Antinomian doctrines so feared by Baxter. It is only when the death of Christ is isolated from the Trinitarian framework that such issues can become problematic, but this is the kind of speculative discussion which Owen is resolutely set against. The real point at issue here between Owen and Baxter is not commercialism, limited atonement, etc. but 'Does the death of Christ have meaning only if set within a context which points to its particularity?' For Baxter the immediate context of the death of Christ is not a particularist covenant of redemption, and thus discussion of it in a meaningful way without having to bring out its particularism is itself a possibility. In his theology, therefore, the *solutio tantidem* distinction can come to play a significant role in its own right. He does not use it, as does Grotius, to allow for an Arminian ordering of decrees, but combines it with the distinction between God's antecedent and consequent will, to produce a soteriology which is distinctly Amyraldian in terms of its decretalism.[70] Because Owen, however, makes Christ's satisfaction a function of his mediatorial office and thus of the covenant of redemption, he simply cannot isolate his doctrine of atonement from that covenant, or, therefore, from its particularity.[71]

---

[70] On the distinction in God's will, and its soteriological implications, see *Catholick Theologie* 2, pp. 54–8. Also, Boersma's book is excellent on Baxters' views, especially on this point.

[71] It is hard not to suspect that behind Clifford's critique of the commercial theory of the atonement is a belief that this somehow involves a crudely quantitative view of sin, whereby, if there had been more sin in the world, the satisfaction would have had

The decree of election and the appointment of Christ as Mediator are part of one and the same thing, and it is this that forms the basis for the particularism of Christ's death.

Conclusion

There are two points which emerge very clearly from studying Owen's theology of satisfaction in its seventeenth-century context. The first is that it is framed to a large extent in opposition to a number of contemporary positions as defined by, amongst others, the Socinians, Grotius, Baxter, and the Antinomians. As such, in terms of its specific formulation, it cannot be abstracted from its historical context and brought into direct relation to its sixteenth-century antecedents. The situation, historically and theologically, is too complex for such an approach to yield results that reflect in any accurate way the points which Owen is attempting to establish. Calvin and his contemporaries never faced Grotius or the Antinomians, and thus never had to take their insights or criticisms into account. For Baxter and Owen the situation is far different, and to deny this, by drawing direct comparisons between the sixteenth and the seventeenth centuries, or by failing to discuss the context of the Grotian theory, is not a sound historical approach.

The second point that emerges so clearly from Owen's disagreements with Grotius, Baxter, etc. over satisfaction is once again the decisive role played in his thinking by the Trinitarian

---

Footnote 71 (*continued*) to be that much greater: see his comments, *Atonement and Justification*, p. 126. The evidence he cites from Owen to prove this point is the latter's use of a particular metaphor. It is, of course, not sound methodology to understand specific non-metaphorical theological formulations in terms of the metaphors used to elucidate them; rather, one should understand the metaphors as being subordinate to the doctrinal formulations upon which they shed light. If account is taken of the Christological and soteriological context of the debtor-creditor metaphor, such a crudely quantitative view of sin and satisfaction cannot be imputed to Owen. Indeed, the interpretation offered by Clifford does not take sufficient account of the infinite internal value of the death of Christ which derives from Christ's person, a point quite clear in Anselm's classic formulation of the argument in *Cur Deus Homo?* 2.14, and which is preserved in the Christological and soteriological arguments put forward by Reformed Orthodox such as Owen and Goodwin.

covenant of redemption. This comes as no surprise given all that has been said so far about the Trinitarian-Christological structure of salvation. From the point of view of pure Christology the satisfaction of Christ is infinite by virtue of the communication of properties within his divine–human person. Nevertheless, the context of Christ's satisfaction, the point at which his work of satisfaction comes into positive relation with God's salvific will and therefore becomes efficient for salvation, is the covenant of redemption. It is this that appoints him as Mediator and it is this that determines which humans are elect and which are not. Thus, the atonement is 'limited' by the covenant. In fact, 'limited atonement' is perhaps a misleading word in this context, pointing towards crudely quantitative views of sin and satisfaction and an abstraction of Christ's death from its proper context – none of which are appropriate as hermeneutical keys to Owen's thinking. In light of this, 'particular redemption' is perhaps more faithful to Owen's purpose, drawing attention to the way in which the infinite value of Christ's sufferings is only aimed at the salvation of particular individuals.

Christ's satisfaction is the focal point of Owen's whole theology, and indicates the pyramidic structure of his thought which this book has attempted to highlight: his understanding of God is the context in which Christology must be understood; and his understanding of Christology provides the context within which Christ's satisfaction must be understood. To divorce satisfaction from its proper context, in Christology and in the doctrine of God, is to indulge in the kind of speculative doctrinal discussion which is absent from Owen's work, and to do violence to his thinking. As such, it is doomed to lead to a misunderstanding of his thought. Owen's understanding of Christ's death may be unacceptable – but it must be understood not as a straightforward Aristotelian perversion of some static doctrinal ideal, but as part of his attempt to stand within the ongoing Western tradition which sought to draw out the implications of a rich, Trinitarian theology for the economy of salvation.

Six

The Man Who Wasn't There

As I was going up the stair,
I met a man who wasn't there
He wasn't there again today.
Oh! How I wish he'd go away!

It is a remarkable fact, but the secondary literature surrounding the Protestantism of the late sixteenth and seventeenth centuries is populated by men who were not actually there – not actually in those centuries, that is. It may well be that scholars were on the whole never foolish enough to subscribe to the popular myths about Calvinism epitomized in Mencken's definition of Puritanism as a 'haunting fear that someone, somewhere, may be happy', but they have generated enough myths and factoids of their own to fill the void. Whether it is Beza, playing Stalin to Calvin's Lenin and almost single-handedly perverting the Reformed faith, or Zanchi rationalizing Reformed theology into a *centraldogma* based upon a rigid form of Aristotelianism, or Perkins taking English Reformed thought out into the wasteland of despair created by voluntarist notions of faith[1] – scholars have found no shortage of villains to blame for the directions taken by Reformed thought in the late-sixteenth and seventeenth centuries.

---

[1] For examples of these views, see Bizer, *Frühorthodoxie und Rationalismus*; J. Dantine, 'Les Tabelles de la Prédestination par Theodore de Bèze', *Revue de Théologie et de Philosophie* 16 (1966), 365–77; and Kendall, *Calvin and English Calvinism*. For evidence of the continuance of the old school of scholarship up to the present day, see Otto Gründler's article, 'Zanchi, Girolamo', in Hans J. Hillerbrand (ed.), *The Oxford Encyclopedia of the Reformation*, 4 vols. (Oxford: OUP, 1996).

It is, however, becoming increasingly clear that these sinister villains who prowl through the pages of the secondary scholarship bear little resemblance to the theologians who led the Reformed churches of their day. Indeed, as far as their 'crimes' are concerned, they have, to use a crude modern colloquialism, been 'framed'. The scholarly evidence that this is the case is now overwhelming. The work of Kristeller and Schmitt has debunked many of the myths surrounding the Scholasticism and Aristotelianism of the Renaissance and post-Renaissance worlds. The work of Donnelly and Muller, amongst a growing band of others, has put to death the notion that the theology of Reformed Orthodoxy is fundamentally discontinuous with the theology of the Reformation. Most important of all, the establishment of a proper developmental model of interpretation based upon historical criteria and careful analysis of primary texts has exposed the fact that much of the older school of scholarship on Reformed Orthodoxy assumed models of interpretation which were based upon anachronistic agendas, whether Barthian, neo-Calvinist, Amyraldian, or whatever.[2] Once one has read the primary texts from a historical perspective, reading the analyses of such as Beza, etc. given by the old school is an experience not dissimilar from that described by the author of the above rhyme: it is like meeting a man who wasn't there, and whose continued presence is a source only of irritation and frustration.

To the ever-growing list of men who weren't there can now be added John Owen – the John Owen, that is, whose theology, particularly his view of atonement, is supposed to be based upon, and therefore explicable in terms of, Aristotelian teleology. If nothing else, the above pages should have demonstrated that the real John Owen, the man who *was there* in the seventeenth century, was someone whose theological works are clearly of a sophistication to defy reduction to a few simplistic categories. For example, the framework within which he understands even a single doctrine such as Christ's atonement is too complex, too dependent upon other doctrines, to be abstracted

---

[2] See Muller, 'Calvin and the "Calvinists"'.

from its position within the overall theological context without serious distortion of its content. Furthermore, his theology draws upon a multiplicity of sources which is reflected in his extensive knowledge of patristic and medieval theology. Indeed, the catholicity of his library catalogue is reflected in the catholicity of his thought: his understanding of Trinitarianism and his discussion of key doctrinal loci, such as providence, predestination, and the necessity of satisfaction, all reveal a man who has read widely in the relevant theological literature of his own day and of previous ages. That he assumes the validity of Aristotelian logic and physics, and that he uses the language of Aristotle in order to give his doctrinal formulations a precision and coherence they would otherwise lack, merely indicate that he was a man of his age. In his use of 'the Philosopher', he was at one with his greatest opponent, Richard Baxter, and, as a seventeenth-century figure, he was unremarkable, simply a Reformed Orthodox thinker operating within the accepted canons and conventions of contemporary theological discourse.

What is perhaps more significant, especially in light of interpretations of Owen which stress the 'rationalistic' bent of his thinking, is the rigorous way in which his entire soteriological scheme is actually an extended, and consistent, reflection upon the implications of Western Trinitarianism for an anti-Pelagian understanding of salvation. This in itself should be enough to suggest that Owen is no 'rationalist' in any modern sense of the word, since Owen, unlike Baxter, stands firmly within the Reformed tradition which emphasized the Trinity as a revealed truth of faith which had no analogy to the natural world. As he reflects upon the relationship between the trinity and the anti-Pelagian view of salvation which he wishes to maintain, he elaborates at length upon, among other things, the nature of theology and revelation, the constitution of Christ's person, the relation of the Trinitarian acts *ad intra* to the Trinitarian acts *ad extra*, the importance of the dual procession of the Spirit, and the necessity of incarnation and atonement for the maintenance of the Christological focus of his soteriological scheme. His arguments concerning all of these issues serve to locate him firmly within the broad Western catholic tradition of theology which extends right back from the seventeenth century, through the Middle Ages, to the early church. Indeed, Owen stands as a classic example of that which Paul Tillich found so praiseworthy in seventeenth-century Orthodoxy: one who remained in dialogue with all periods of the church's historical tradition. Only by a remarkable feat of historical and theological myopia can he be turned into a direct forerunner of those modern British neo-Calvinists or fundamentalists who show no interest in the patristic or medieval theology upon which Owen himself drew so positively. Rather, Owen, like Baxter, stands as one of the most theologically gifted and articulate Englishmen of the seventeenth century. That their side ultimately 'lost' the political and ecclesiastical battles of the age, and that they were subsequently excluded from the canon of English theologians considered worth studying, should not be taken as any sign of their intrinsic mediocrity. Like their continental counterparts, it was their misfortune to be the intellectual giants of a world which was about to disappear forever in the critical light of Enlightenment philosophy.

This fundamental insight – that the Puritans are important representatives of Western theology on their own terms – will, of course, never be appreciated while scholarship remains preoccupied with judging the seventeenth century by standards other than those which were set within its own day. If one is looking for a Barth, or a Calvin, one must look in the twentieth, or the sixteenth century, respectively; it is pointless to search for one in seventeenth-century England, and even more pointless to express dismay at, or even harsh criticism of, those theologians one does find there on the grounds that they do not measure up to standards which were irrelevant in their own day. This is crucial if studies of seventeenth-century theology are ever to come of age – after all, it was only when sixteenth-century studies moved beyond the terms of debate set by the theological presuppositions of the Catholic–Protestant divide, that real progress was made in understanding the true intellectual dynamics of the age. Indeed, the results there have been revolutionary, as evidenced by the work of Oberman, Steinmetz, and their students. The creative possibilities for studies of seventeenth-century thought, once the distorting influence of unhistorical presuppositions has been deleted, are, if anything, even greater than they were for Reformation studies.

The caricature of Owen and those like him as terrible perverters of some imagined perfect Calvinism is not a helpful model of historical interpretation, depending as it does upon unhistorical presuppositions and an arbitrary theological positivism which sets up the thought of one or two thinkers as the norm by which all others, regardless of context, are to be judged. Such an approach not only involves breathtaking anachronism, it also narrows the field of scholarly investigation in a way that prevents exploration of the relationship of Reformed Orthodoxy and Puritanism to the broader Western tradition which, as we have seen, provided much that was useful for men such as Owen. As such, this model can only lead to an impoverished understanding of Owen and his contemporaries which fails to see the depth and sophistication of their approach to the theological task; it has therefore surely outlived what limited usefulness it ever had.

Freed from the partisan agenda of the 'Calvin against the Calvinists' school, we are able to assess Owen according to the criteria of his own day. When this is done, he stands not as one who implicitly repudiated his Reformation heritage by developing an arid form of theological rationalism but as one who sought to discover and elucidate the inner rationality of that heritage through careful study of the great theologians of the past and judicious application of the methods of the present. His is a theology which seeks all means at its disposal to place Christ at the centre of a soteriological scheme determined by the Trinitarian God. Whether he was successful or not by the standards of the sixteenth, or the twentieth, century is irrelevant; and he would certainly never have claimed any ultimate authority, in any sense, for his own theological formulations. As the closing words of his treatise on the glory of Christ indicate, Owen knew that there comes a point when theological speculation must confess its own inadequacy in the face of God's mystery and give way to humble and silent adoration:

There is nothing farther for us to do herein but that now and always we shut up all our meditations concerning it with the deepest self-abasement, out of a sense of our unworthiness and insufficiency to comprehend those things, admiration of that excellent glory which we cannot comprehend, and vehement longings for that season when we shall see him as he is, be ever with him, and know him ever as we are known.[3]

---

[3] *Works* 1, p. 415.

Appendix One

The Role of Aristotelian Teleology in Owen's Doctrine of Atonement

In his book *Atonement and Justification* Alan Clifford sees Owen's arguments in one of his most important treatises, *The Death of Death in the Death of Christ* (1647), as controlled by an Aristotelian philosophy which leads to nothing less than a betrayal of biblical teaching and a hopelessly inconsistent view of grace. Another scholar, Hans Boersma, has also adopted Clifford's argument. In *A Hot Peppercorn: Richard Baxter's Doctrine of Justification in Its Seventeenth Century Context of Controversy*, he is primarily concerned with Richard Baxter but, when dealing with Owen, he openly argues along the lines laid down by Clifford. Clifford's argument, if correct, clearly has important implications for any assessment of Owen's theology but a close examination of his thesis reveals a number of fundamental problems in his interpretation of Owen.

Clifford's argument about Owen's view of atonement, which is adopted with little alteration by Boersma, falls into two distinct halves: the first concerns the impact of Aristotle upon Owen's theology of atonement; the second concerns Owen's adherence to a commercial view of atonement. The latter has been discussed in the main text, so only the former need concern us here. His thesis runs as follows: Owen construes the atonement as governed by a 'one-end teleology', derived from Aristotle, whereby it has only one exclusive end, i.e. the salvation of the elect; thus, other 'ends', such as common grace, are logically excluded.[1]

---

[1] *Atonement and Justification*, pp. 96–8; cf. Boersma, *A Hot Peppercorn*, 211–12.

While Clifford does allow that Owen's theology gives some room to 'common grace', he regards this as the result of a basic inconsistency in Owen's arguments and, in the light of his view of atonement, as fundamentally incoherent.[2]

The first problem is the implicit assumption that Clifford apparently makes concerning the deleterious impact of Aristotelianism *per se* on theology. The general problem of the relationship of Aristotelian language to the content of theology has already been discussed and so need not delay us here.[3] Nevertheless, it is worth noting that Clifford seems to presuppose that the presence of Aristotelian categories indicates that Owen gives them equal standing with, or even priority over, the biblical data or the doctrinal tradition. At no point in his book is there any discussion of the notion, commonplace amongst theologians of the seventeenth century, that philosophy was a tool which could be used within the framework of the church's credo in order to elucidate the inner structure of doctrines, without it being made in any way equal, or, even worse, superior, to biblical revelation.[4] Of course, this may not be the case with Owen's use of Aristotle here, but that is for scholars to prove with evidence, not presuppose as basic from the outset. The failure to entertain this even as a possibility suggests that Clifford has come to Owen with an a priori framework which rejects it out of hand.[5]

More significantly, the notion that an Aristotelian 'one-end teleology' governs Owen's approach needs both clarification and modification. First, Clifford assumes that Owen's use of the

---

[2] Ibid., pp. 102–3.

[3] See Ch. 2 above.

[4] Contrast the findings of Richard A. Muller, '*Vera Philosophia cum sacra theologia nusquam pugnat*: Keckermann on Philosophy, Theology and the Problem of Double Truth', *SCJ* 15 (1984), 341–65.

[5] Particularly suggestive of Clifford's hostility to any use of Aristotle in theology is the following comment: 'Indeed, when justifying the reality of devotion to Christ, why does he feel the need to quote "the philosopher"?' *Atonement and Justification*, p. 98. The references supplied are to *Works* 2, p. 343, and *Works* 12, p. 112. In neither case is Owen using Aristotle to justify the reality of devotion to Christ: in the first, he uses Aristotle as a source for the definition of love; in the second, as a source for the definition of hate. Such use of pagan sources as linguistic aids was scarcely exceptional in the sixteenth and seventeenth centuries, as Calvin's often positive use of quotations from Cicero and Seneca shows.

language of Aristotelian teleology makes him vulnerable to the same philosophical criticisms as Aristotle himself.[6] This is simply another instance of the 'root-fallacy' whereby it is assumed that two thousand years of linguistic, philosophical, and cultural history have made no substantial difference to the way in which Aristotle is understood and his terminology employed. Of course, there is a slight possibility that this is the case, but one cannot simply assume that it is so without first discussing, or at least referring to, the scholarly literature on the development of Aristotelianism within the late classical, medieval, and Renaissance periods. After all, if one is to make such great play of Owen's use of Aristotle, one must surely ask if the Aristotle of Owen is that of the Suarezian school, the Paduan school, his Oxford mentors, etc. If Aristotelianism is to be used as an a priori category it must be acknowledged that it is a term that requires a precise definition of a kind which Dr Clifford nowhere supplies. The use of Aristotelian language, as we noted in Ch. 2, is absolutely standard for seventeenth-century thinkers of all descriptions, and in itself gives no insight into the content of their views prior to analysis of the use of the terms in their context.

Furthermore, the 'one, single end' in Owen's theology of atonement is inclusive, not exclusive, and allows for at least one intermediate end: the final end, the glory of God, does not preclude the existence of an intermediate end, the salvation of the elect.[7] Clifford himself appears to misinterpret Owen as regarding the salvation of the elect, rather than the glory of God, being the ultimate end of Christ's death, and provides evidence in the form of a quotation:

> By the end of the death of Christ, we mean in general, both – first, that which his Father and himself intended in it; and secondly, that which was effectually fulfilled and accomplished by it . . . the end of Christ's

---

[6] See *Atonement and Justification*, p. 107, notes 13 and 15.

[7] *Works* 10, pp. 201–202. Clifford, unlike Boersma, makes no allowance for the distinction Owen makes between the final end (God's glory) and the intermediate end (salvation of the elect) of Christ's death, and appears to identify the salvation of the elect as the final end of Christ's death. Nevertheless, Boersma still does not draw out the implications of this distinction: cf. *Atonement and Justification*, pp. 96–7 and *A Hot Peppercorn*, p. 212.

[8] *Atonement and Justification*, p. 96.

obtaining grace and glory with his Father was, that they might be certainly bestowed upon all those for whom he died . . .[8]

In fact, this quotation is taken from two passages of Owen which are separated by 45 pages of text! The first half is taken from page 157, the second from page 202. If this approach is legitimate, then one might as well argue that 'Judas went and hanged himself . . . Go and do thou likewise' is a command explicitly taught in the Bible.

Set in context, the second sentence comes from a passage which is dealing explicitly with 'intermediate and subservient' ends, under which category falls the salvation of the elect. This crucial distinction makes it obvious that the term 'one-end teleology', unless applied to an understanding of God's salvation of the elect, or even of God's glory, as an inclusive end, is thoroughly misleading. Even if one interprets Aristotelian teleology as implying one ultimate goal, this does not preclude the existence, or importance, of intermediate goals subordinate to that end. The fact that Owen himself adopts a distinction between the final end and the intermediate ends of Christ's death indicates his assumption of a hierarchy of ends within his teleology.

Clifford himself appears to make some attempt to allow for this in a footnote, where he declares that '[i]n Owen's case, this is not to question his valid admission of constituent "sub-ends" within the "end" of the atonement . . . but to reject his thesis of a single, exclusive end'.[9] The sentiments contained within this statement are at best obscure, at worst self-contradictory. Owen's admission of 'sub-ends' automatically means that he does not hold to a single *exclusive* end, but a single *inclusive* end: the glory of God. As for this being a *single* inclusive end, it is tempting to ask what other kind of teleology there is. The principle of teleology as understood in the seventeenth century demands that there be only one ultimate end, and the applicability of teleology as an organizational or heuristic principle for demonstrating the coherence of theology was generally accepted, by all – by Baxter as well as Owen.[10]

---

[9]   Ibid., p. 107, n. 15.

[10] Baxter himself states the principle with as much, if not more, force and clarity than Owen: 'It is an injury to God unworthy of a Divine, to make God have as many distinct ends, as they think there are particular aptitudes or tendencies in the means. For undoubtedly we must feign in God no more ultimate *ends than one*. And undoubtedly

This realization that the glory of God is the ultimate end of Christ's death, and that all other ends are intermediate then allows us to dispose of another problem raised by Clifford's thesis: Owen's adherence to common grace. Clifford argues that Owen's two references to common grace in *The Death of Death* betray a basic incoherence within his theology of atonement: how can the purchase of common grace be reconciled with an atonement whose exclusive end is the glorification of God in the salvation of the elect?[11] The answer is that it can easily be done if we accept that Owen's teleology is inclusive. There is then nothing to stop us taking Owen's statements about common grace at face value:

> The fruits of Christ's mediation have been distinguished by some into those that are more general and those which are more peculiar, which, in some sense, may be tolerable . . .[12]
>
> [T]here are no spiritual distinguishing fruits of redemption ascribed to these false teachers, but only common gifts of light and knowledge, which Christ hath purchased for many for whom he did not make his soul a ransom.[13]

It is quite clear from the second quotation that Owen does allow that Christ's atonement involves the provision of common grace, even if the details of how they relate to each other are omitted – although the notions of a universal internal sufficiency point towards a possible resolution: we must not forget that even in

---

Footnote 10 (*continued*) the *means* consisting of innumerable parts, make up one perfect *whole*, in which God's Glory shineth so, as it doth not in any part alone. And he that will cut God's frame into scraps and shreds, and set up the *parts* as so many *wholes*, will more dishonour him than he that would so mangle a Picture, or a Watch, or Clock, or House, or the pipes of an Organ, or the strings of a Lute, and tell you of their beauty and Harmony only distinctly. Well therefore did Dr *Twisse* reduce all the *Decrees de mediis* to one: But they are one in their *apt composition* for *one end*: And the Glory of Sun, and Stars, and Angels, and the whole Creation is a part, and the glory of our salvation and damnation is but another part.' *Catholick Theologie*, p. 62.

[11] *Atonement and Justification*, p. 102. Again, he states that the ' "exclusive" end of the death of Christ is to supply grace for the elect alone'. The references he provides on p. 109, n. 48 nowhere exclude the notion of common grace from Owen's theology, nor do they declare that the procurement of grace for the elect is the *exclusive* end of the atonement in the sense intended by Clifford.

[12] *Works* 10, p. 189.

[13] Ibid., p. 362.

The Death of Death Owen seems to presuppose the substance of the sufficient/efficient distinction, with the former being universal in scope.[14]

Faced with such statements, advocates of the 'one-end teleology' approach as it is formulated by Clifford have two options. First, they can argue that the theology of these texts referring to common grace is inconsistent with Owen's adherence to one-end teleology. This is what Clifford does, but it is clearly not a methodologically sound response to raise the model of interpretation above the text which it is supposed to interpret and to use it as a way of dismissing any evidence that might falsify it as a thesis. Surely the validity of Clifford's model must depend upon its ability to account for all the aspects of *The Death of Death*? Yet, these texts prove the inapplicability of the model which he uses and obviously require at the very least its substantial revision. To dismiss the very texts that would appear to falsify the thesis as signs of Owen's being logically inconsistent betrays a methodological apriorism indicative of an agenda based not on historical criteria but on systematic theological concerns, and aimed at bringing in a verdict of 'guilty as charged' against Owen whatever the evidence might suggest to the contrary. One could just as easily proceed to prove that Owen was a Pelagian if his references to human responsibility and freedom were taken as basic, and his other statements about total depravity, predestination, causality, etc. were dismissed as being aberrations and inconsistencies.

The alternative response is to see in these texts evidence that Owen did indeed regard the atonement as including other dimensions than those summarized by God's glory in the salvation of the elect. While Owen never explicitly refers to these aspects of common grace as an 'end' of the atonement in *The Death of Death*, there is no reason for us to expect him to do so: the treatise is not in the genre of dispassionate, systematic and exhaustive treatments of doctrine but is a highly-charged polemical work which focuses on specific points of controversy. The issue at stake

---

[14] 'If you mean that there is a sufficiency in the merit of Christ to save them [the non-elect] if they should believe, we grant it, and affirm that this sufficiency is the chief ground of the proposing it unto them', *Works* 10, p. 383. Cf. *Works* 12, p. 431.

is the efficacy of the atonement for salvation, not the provision of common grace. That such a treatise deals with the topic immediately in hand and refers rarely, if at all, to other issues, no matter how closely related, cannot form the basis for positive assertions about Owen's views in these other areas.

In fact, of course, Owen's distinction between final and intermediate ends, with its implications of a hierarchical, inclusive teleology, means that there is plenty of room for a doctrine of common grace in his theology, and that such a notion is not necessarily excluded by the structure of his thought. When freed from the strait-jacket of the 'one-end teleology' model, the two texts cited above can act as decisive proof that this is in fact the case, even within *The Death of Death*.[15]

While it is clear from the textual evidence that the one-end teleology argument needs radical revision if it is to be at all useful in elucidating Owen's arguments in *The Death of Death*, a careful reading of the treatise as a whole indicates that the emphasis placed by this argument upon the primacy of Aristotelian categories is entirely misplaced and represents a serious misreading of Owen's work. This comes out most clearly if one compares Clifford's summary of the work with the analysis which prefaces the Goold edition.[16] Whereas Clifford places all his emphasis upon the Aristotelian aspects of the work, Goold emphasizes the theological structure of the treatise in which the logic of Aristotle serves as a heuristic device which elucidates but does not construct. As we have noted throughout the main text of this work, it is the Trinitarian structure of the economy of salvation which provides the basis for Owen's understanding of Christ's work,

---

[15]   Owen does make the following comment which might appear to support Clifford's radical 'one-end teleology' thesis: 'That there is any other end of the death of Christ, besides the fruit of his ransom and propitiation, directly intended, and not by accident attending it, is utterly false. Yea, what other end the ransom paid by Christ and the atonement made by him can have but the fruits of them, is not imaginable. The end of any work is the same with the fruit, effect, or product of it.' *Works* 10, p. 216. Upon close examination, however, the statement is clearly dealing with the end Christ's death *as it is a ransom*, and, as has been demonstrated above, Christ's death gains its character as a ransom, as well as its particularity, from the covenant of redemption between Father and Son, not from Owen's understanding of Aristotelian philosophy.
[16]   Cf. *Atonement and Justification*, p. 107 with *Works* 10, pp. 142–4.

and thus for his understanding of the nature of the atonement. One may not like the results of this structure, one may feel they prejudice exegesis; one may, if one wishes, even regard them as little short of blasphemy, but one should then blame this upon Owen's understanding of the Trinitarian nature of theology, not upon a philosopher who had been dead for two thousand years and whose philosophy was used in the seventeenth century to prove all manner of mutually contradictory positions.

Appendix Two

Owen, Baxter, and the Threefold Office

One fundamental point of contrast between the Christology of Owen and that of Baxter is the virtual absence of the threefold office from Baxter's discussion of Christ's work as Mediator, as opposed to its centrality to Owen's argument. In neither of his major systematic expressions of doctrine, *Catholick Theologie* (1675) or *Methodus Theologiae* (1681), does Baxter develop the notion of Christ's mediation in terms of the threefold office or, more specifically, in terms of priesthood. The same is true of his extended discussion of the relationship of Christ's death to salvation, *Universal Redemption* (1694). Furthermore, it is not a major theme in the *Aphorismes of Justification* (1649), a work which engages directly with Owen's *Death of Death* in an Appendix, and yet ignores the importance of Christ's role as Mediator to Owen's argument, thereby missing a central plank of the treatise's argument. Whether the omission is intentional or not is a matter for pure speculation. What is significant is the fact that something of such importance to Owen's argument is simply bypassed by his great opponent.

Such a distinct difference between the two men's approaches should be enough to alert the reader to the fact that there is possibly something here which indicates more than just a simple disagreement over the nature and extent of Christ's death. It is, of course, true that the threefold office, rather like Aristotelian terminology, does not necessarily import a particular doctrinal content: the fact that both Reformed Orthodox and Socinians could use it as a basic organizational framework for Christological discussion should be sufficient to indicate that it may not be such a significant difference in approach. It is possible that its absence from Baxter might simply indicate an organizational or terminological difference with Owen and not something more significant. There is, however, a sound reason for believing from the outset that this is not the case: for Owen, Christ's mediation, his threefold office, and especially his priesthood do indeed function as loci for the convenient presentation of key aspects of Christ's work; but they have also profound theological and hermeneutical significance, for they draw attention to the causal foundation of the whole scheme in the intratrinitarian covenants and to the relationship between Old Testament priesthood and the work of Christ, which allows for the development of those arguments concerning the relationship of oblation and intercession that are so central to Owen's basic argument. In addition, the absence of the threefold office as a key part of Baxter's argument means that Baxter's approach, unlike that of Owen, represents a significant deviation from the more traditional Reformed approach to Christology which uses the two states/threefold office motifs as basic organizational principles. These structures are clearly important in the *Institutes* of John Calvin and, by the time of Perkins and beyond, have become basic organizational principles for discussing the work of Christ.[1] Owen's work uses this tradition positively to build his Christology, but Baxter has little to say on the issue.

Why is it, then, that Baxter both breaks with Reformed tradition and gives little attention to the biblical and historical concept of priesthood, in contrast to Owen's attempt to articulate his theology within the traditional categories? The answer must lie in the fact that Baxter considers that his own distinctive concerns could be better expressed without using the traditional framework and the biblical patterns. These concerns can be determined from a reading of *Catholick Theologie*, Part 2, sect.3 'Of Christ's Incarnation and our Redemption'.[2] The argument here can be broken down into a number of subsections: Christ's appointment as Mediator; a denial that Christ was a real representative of humans, as, say, a servant is of his master; an assertion that

---

[1]   Calvin, *Inst.* 2.12–16; Perkins, *Workes* 1, pp. 26–31.
[2]   *Catholick Theologie*, pp. 37–42.

Christ did suffer for sinners, but not so that sinners might say that they had, in a legal sense, suffered the penalty in his person; and an assertion that Christ's sufferings were a sufficient satisfaction for all sin but were not in stead of all the sufferings due to those for whom he died. This last point is supported by a discussion of the nature of Christ's sufferings which reflects the Grotian discussions over *solutio tantidem* and *solutio eiusdem* which Baxter first articulates in his *Aphorismes*.[3]

The same basic pattern is evident in the *Methodus Theologiae*, where Baxter's discussion of Christ's work in Part Three starts with an extended discussion of Christ's sacrifice in terms of both the nature of Christ's representation of humanity and the relationship between Christ's sufferings and the punishment due to sinners. Indeed, this whole discussion covers some 53 folio pages and precedes all other discussion of Christ's role in salvation.[4] It is only after this that Baxter introduces the ideas of the two states and the threefold office, a discussion which takes barely two pages and which occurs in the context of clarifying the relationship of Christ as God to the economy of salvation, and of emphasizing the historical movement within the incarnation. He does not introduce these themes as ways of developing his understanding of the content of Christ's work of mediation; that has already been done in the previous chapter.[5]

The arguments of *Catholick Theologie* and *Methodus Theologiae*, particularly the structural arrangement of the latter, are most revealing as they clearly highlight the focal points of concern in Baxter's Christology. These centre on the nature of Christ's representation of sinful humanity, and the nature of his sufferings. They thus reflect an agenda which is set not by the

---

[3] For a full discussion of this distinction, see Ch. 5 above.

[4] *Methodus Theologiae* 3a.1.1–18, pp. 9–61.

[5] See the chart, *Methodus Theologiae* 3a.2, pp. 62–3; 'Etiam in sua Infantia Christus erat Ecclesiae Caput, Propheta, Rex, Sacerdos; Quoad designationem scilicet ad opus postea praestandum, et Relationem inde resultantem: Persona quippe fuit in incunabulis ex natura divina et *humana*, et patris missione, et sui ipsius sponsione ad opus hoc praestandum adaptata; quanquam ad opera mediatoria plene exequenda, ad docendum scilicet, et justitiam omnem actu adimplendam, humana eius natura non fuit idonea donec ad maturitatem quadantenus adolevit.' *Methodus Theologiae* 3a.2.1.2, p. 63. See also the continuation of this discussion on p. 64.

internal dynamics of the Reformed tradition, but by the Grotian response to Socinianism and by the problems raised for Orthodoxy by the development of Antinomian tendencies in the doctrine of justification.[6] Needless to say, this is not the primary agenda for Owen, and is not the point at which he starts his discussion. For him the concerns are, theologically, the relationship of the Trinity to the economy of salvation, and, polemically, the efficacy of Christ's atonement for salvation, both issues which can be conveniently addressed using the models which the Reformed tradition had developed for just this purpose. Issues such as those which hold centre stage for Baxter can only be addressed by Owen once the basic framework of mediation has been established.

With Baxter, we have a theologian whose basic motivation in the theological task is different from that of Owen. As a self-appointed ecumenist, his approach to theology in works such as *Catholick Theologie,* is determined by the need to find a middle ground for the reconciliation of opposites. Thus his approach tends to be governed by taking as his starting point the unacceptable results of the theological arguments of others and then moving to positive formulation by way of a critique of established, but in his view incorrect or inadequate, positions. This supplies the whole ethos of *Catholick Theologie*, and is nowhere clearer than in *Universal Redemption*. In this latter work the lynchpin of the argument can be found in Chapter Four, where the proposition is affirmed that 'Christ in suffering did not strictly and properly bear and represent the person of the Sinner, so as *Civiliter, Moraliter, Legislater*, it might be said that "We either satisfied of suffered in or by Christ"'.[7] If this premise does not hold, the whole Baxterian edifice collapses. What is interesting is the method used to establish its validity: a series of propositions of the form 'Any doctrine which denies x cannot be true', where x is a necessary implication of Baxter's premise; this is then followed by a demonstration that a denial of x is indeed demanded by some aspect of the Orthodox theory of atonement. The result is that his positive theological constructions are some-

---

[6] See Ch. 5 above.

[7] *Universal Redemption* (London, 1694), p. 67.

what reminiscent of the old adage of Sherlock Holmes, 'When you have eliminated the impossible, whatever is left, however improbable, must be the truth.'

Two observations about the respective methodologies of Owen and Baxter are thus in order at this point. First, there is the contrast in basic purpose. Owen's concern is to use the resources of the Reformed tradition as a basis for polemical refutation of opponents. He does this primarily by showing the basic coherence of Reformed Orthodox theology, focusing on the relationship between God's Trinitarian acts *ad intra* and those *ad extra*, particularly as they centre in the person and work of the Mediator. Baxter, however, convinced that the Reformed Orthodox tradition is fundamentally flawed at certain points, is more concerned to take seriously some of the criticisms made of the Orthodox theology, and he thus focuses on such criticisms as the starting point for his reconstruction of, for example, the death of Christ. Traditional Reformed structures, such as the threefold office and, one might add, vigorous Reformed Trinitarianism, are thus less significant to him because they do not immediately facilitate the kind of ecumenical theological task to which he has committed himself.

The second point relates to a contrast in argumentation. Owen's arguments are positive, in that they work directly from the tradition to refutation of opponents. Baxter's arguments, however, often seem as if they succeed by default: positive doctrinal statement is built simply upon the fact that the available alternatives are, within Baxter's frame of reference, absurd. Unless this basic difference is noted, no end of problems arise for those attempting to compare the views of the two men. It simply cannot be done directly, but must take into account the basic differences in context and purpose which underlie their respective statements. Owen is ultimately concerned with developing a powerful Trinitarianism; Baxter with articulating a theological ecumenism.

Bibliography

Primary Sources

Ames, W. *The Marrow of Theology*. Translated by J. D. Eusden. Durham: Labyrinth, 1983.

Aquinas, T. *Thomae Aquinatis Opera Omnia cum hypertextibus in CD-ROM*. Edited by R. Busa. Milan: Editoria Elettronica Editel, 1992.

Arminius, J. *The Works of James Arminius*. Translated by J. and W. Nichols. 3 vols. Grand Rapids: Baker, 1986.

Aureole, P. *Scriptum super primum sententiarum*. New York: Franciscan Institute, 1952.

Baxter, R. *Aphorismes of Justification*. London, 1649.

— *Catholick Theologie*. London, 1675.

— *Methodus Theologiae*. London, 1681.

— *Universal Redemption of Mankind*. London, 1694.

— *Practical Works*. 4 vols. London, 1707.

— *The Reformed Pastor*. Edinburgh: Banner of Truth, 1974.

— *The Autobiography of Richard Baxter*. Mobile: RE Publications, n.d.

— *Calendar of the Correspondence of Richard Baxter*. Edited by N. H. Keeble and G. F. Nuttall. 2 vols. Oxford: Clarendon Press, 1991.

Biddle, J. *A Twofold Catechism*. London, 1654.

Boethius *Tractates and The Consolation of Philosophy*. Cambridge: Harvard University Press, 1973.

Calvin, J. *Institutes of the Christian Religion*. Translated by F. L. Battles. 2 vols. Philadelphia: Westminster, 1960.

— *Opera quae supersunt omnia.* Edited by Baum, Cunitz, and Reuss. Brunswick: Schwetschke, 1863–1900.

Campanella, T. *Metaphysica.* Edited by L. Firpo. Turin: Bottega d'Erasmo, 1961.

Crellius, J. *De Uno Deo Patre.* Cracow, 1631.

Crisp, T. *Christ Alone Exalted.* Edited by J. Gill. 2 vols. London: John Bennett, 1832.

Davenant, J. *A Dissertation on the Death of Christ.* London: Hamilton, 1832.

Goodwin, T. *The Works of Thomas Goodwin.* 12 vols. Eureka: Tanski Publications, 1996.

Grotius, H.*Opera omnia theologica.* 3 vols. Amsterdam, 1679.

— *A Defence of the Catholic Faith.* Translated by F. H. Foster. Andover: Draper, 1889.

Junius, F. *Opera Theologica.* Geneva, 1613.

Library of Ante-Nicene, Nicene, and Post-Nicene Fathers. Reprinted in 38 vols. Grand Rapids: Eerdmans, 1993.

Lombard, P. *Magistri Petri Lombardi Parisiensis Episcopi Sententiae in IV Libros Distinctae.* 2 vols. Grottaferrata: Collegii S Bonavenurae, 1971–81.

Molina, L. *On Divine Foreknowledge.* Translated with an introduction by A. J. Freddoso. Ithaca: Cornell University Press, 1988.

Owen, J. *The Works of John Owen.* 24 vols. London: Johnstone and Hunter, 1850–5.

— *Bibliotheca Oweniana.* London, 1684.

— *The Correspondence of John Owen.* Edited by P. Toon. Cambridge: James Clarke, 1970.

Perkins, W. *The Workes of . . . William Perkins.* 3 vols. Cambridge, 1609.

Pococke, E. *Porta Moris.* Oxford, 1655.

Racovian Catechism. Translated by T. Rees. London: Longman, 1818.

Rutherford, S. *Disputatio Scholastica de Providentia.* Edinburgh, 1643.

— *Christ Dying and Drawing Sinners to Himselfe.* London, 1647.

Saltmarsh, J. *Free Grace.* London, 1646.

— *Sparkles of Glory.* London: E Huntington, 1811.

Schaff, P. (ed.) *The Creeds of Christendom*. 3 vols. Grand Rapids: Baker, 1983.

Scotus, Duns J. *Opera Omnia*. 26 vols. Paris: Vives, 1891–5.

Socinus, F. *De Jesu Christo Servatore*. Cracow, 1594.

Synopsis Purioris Theologiae. Edited by H. Bavinck. Leiden: Donner, 1881.

TG *The True Idea of Jansenisme*. Preface by John Owen. London, 1669.

Turretin, F. *Institutes of Elenctic Theology*. Vol. 1. Translated by G. M. Giger and edited by J. T. Dennison Jr. Phillipsburg: Presbyterian and Reformed, 1992.

Twisse, W. *A Discovery of D Jacksons vanitie*. London, 1631.

— *Vindiciae Gratiae, Potestatis, ac Providentiae Dei*. Amsterdam, 1632.

— *Dissertatio de Scientia Media*. Arnhem, 1639.

— *The Scriptures Sufficiency*. London, 1656.

Ursinus, Z. *Commentary on the Heidelberg Catechism*. Translated by G. W. Williard. Phillipsburg: Presbyterian and Reformed, n.d.

Ussher, J. *A Body of Divinitie*. London, 1653.

Watson, T. *A Body of Divinity*. Edinburgh: Banner of Truth Trust, 1883.

Secondary Sources

Althaus, P. *Die Prinzipien der deutschen reformierten Dogmatik im Zeitalter der aristotelischen Scholastik*. Leipzig: Deichertsche, 1914.

Anonymous 'Richard Baxter's "End of Controversy".' *Bibliotheca Sacra and American Biblical Repository* 12 (1855), 348–85.

Armstrong, B. G. *Calvinism and the Amyraut Heresy*. Madison: University of Wisconsin Press, 1969.

Backus, I. ' "Aristotelianism" in some of Calvin's and Beza's Expository Exegetical Writings on the Doctrine of the Trinity.' In *Histoire de l'exégèse au XVIe siècle. Textes du Colloque International tenu à Genève en 1976. Réunis par Olivier Fatio et Pierre Fraenkel*. Geneva: Librarie Droz, 1978, pp. 351–60.

Baker, D. (ed.)*Reform and Reformation: England and the Continent c. 1500–c.1750*. Oxford: Blackwell, 1979.

Baker, J. W. and McCoy, C. S. *Fountainhead of Federalism: Heinrich Bullinger and the Covenantal Tradition*. Louisville: Westminster, 1991.

Barr, J. *The Semantics of Biblical Language*. Oxford: Oxford University Press, 1961.

Barth, K. *Church Dogmatics* 2.2. Translated by G. W. Bromiley *et al.* Edinburgh: T and T Clark, 1957.

Bass, W. W. 'Platonic Influences on Seventeenth Century English Puritan Theology as expressed in the thinking of John Owen, Richard Baxter, and John Howe.' Unpubl. PhD diss. University of Southern California, 1958.

Bavinck, H. *The Doctrine of God*. Translated by W. Hendriksen. Edinburgh: Banner of Truth, 1977.

Bebbington, D. W. *Evangelicalism in Modern Britain*. London: Unwin, 1989.

Beeke, J. R. *Assurance of Faith: Calvin, English Puritanism, and the Dutch Second Reformation*. New York: Peter Lang, 1991.

Bell, M. D. '*Propter Potestatem, Scientiam, ac Beneplacitum Dei*: The Doctrine of the Object of Predestination in the Theology of Johannes Maccovius.' Unpubl. ThD diss. Westminster Theological Seminary, 1986.

Berkhof, L. *Systematic Theology*. Grand Rapids: Eerdmans, 1949.

Berkouwer, G. C. *Holy Scripture*. Translated by J. B. Rogers. Grand Rapids: Eerdmans, 1975.

Bierma, L. D. 'Federal Theology in the Sixteenth Century: Two Traditions?' *Westminster Theological Journal* 45 (1983), 304–21.

Bizer, E. *Fruhorthodoxie und Rationalismus*. Zurich: EVZ, 1963.

Boersma, H. *A Hot Peppercorn: Richard Baxter's Doctrine of Justification in Its Seventeenth-Century Context of Controversy*. Zoetermeer: Boekencentrum, 1993.

Bonansea, B. M. 'Duns Scotus' Voluntarism.' In B. M. Bonansea and J. K. Ryan (eds.), *John Duns Scotus, 1265–1965*. Washington: Catholic University of America Press, 1965.

— *Tommaso Campanella: Renaissance Pioneer of Modern Thought*. Washington: Catholic University of America Press, 1969.

Boughton, L. C. 'Supralapsarianism and the Role of Metaphysics in Sixteenth Century Reformed Theology.' *Westminster Theological Journal* 48 (1986), 63–96.

Brauer, J. C. 'Reflections on the Nature of English Puritanism.' *Church History* 23 (1954), 99–108.

Brunner, E. *Truth as Encounter*. Translated by A. Loos and D. Cairns. Philadelphia: Westminster, 1964.

Clark, R. Scott *See* Trueman, Carl R.

Clifford, A. C. *Atonement and Justification: English Evangelical Theology 1640–1790, An Evaluation*. Oxford: Clarendon Press, 1990.

Cohen, C. L. *God's Caress: The Psychology of Puritan Religious Experience*. Oxford: Oxford University Press, 1986.

Collinson, P. *The Elizabethan Puritan Movement*. Oxford: Clarendon Press, 1967.

—— *Godly People: Essays on English Protestantism and Puritanism*. London: Hambledon, 1982.

—— 'England and International Calvinism 1558–1640.' In M. Prestwich (ed.), *International Calvinism*. Oxford: Clarendon Press, 1985, pp. 197–223.

Coolidge, J. S. *The Pauline Renaissance in England*. Oxford: Clarendon Press, 1970.

Copleston, F. *A History of Philosophy*. 9 vols. London: Burns Oates and Washbourne, 1946–75.

Costello, W. T. *The Scholastic Curriculum at Seventeenth Century Cambridge*. Cambridge: Harvard University Press, 1958.

Craig, W. L. *The Problem of Divine Knowledge and Future Contingents from Aristotle to Suarez*. Leiden: E J Brill, 1988.

Crilly, W. H. 'Scholastic Philosophy.' In *New Catholic Encyclopedia* 12, 1146–7.

Cumming, G. J. (ed.) *Studies in Church History* 2. London: Nelson, 1965.

Daniel, C. 'Hypercalvinism and John Gill.' Unpubl. PhD diss. University of Edinburgh, 1983.

Dantine, J. 'Les Tabelles sur la Doctrine de la Prédestination par Theodore de Bèze.' *Revue de Theologie et de Philosophie* 16 (1966), 365–77.

Dekker, E. 'Was Arminius a Molinist?' *Sixteenth Century Journal* 27 (1996), 337–52.

Denzinger, H. *Enchiridion Symbolorum*. Freiburg: Herder, 1937.

Donnelly, J. P. *Calvinism and Scholasticism in Vermigli's Doctrine of Man and Grace*. Leiden: E J Brill, 1975.

— 'Italian Influences on Calvinist Scholasticism.' *Sixteenth Century Journal* 7 (1976), 81–101.

Dowey, E. A. *The Knowledge of God in Calvin's Theology*. Grand Rapids: Eerdmans, 1994.

Duffield, G. E. (ed.) *John Calvin*. Grand Rapids: Eerdmans, 1966.

Elert, W. *The Structure of Lutheranism*. Translated by W. A. Hansen. St Louis: Concordia, 1962.

Evans, G. R., McGrath, A.E., Galloway, A.D. *The History of Christian Theology 1: The Science of Theology*. Grand Rapids: Eerdmans, 1986.

Fatio, O. *Méthode et Théologie: Lambert Daneau et les debuts de la scolastique reformée*. Geneva: Librairie Droz, 1976.

Ferguson, S. B. *John Owen on the Christian Life*. Edinburgh: Banner of Truth, 1987.

Fisher, G. P. 'The Theology of Richard Baxter.' *Bibliotheca Sacra and American Biblical Repository* 9 (1852), 135–69.

— 'The Writings of Richard Baxter.' *Bibliotheca Sacra and American Biblical Repository* 9 (1852), 300–29.

Fraenkel, P. *Testimonia Patrum: The Function of the Patristic Argument in the Theology of Philip Melanchthon*. Geneva: Librairie Droz, 1961.

Gerrish, B. A. 'Biblical Authority and the Continental Reformation.' *Scottish Journal of Theology* 10 (1957), 337–60.

Gleason, R. *John Calvin and John Owen on Mortification*. New York: Peter Lang, 1995.

Godbeer, L. *The Devil's Dominion: Magic and Religion in Early New England*. Cambridge: Cambridge University Press, 1992.

Godfrey, W. R. 'Tensions Within International Calvinism: The Debate on the Atonement at the Synod of Dordt.' Unpubl. PhD diss. Stanford University, 1974.

Gomes, A. W. '*De Jesu Christo Servatore*: Faustus Socinus on the Satisfaction of Christ.' *Westminster Theological Journal* 55 (1993), 209–31.

Graham, W. F. (ed.) *Later Calvinism: International Perspectives*. Kirksville: Sixteenth Century Essays and Studies, 1994.

Grillmeier, A. *Jesus der Christus im Glauben der Kirche* 2.2. Freiburg: Herder, 1989.

Gründler, O. 'Zanchi, Girolamo.' In Hans J Hillerbrand (ed.), *The Oxford Encyclopedia of the Reformation*. 4 vols. Oxford: Oxford University Press, 1996. 4, pp. 305–6.

Gundry, S. N. 'John Owen on Authority and Scripture.' In J. D. Hannah (ed.), *Inerrancy and the Church*. Chicago: Moody Press, 1984.

Hall, B. 'Puritanism: The Problem of Definition.' In G. J. Cumming, (ed.) *Studies in Church History* 2. London: Nelson, 1965. pp. 283–96.

— 'Calvin against the Calvinists.' In G. E. Duffield (ed.), *John Calvin*, pp. 19–37.

Haller, W. *The Rise of Puritanism*. New York: Columbia, 1955.

Headley, J. M. 'Tommaso Campanella and the end of the Renaissance.' *Journal of Medieval and Renaissance Studies* 20 (1990), 157–74.

— 'Tommaso Campanella and Jean de Launoy: The Controversy over Aristotle and his Reception in the West.' *Renaissance Quarterly* 43 (1990), 529–50.

Helm, P. *Calvin and the Calvinists*. Edinburgh: Banner of Truth, 1982.

— 'Calvin (and Zwingli) on Divine Providence.' *Calvin Theological Journal* 29 (1994), 388–405.

Heppe, H. *Reformed Dogmatics Set Out and Illustrated from the Sources*. Translated by G. T. Thomson. Grand Rapids: Baker, 1978.

Heyd, M. 'From Rationalist Theology to Cartesian Voluntarism.' *Journal of the History of Ideas* 40 (1979), 527–42.

Hill, C. *Society and Puritanism in Pre-Revolutionary England*. London: Secker and Warburg, 1967.

— *The World Turned Upside Down*. London: Pelican, 1975.

— *Milton and the English Revolution*. New York: Viking, 1978.

— *A Turbulent, Seditious, and Factious People*. Oxford: Oxford University Press, 1988.

— *The Experience of Defeat: Milton and some contemporaries*. London: Bookmarks, 1994.

Holtrop, P. C. 'Decrees of God.' In D. McKim (ed.), *Encyclope-*

dia of the Reformed Faith. Edinburgh: St Andrew Press, 1992, pp. 97–9.

Hutton, S. 'Thomas Jackson, Oxford Platonist, and William Twisse, Aristotelian.' *Journal of the History of Ideas* 39 (1978), 635–52.

Jansen, J. F. *Calvin's Doctrine of the Work of Christ*. Edinburgh: James Clarke, 1956.

Keeble, N. H. *Richard Baxter: Puritan Man of Letters*. Oxford: Clarendon Press, 1982.

Kendall, R. T. *Calvin and English Calvinism to 1649*. Carlisle: Paternoster Press, 1997.

Kenny, A. *Wyclif*. Oxford: Oxford University Press, 1985.

— *Aquinas on Mind*. London: Routledge, 1993.

Kevan, E. F. *The Grace of Law: A Study in Puritan Theology*. Ligonier: Soli Deo Gloria, 1993.

Klauber, M. I. 'Reason, Revelation, and Cartesianism: Louis Tronchin and Enlightened Orthodoxy in Late Seventeenth-Century Geneva.' *Church History* 59 (1990), 326–39.

— 'The Drive Toward Protestant Union in Early Eighteenth--Century Geneva: Jean-Alphonse Turretin on the "Fundamental Articles" of the Faith.' *Church History* 61 (1992), 334–49.

— 'Between Protestant Orthodoxy and Rationalism: Fundamental Articles in the Early Career of Jean LeClerc.' *Journal of the History of Ideas* 54 (1993), 611–36.

— *Between Reformed Scholasticism and Pan-Protestantism: Jean-Alphonse Turretin (1671-1737) and Enlightened Orthodoxy at the Academy of Geneva*. Selinsgrove: Susquehanna University Press, 1994.

— 'Reformed Orthodoxy in Transition: Benedict Pictet (1655–1724) and Enlightened Orthodoxy in Post-Reformation Geneva.' In W. F. Graham, *Later Calvinism*, pp. 93–113.

— and Sunshine, G. S.'Jean-Alphonse Turretin on Biblical Accommodation: Calvinist or Socinian?' *Calvin Theological Journal* 25 (1990), 7–27.

Knappen, M. M. *Tudor Puritanism*. Chicago: University of Chicago Press, 1939.

— *Two Elizabethan Puritan Diaries*. Gloucester: Peter Smith, 1966.

Kneale, W. M. and J. *The Development of Logic*. Oxford: Clarendon Press, 1962.

Kristeller, P. O. *Renaissance Thought: The Classic, Scholastic, and Humanist Strains*. New York: Harper and Row, 1961.

Kvacala, J. *Thomas Campanella: Ein Reformer der Ausgehenden Renaissance*. Berlin: Trowitzsch, 1973.

Ladd, G. E. *A Theology of the New Testament*. Revised edition. Grand Rapids: Eerdmans, 1993.

Lane, A. N. S. 'Sola Scriptura? Making Sense of a Post-Reformation Slogan.' In P. E. Satterthwaite and D. F. Wright (eds.), *A Pathway into the Holy Scripture*. Grand Rapids: Eerdmans, 1994, pp. 297–327.

Lane, A. N. S. (ed.) *Interpreting the Bible*. Leicester: Apollos, 1997.

Lerner, M-P. 'Campanella, Juge d'Aristote.' In M Gandillac (ed), *Platon et Aristote à la Renaissance*. XVI Colloque International de Tours. Paris: Librarie Philosophique J Vrin, 1976.

McDonald, William J. et al. (eds.) *The New Catholic Encyclopedia*. 15 vols. New York: McGraw-Hill, 1967.

McGiffert, M. 'American Puritan Studies in the 1960s.' *William and Mary Quarterly*, Series 3, 27 (1970), 36–67.

McGrath, A. E. *A Life of John Calvin*. Oxford: Blackwell, 1990.

McGrath, G. J. 'Puritans and the Human Will: Voluntarism within Mid-Seventeenth Century English Puritanism As Seen in the Thought of Richard Baxter and John Owen.' Unpubl. PhD diss. University of Durham, 1989.

McKim, D. K. 'John Owen's Doctrine of Scripture in Historical Perspective.' *Evangelical Quarterly* 45 (1973), 195–207.

—— and Rogers, J. B. *The Authority and Interpretation of the Bible: An Historical Approach*. San Francisco: Harper and Row, 1979.

McLachlan, H. J. *Socinianism in Seventeenth-Century England*. Oxford: Oxford University Press, 1951.

MacLeod, J. N. 'John Owen and the Death of Death.' In *Out of Bondage*, Proceedings of the Westminster Conference. Nottingham, 1984.

Marsden, G. M. 'Perry Miller's Rehabilitation of the Puritans.' *Church History* 39 (1970), 91–105.

Miller, P. *The New England Mind: The Seventeenth Century.* Cambridge: Harvard University Press, 1939.

— *Errand into the Wilderness.* New York: Harper and Row, 1956.

Møller, J. G. 'The Beginnings of Puritan Covenant Theology.' *Journal of Ecclesiastical History* 14 (1963), 46–67.

Mueller, J. T. *Christian Dogmatics.* St Louis: Concordia, 1934.

Muhl, M. 'Der *logos endiathetos* und *prophorikos* von der alteren Stoa bis zur Synode von Sirmium 351.' *Archiv für Begriffsgeschichte* 7 (1962), 7–56.

Muller, R. A. 'Perkins' *A Golden Chaine*: Predestinarian System or Schematized Ordo Salutis?' *Sixteenth Century Journal* 9 (1978), 69–81.

— '"*Duplex cognitio dei*" in the Theology of Early Reformed Orthodoxy.' *Sixteenth Century Journal* 10 (1979), 51–61

— 'The Debate over the Vowel Points and the Crisis in Orthodox Hermeneutics.' *Journal of Medieval and Renaissance Studies* 10 (1980), 53–72.

— 'Christ in the Eschaton: Calvin and Moltmann on the Duration of the *Munus Regium*.' *Harvard Theological Review* 74 (1981), 31–59.

— 'The Federal Motif in Seventeenth Century Arminian Theology.' *Nederlands Archief voor Kerkgeschiedenis* 62 (1982), 102–22.

— '*Vera Philosophia cum sacra Theologia nusquam pugnat*: Keckermann on Philosophy, Theology, and the Problem of Double Truth.' *Sixteenth Century Journal* 15 (1984), 341–65.

— *Dictionary of Latin and Greek Theological Terms.* Grand Rapids: Baker, 1985.

— *Christ and the Decree: Christology and Predestination from Calvin to Perkins.* Durham: Labyrinth, 1986.

— *Post-Reformation Reformed Dogmatics 1: Prolegomena to Theology.* Grand Rapids: Baker, 1987.

— 'The Christological Problem in the Thought of Jacobus Arminius.' *Nederlands Archief voor Kerkgeschiedenis* 68 (1988), 145–63.

— *God, Creation, and Providence in the Thought of Jacob Arminius.* Grand Rapids: Baker, 1991.

— *Post-Reformation Reformed Dogmatics 2: Holy Scripture –*

The Cognitive Foundation of Theology. Grand Rapids: Baker, 1993.

— 'God, Predestination, and the Integrity of the Created Order: A Note on Patterns in Arminius's Theology.' In W. F. Graham (ed.), *Later Calvinism*, pp. 431–50.

— 'Grace, Election, and Contingent Choice: Arminius's Gambit and the Reformed Response.' In T. R. Schreiner and B. A. Ware (eds.), *The Grace of God and the Bondage of the Will*. Grand Rapids: Baker, 1995, pp. 251–78.

— 'Calvin and the "Calvinists": Assessing Continuities and Discontinuities between the Reformation and Orthodoxy.' *Calvin Theological Journal* 30 (1995), 345–75; 31 (1996), 125–60.

Murray, J. *Collected Writings*. 4 vols. Edinburgh: Banner of Truth, 1976–82.

Neuser, W. H. (ed.) *Calvinus Sacrae Scripturae Confessor*. Grand Rapids: Eerdmans, 1994.

Nuttall, G. F. *Richard Baxter and Philip Doddridge: A Study in Tradition*. London: Oxford University Press, 1951.

— 'A Transcript of Richard Baxter's Library Catalogue: A Bibliographical Note.' *Journal of Ecclesiastical History* 2 (1951), 207–21.

— 'A Transcript of Richard Baxter's Library Catalogue (Concluded).' *Journal of Ecclesiastical History* 3 (1952), 74–100.

— *Richard Baxter*. London: Nelson, 1965.

— *The Holy Spirit in Puritan Faith and Experience*. Chicago: University of Chicago Press, 1992.

Oakley, F. *Omnipotence, Covenant, and Order: an Excursion in the History of Ideas from Abelard to Leibniz*. Ithaca: Cornell University Press, 1984.

Oberman, H. A. *The Masters of the Reformation*. Cambridge: Cambridge University Press, 1981.

— *The Harvest of Medieval Theology: Gabriel Biel and Late Medieval Nominalism*. Durham: Labyrinth, 1983.

— *The Dawn of the Reformation*. Edinburgh: T and T Clark, 1986.

— *The Impact of the Reformation*. Grand Rapids: Eerdmans, 1994.

Ong, W. J. *Ramus, Method, and the Decay of Dialogue*. Cambridge: Harvard University Press, 1958.

Packer, J. I. 'The Redemption and Restoration of Man in the Thought of Richard Baxter.' Unpubl. DPhil diss. University of Oxford, 1954.

— *Among God's Giants: The Puritan Vision of the Christian Life.* Eastbourne: Kingsway, 1991.

Pannenberg, W. *Theology and the Philosophy of Science.* Translated by F. McDonagh. Philadelphia: Westminster, 1976.

Patterson, R. L. *The Conception of God in the Philosophy of Aquinas.* London: George Allen and Unwin, 1933.

Platt, J. E. 'Eirenical Anglicans at the Synod of Dordt.' In D. Baker, *Reform and Reformation,* pp. 221–43.

— *Reformed Thought and Scholasticism: The Arguments for the Existence of God in Dutch Theology,* 1575–1650. Leiden: E J Brill, 1982.

Popkin, R. H. *The History of Scepticism from Erasmus to Spinoza.* Berkeley: University of California Press, 1979.

Powicke, F. J. *A Life of the Reverend Richard Baxter 1615–1691.* New York: Hought Mifflin Co., n.d.

Preus, R. D. *The Theology of Post-Reformation Lutheranism.* 2 vols. St Louis: Concordia, 1970–2.

Rainbow, J. H. *The Will of God and the Cross: An Historical and Theological Study of John Calvin's Doctrine of Limited Redemption.* Allison Park: Pickwick, 1990.

Raitt, J. *The Eucharistic Theology of Theodore Beza.* Chambersburg: American Academy of Religion, 1972.

Rehnman, S. 'Theologia Tradita: A Study in the Prolegomenous Discourse of John Owen (1616–1683).' Unpubl. DPhil diss. University of Oxford, 1997.

Ricard, L. B. 'New England Puritan Studies in the 1970's.' *Fides et Historia* 15 (1983), 6–27.

Rolston III, H. *John Calvin versus the Westminster Confession.* Richmond: John Knox, 1972.

Ryken, P. G. 'Scottish Reformed Scholasticism.' In Trueman and Clark, *Protestant Scholasticism.*

Schaefer, P. R. Jr. 'The Spiritual Brotherhood on the Habits of the Heart: Cambridge Protestants and the Doctrine of Sanctification from William Perkins to Thomas Shepard.' Unpubl. DPhil diss. University of Oxford, 1994.

— 'Protestant Scholasticism at Elizabethan Cambridge: William Perkins and a Reformed Theology of the Heart.' In Trueman and Clark, *Protestant Scholasticism*.

Schmid, H. *The Doctrinal Theology of the Evangelical Lutheran Church*. Translated by C. A. Hay and H. E. Jacobs. Minneapolis: Augsburg, 1961.

Schmitt, C. B. *Studies in Renaissance Philosophy and Science*. London: Variorum Reprints, 1981.

— *John Case and Aristotelianism in Renaissance England*. Kingston: McGill-Queen's University Press, 1983.

Schoneveld, C. W. *Intertraffic of the Mind: Studies in Seventeenth-Century Anglo-Dutch Translation with a Checklist of Books Translated from English into Dutch, 1600–1700*. Leiden: E J Brill, 1983.

Schreiner, S. E. *The Theater of His Glory: Nature and the Natural Order in the Thought of John Calvin*. Grand Rapids: Baker, 1995.

Sinnema, D. 'The Issue of Reprobation at the Synod of Dordt (1618–19) in Light of the History of this Doctrine.' Unpubl. PhD diss. Toronto School of Theology, 1985.

— 'Aristotle and Early Reformed Orthodoxy: Moments of Accommodation and Antithesis.' In W. E. Helleman (ed.), *Christianity and the Classics: The Acceptance of a Heritage*. New York: University Press of America, 1990, pp. 119–48.

Sprunger, K. L. 'Ames, Ramus and the Method of Puritan Theology.' *Harvard Theological Review* 59 (1966), 133–51.

— *The Learned Doctor William Ames: Dutch Backgrounds of English and American Puritanism*. Chicago: University of Illinois, 1972.

— *Dutch Puritanism: A History of English and Scottish Churches of the Netherlands in the Sixteenth and Seventeenth Centuries*. Leiden: E J Brill, 1982.

— *Trumpets from the Tower: English Puritan Printing in the Netherlands 1600–1640*. Leiden: E J Brill, 1994.

Steinmetz, D. C. *Luther and Staupitz: An Essay in the Intellectual Origins of the Protestant Reformation*. Durham: Duke University Press, 1980.

— *Luther in Context*. Grand Rapids: Baker, 1995.

— *Calvin in Context*. New York: Oxford University Press, 1995.

Stephens, W. P. *The Theology of Huldrych Zwingli*. Oxford: Clarendon Press, 1986.

Stout, H. S. *The New England Soul: Preaching and Religious Culture in Colonial New England*. Oxford: Oxford University Press, 1986.

Studer, B. *Trinity and Incarnation*. Translated by M. Westerhoff and edited by A. Louth. Minnesota: Liturgical Press, 1993.

Thiselton, A. C. *The Two Horizons*. Carlisle: Paternoster, 1980.

Thomas, K. *Religion and the Decline of Magic*. New York: Scribners, 1971.

Tillich, P. *A History of Christian Thought*. Edited by C. E. Braaten. New York: Simon and Schuster, 1968.

Toon, P. *Hypercalvinism*. London: Olive Tree, 1967.

— *God's Statesman: The Life and Work of John Owen*. Exeter: Paternoster, 1971.

Torrance, J. B. 'The Incarnation and "Limited Atonement".' *Evangelical Quarterly* 55 (1982), 83–94

— 'Strengths and Weaknesses of the Westminster Theology' in A. I. C. Heron (ed.), *The Westminster Confession in the Church Today*. Edinburgh: St Andrew Press, pp. 40–54.

— 'The Concept of Federal Theology – Was Calvin a Federal Theologian?' In W. H. Neuser, *Calvinus Sacrae Scripturae Confessor*, pp. 15–40.

Torrance, T. F. 'One Aspect of the Biblical Conception of Faith.' *Expository Times* 68 (1956–57), 111–14.

Trinterud, L. J. 'The Origins of Puritanism.' *Church History* 20 (1951), 37–57.

Trueman, Carl R. *Luther's Legacy: Salvation and English Reformers, 1525–1556*. Oxford: Clarendon Press, 1994.

— 'Heaven and Hell (12): In Puritan Theology.' *Epworth Review* 22.3 (1995), 75–85.

— 'Protestant Scholasticism, Jews, and Judaism: Some Notes on their Connection.' *Journal of Progressive Judaism* 4 (1995). 61–76.

— 'Faith Seeking Understanding: Some Neglected Aspects of John Owen's Understanding of Scriptural Interpretation.' In A. N. S. Lane (ed.), *Interpreting the Bible: Historical and*

Theological Studies in Honour of David F. Wright. Leicester: Apollos, 1997, pp. 147–62.

— 'A Small Step Towards Rationalism: The Impact of the Metaphysics of Tommaso Campanella on the Theology of Richard Baxter.' In Trueman and Clark (eds.), *Protestant Scholasticism.*

— 'John Owen's *Dissertation on Divine Justice*: an Exercise in Christocentric Scholasticism.' *Calvin Theological Journal*, forthcoming.

— and Clark, R.S. (eds.) *Protestant Scholasticism: Essays in Reassessment.* Carlisle: Paternoster, 1997.

Tyacke, N. *Anti-Calvinists: The Rise of English Arminianism c.1590–1640.* Oxford: Clarendon Press, 1987.

van Asselt, W. J. 'Studie van de Gereformeerde Scholastiek: Verleden en Toekomst.' *Nederlands Theologisch Tijdschrift* 50 (1996), 290–312.

van Ruler, J. A. 'New Philosophy to Old Standards: Voetius' Vindication of Divine Concurrence and Secondary Causality.' *Nederlands Archief voor Kerkgeschiedenis* 71 (1991), 58–91.

von Rohr, J. *The Covenant of Grace in Puritan Thought.* Atlanta: Scholars Press, 1986.

Wallace, D. D. *Puritans and Predestination: Grace in English Protestant Theology.* Chapel Hill: University of North Carolina Press, 1982.

Wallace, R. S. *Calvin's Doctrine of Word and Sacrament.* Edinburgh: Oliver and Boyd, 1953.

Weber, H-E. *Reformation, Orthodoxie, und Rationalismus.* Gutersloh: Bertelsmann, 1951.

Weber, O. *Foundations of Dogmatics.* Translated by D. L. Guder. 2 vols. Grand Rapids: Eerdmans, 1981.

Weisheipl, J. A. 'Scholastic Method.' In New Catholic Encyclopedia 12, 1145–6.

White, P. *Predestination, Policy and Polemic: Conflict and Consensus in the English Church from the Reformation to the Civil War.* Cambridge: Cambridge University Press, 1992.

Willis, E. D. *Calvin's Catholic Christology.* Leiden: E J Brill, 1966.

Index